BILINGUAL
VISUAL
DICTIONARY

ㅂㅈㄷㄱㅅㅛㅕㅑㅐㅔ
ㅁㄴㅇㄹㅎㅗㅓ;ㅣ
ㅋㅌㅊㅍㅠㅜㅡ,./

BILINGUAL
VISUAL
DICTIONARY

FIRST EDITION
Managing Editor Christine Stroyan
Managing Art Editor Anna Hall
Translations by Andiamo! Language Services Ltd

REVISED EDITION
DK LONDON
Senior Editors Christine Stroyan, Ankita Awasthi Tröger
Designer Thomas Keenes
Managing Editor Carine Tracanelli
Managing Art Editor Anna Hall
Senior Production Controller Rebecca Parton
Senior Jacket Designer Surabhi Wadhwa Gandhi
Publisher, DK Learning Sarah Forbes
Managing Director, DK Learning Hilary Fine

Translations by Planet Languages Ltd

DK INDIA
Editor Alka Thakur-Hazarika
Desk Editors Pankhoori Sinha, Joicy John
DTP Designers Anurag Trivedi, Rakesh Kumar
Assistant Picture Researchers Geetam Biswas, Shubhdeep Kaur
Senior Art Editor Vikas Chauhan
Senior Jacket Designer Suhita Dharamjit
Managing Editor Saloni Singh
Managing Art Editor Govind Mittal
DTP Coordinator Tarun Sharma
Preproduction Manager Balwant Singh
Senior Jacket Coordinator Priyanka Sharma Saddi

This American Edition, 2025
First American Edition, 2019
Published in the United States by DK Publishing,
a division of Penguin Random House LLC
1745 Broadway, 20th Floor, New York, NY 10019

Copyright © 2019, 2025 Dorling Kindersley Limited
A Penguin Random House Company
25 24 23 22 21 20 10 9 8 7 6 5 4 3 2 1
001–340371–Apr/2025

All rights reserved.

Published in Great Britain by Dorling Kindersley Limited

A catalog record for this book
is available from the Library of Congress.

DK books are available at special discounts when purchased
in bulk for sales promotions, premiums, fund-raising,
or educational use.
For details, contact: DK Publishing Special Markets,
1745 Broadway, 20th Floor, New York, NY 10019
SpecialSales@dk.com

ISBN 978-0-5939-6346-3

**The corresponding free audio is available for a period
of at least 5 years from publication of this edition.**

Printed and bound in China

www.dk.com

MIX
Paper | Supporting
responsible forestry
FSC™ C018179

This book was made with Forest
Stewardship Council™ certified
paper — one small step in DK's
commitment to a sustainable future.
Learn more at
www.dk.com/uk/information/sustainability

목차
mogcha
contents

사람 saram • people

외모 waemo appearance

건강 geongang health

가정 gajeong • home

서비스 seobiseu services

쇼핑 shoping shopping

식품 sikpoom • food

외식 waesik eating out

이 사전에 대하여

입증된 이론에 의하면, 그림(사진)은 정보 이해와 기억에 도움이 됩니다. 이러한 원칙에 따라, 저희는 본 영한 시각 사전에 상세한 그림 및 사진과 광범위하고 유용한 단어을 포함했습니다.

이 사전은 주제별로 구분되어 있고 일상생활에 쓰이는 거의 모든 단어를 찾을 수 있습니다. 또한 대화에서 활용할 수 있고 어휘를 늘리기 위한 단어 및 문구를 추가적으로 포함했습니다.

이 사전은 언어에 관심이 있는 사람들을 위해 준비되었으며, 실용적이고, 고무적이며 사용하기 쉽게 디자인된 필수 도구입니다.

언어 관련 참고사항

이 사전에서 한국어는 대한민국(남한) 및 조선민주주의인민공화국(북한)의 공식 표기 체계인 한글로 표시되었습니다.

발음은 표준말의 원칙을 따랐으며, 한글의 영어 표기는 최근에 가장 많이 이용되는 로마자로 표기했습니다.

각 항목은 한국어, 한국어 로마자 표기, 영어순으로 일관적으로 제시됩니다.

안전 벨트
anjeon belteu
seat belt

점심
jeomsim
lunch

동사는 영어 단어 옆에 (v) 로 표시되고 있습니다. 예를 들어서,

수확하다 soohwakhada **I harvest (v)**

영어와 한국어의 색인은 이 사전의 끝 부분에서 찾을 수 있습니다. 색인에서 영어 또는 한국어 로마자 표기로 단어를 찾을 수 있으며, 해당 단어가 등장하는 페이지가 각 단어 옆에 제시되고 있습니다. 특정 단어에 대한 한국어 표현을 확인하기 위해, 한국어 로마자 표기 또는 영어 색인을 찾아 보고 관련 페이지로 이동하시면 됩니다.

이 사전의 활용 방법

사업, 취미, 여행을 위해 새로운 언어를 배우거나, 이미 잘 알고 있는 언어의 단어 실력을 향상시키고 싶은 사람들 모두가 다양한 방법으로 활용할 수 있는 이 사전은 매우 가치 있는 학습 도구로 자리매김할 것입니다.

새로운 언어를 배울 때, 어원(다른 언어들에 존재하는 유사 단어) 및 파생어(특정 언어에서 같은 어원에서 파생한 단어)를 찾으십시오. 또한, 여러분들은 어떤 상황에서 여러 언어들이 서로에게 영향을 주는지 이해할 수 있습니다. 예를 들어, 음식에 대한 영어 단어 중에는 한국어의 영향을 받은 것들이 있습니다. 또한 테크놀로지 및 대중 문화에 대한 영어 단어를 다른 언어에서 채택하기도 합니다.

실용적인 학습 활동

• 집, 직장 또는 대학에 있을 때 해당 환경과 관련한 표현을 이 사전에서 찾아보세요. 그리고, 사전을 닫고 주변을 둘러보면서 몇 개의 대상 및 특징들에 대한 표현을 기억할 수 있는지 스스로 시험해 보세요.

• 단어 카드를 준비하세요. 카드의 각 면에 한국어와 영어 뜻을 쓰세요. 이 카드들을 항상 소지하고, 시간이 날 때마다 본인의 언어 실력을 시험해 보세요. 카드들의 차례를 자주 섞는 것을 잊지 마세요.

• 특정 페이지에 있는 단어들을 최대한 많이 사용해서 편지, 이야기, 또는 대화를 써 보세요. 이런 방법을 통해 단어 및 철자의 암기력을 향상시킬 수 있습니다. 더 긴 글을 쓰고 싶다면, 한 문단에 2~3개의 단어를 한꺼번에 사용해 보세요.

• 시각적 암기력을 가지고 있다면, 이 사전에 있는 항목을 그림으로 그리고, 사전을 닫고 각 그림에 해당되는 표현을 그림 아래에 적어 보세요.

• 자신감이 더 생기면, 영어 색인목록에서 단어를 골라서, 해당 단어의 한국어 뜻을 생각하고, 이 단어가 나오는 관련 페이지에서 정답을 확인하세요.

무료 오디오 앱

DK Visual Dictionary 오디오 앱에는 이 사전에 있는 모든 단어 및 문구가 포함되어 있습니다. 각 단어 및 문구는 한국어 및 영어 원어민이 직접 발음함으로, 중요한 단어를 배우고 발음을 향상시키는 데 도움이 됩니다. 또한 시리즈의 다른 모든 책을 위한 오디오도 마련되어 있습니다.

오디오 앱 사용 방법

• 태블릿 또는 스마트폰을 이용하여 앱스토어에서 "DK Visual Dictionary" (영한 시각 사전)를 찾아 무료 앱을 다운로드하세요.

• 앱을 열고 책의 에디션을 선택하세요.

• "Choose your book(내 책 선택)" 메뉴에서 책을 선택하세요.

• 목록에서 챕터를 선택하거나 검색창에 페이지 번호를 입력하세요.

• 단어를 영어 알파벳순 또는 숫자 오름차순으로 정렬하세요.

• 목록을 위아래로 스크롤하여 원하는 단어 또는 문구를 찾으세요.

• 소리를 들으려면 단어를 탭하세요.

about the dictionary

The use of pictures is proven to aid understanding and the retention of information. Working on this principle, this highly illustrated English–Korean bilingual dictionary presents a large range of useful current vocabulary.

The dictionary is divided thematically and covers most aspects of the everyday world in detail. You will also find additional words and phrases for conversational use and for extending your vocabulary.

This is an essential reference tool for anyone interested in languages—practical, stimulating, and easy-to-use.

a note on Korean language

The Korean in the dictionary is presented in Hangul script, the official writing system of both the Republic of Korea (South Korea), and the Democratic People's Republic of Korea (North Korea). The pronunciation given follows standard Korean dialect, as spoken around Seoul, and is shown in Revised Romanization of Korean, the most common method of expressing Hangul characters in the English language. The entries are always presented in the same order—Korean, romanized Korean, English; for example:

안전 벨트
anjeon belteu
seat belt

점심
jeomsim
lunch

Verbs are indicated by a **(v)** after the English, for example:

수확하다 soohwakhada **I harvest (v)**

Each language also has its own index at the back of the book. Here you can look up a word in either English or romanized Korean and be referred to the page number(s) where it appears.

More on pronunciation
The pronunciation given in this book is for the Korean dialect which is taught in primary and secondary schools, used in news broadcasts, and most commonly heard in Seoul. Numerous systems for representing Korean in roman script have been developed over the past few decades, but the most recent and widely used has been adopted in this dictionary. Be aware that the pronunciation of native speakers will often vary from that given in the dictionary. The best way to perfect your pronunciation is to listen to the spoken Korean on the app and copy the pronunciation.

Some Korean sounds cannot be fully expressed by romanization. A common one is the "ui" sound, found in words such as:

의사	의자
uisa	uija
doctor	**chair**

This sound is very close to an "e" or "ee" sound in English ("bl<u>ee</u>d," "m<u>e</u>dium," "to l<u>ea</u>d"), but equal emphasis is placed on the "u" and "i." Try to imagine you are saying "bleed," "medium," or "to lead," and then someone presses down hard on your stomach for the "ee" sound. If you feel discomfort trying to pronounce such words, then you are probably doing it correctly! Listen to how these words sound on the app, and practice making the sound.

free audio app

The DK Visual Dictionary audio app contains all the words and phrases in the book, spoken by native speakers in both Korean and English, making it easier to learn important vocabulary and improve your pronunciation. Audio is also available for all other books in the series.

how to use the audio app

• Search for "DK Visual Dictionary" in your chosen app store and download the free app on your smartphone or tablet.
• Open the app and select your edition of the book.
• Select your book from the "Choose your book" menu.
• Select a chapter from the contents list or enter a page number in the search bar.
• Sort the words A–Z in Korean or English.
• Scroll up or down through the list to find a word or phrase.
• Tap a word to hear it.

사람 saram
people

신체 sinchae · **body**

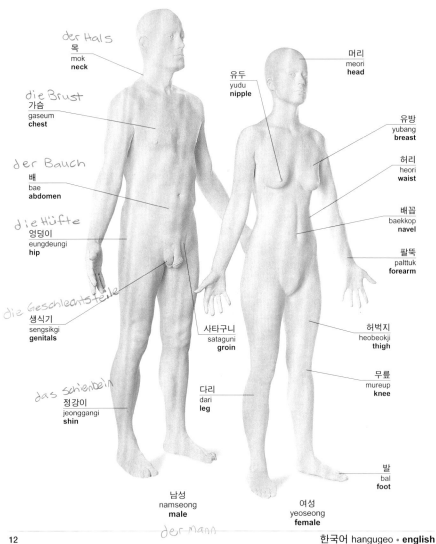

der Hals
목
mok
neck

die Brust
가슴
gaseum
chest

der Bauch
배
bae
abdomen

die Hüfte
엉덩이
eungdeungi
hip

die Geschlechtsteile
생식기
sengsikgi
genitals

das Schienbein
정강이
jeonggangi
shin

유두
yudu
nipple

머리
meori
head

유방
yubang
breast

허리
heori
waist

배꼽
baekkop
navel

팔뚝
palttuk
forearm

사타구니
sataguni
groin

다리
dari
leg

허벅지
heobeokji
thigh

무릎
mureup
knee

발
bal
foot

남성
namseong
male

der Mann

여성
yeoseong
female

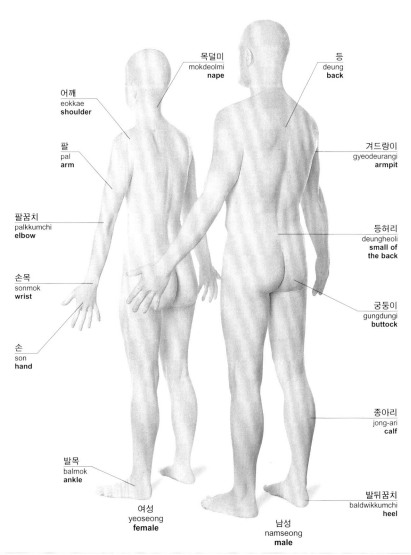

목덜미
mokdeolmi
nape

등
deung
back

어깨
eokkae
shoulder

겨드랑이
gyeodeurangi
armpit

팔
pal
arm

팔꿈치
palkkumchi
elbow

등허리
deungheoli
**small of
the back**

손목
sonmok
wrist

궁둥이
gungdungi
buttock

손
son
hand

종아리
jong-ari
calf

발목
balmok
ankle

발뒤꿈치
baldwikkumchi
heel

여성
yeoseong
female

남성
namseong
male

얼굴 eolgul · **face**

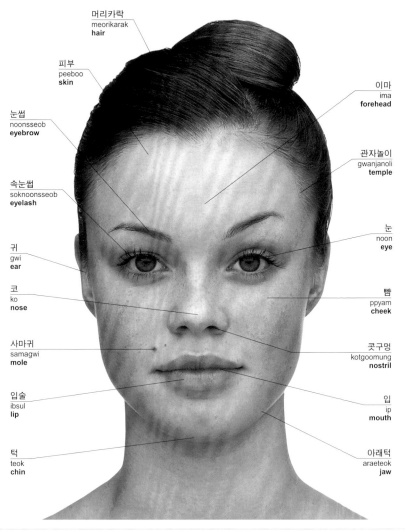

머리카락
meorikarak
hair

피부
peeboo
skin

이마
ima
forehead

눈썹
noonsseob
eyebrow

관자놀이
gwanjanoli
temple

속눈썹
soknoonsseob
eyelash

눈
noon
eye

귀
gwi
ear

코
ko
nose

뺨
ppyam
cheek

사마귀
samagwi
mole

콧구멍
kotgoomung
nostril

입술
ibsul
lip

입
ip
mouth

턱
teok
chin

아래턱
araeteok
jaw

주름살
jureumsal
wrinkle

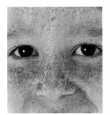

주근깨
joogeunkkae
freckle

모공
mogong
pore

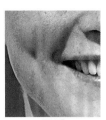

보조개
bojogae
dimple

손 son • **hand**

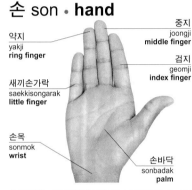

약지
yakji
ring finger

중지
joongji
middle finger

검지
geomji
index finger

새끼손가락
saekkisongarak
little finger

손목
sonmok
wrist

손바닥
sonbadak
palm

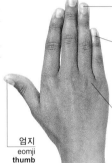

손톱
sontob
nail

각피
gakpi
cuticle

손가락 관절
songarak
gwanjeol
knuckle

엄지
eomji
thumb

주먹
joomeok
fist

발 bal • **foot**

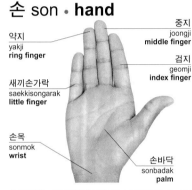

발등 안쪽
baldeung anjjok
instep

발가락
balgarak
toe

발뒤꿈치
baldwikkumchi
heel

발볼
balbol
ball

발바닥
balbadak
sole

발바닥 아치
balbadak achi
arch

엄지발가락
eomjibalgarak
big toe

발톱
baltob
toenail

새끼발가락
saekkibalgarak
little toe

발목
balmok
ankle

근육 geunyook · **muscles**

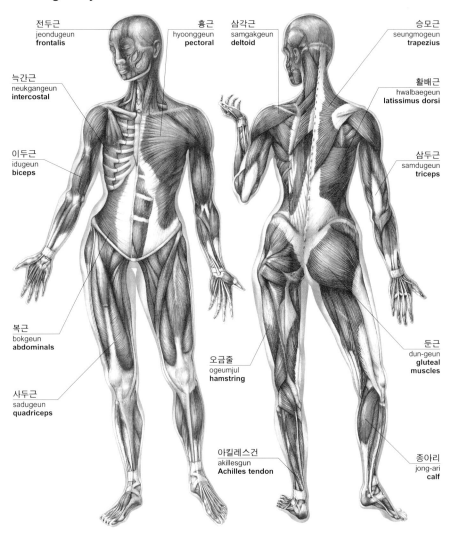

전두근
jeondugeun
frontalis

흉근
hyoonggeun
pectoral

삼각근
samgakgeun
deltoid

승모근
seungmogeun
trapezius

늑간근
neukgangeun
intercostal

활배근
hwalbaegeun
latissimus dorsi

이두근
idugeun
biceps

삼두근
samdugeun
triceps

복근
bokgeun
abdominals

오금줄
ogeumjul
hamstring

둔근
dun-geun
**gluteal
muscles**

사두근
sadugeun
quadriceps

아킬레스건
akillesgun
Achilles tendon

종아리
jong-ari
calf

골격 golgyeok • **skeleton**

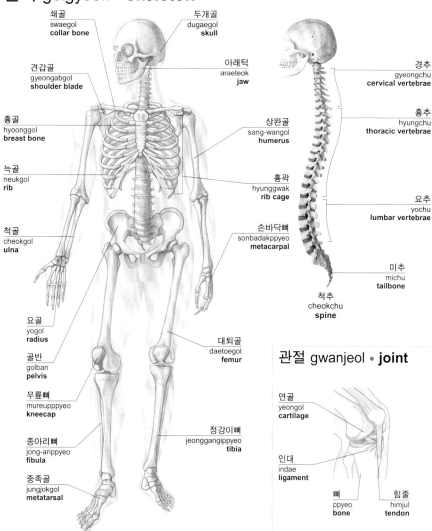

쇄골
swaegol
collar bone

두개골
dugaegol
skull

견갑골
gyeongabgol
shoulder blade

아래턱
araeteok
jaw

흉골
hyoonggol
breast bone

상완골
sang-wangol
humerus

늑골
neukgol
rib

흉곽
hyunggwak
rib cage

척골
cheokgol
ulna

손바닥뼈
sonbadakppyeo
metacarpal

요골
yogol
radius

골반
golban
pelvis

무릎뼈
mureupppyeo
kneecap

대퇴골
daetoegol
femur

종아리뼈
jong-arippyeo
fibula

정강이뼈
jeonggangippyeo
tibia

중족골
jungjokgol
metatarsal

경추
gyeongchu
cervical vertebrae

흉추
hyungchu
thoracic vertebrae

요추
yochu
lumbar vertebrae

미추
michu
tailbone

척추
cheokchu
spine

관절 gwanjeol • **joint**

연골
yeongol
cartilage

인대
indae
ligament

뼈
ppyeo
bone

힘줄
himjul
tendon

장기 jang-gi · **internal organs**

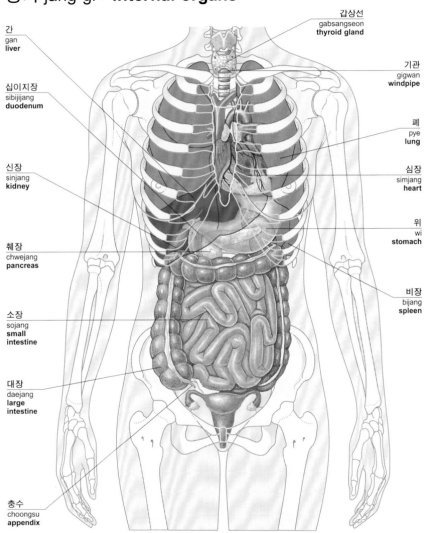

갑상선
gabsangseon
thyroid gland

간
gan
liver

십이지장
sibijijang
duodenum

신장
sinjang
kidney

췌장
chwejang
pancreas

소장
sojang
small intestine

대장
daejang
large intestine

충수
choongsu
appendix

기관
gigwan
windpipe

폐
pye
lung

심장
simjang
heart

위
wi
stomach

비장
bijang
spleen

머리 meori • **head**

뇌
noe
brain

부비강
bubigang
sinus

구개
googae
palate

인두
indu
pharynx

혀
hyeo
tongue

후두
hoodu
larynx

후두개
hudugae
epiglottis

울대뼈
uldaeppyeo
Adam's apple

식도
sikdo
esophagus

성대
seongdae
vocal cords

목구멍
mokgumeong
throat

신체 계통 sinche gyetong • **body systems**

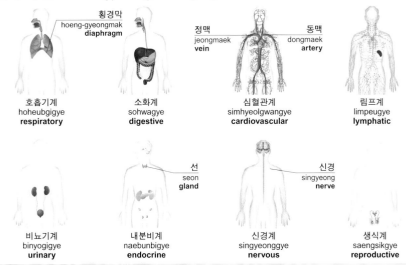

횡경막
hoeng-gyeongmak
diaphragm

정맥
jeongmaek
vein

동맥
dongmaek
artery

호흡기계
hoheubgigye
respiratory

소화계
sohwagye
digestive

심혈관계
simhyeolgwangye
cardiovascular

림프계
limpeugye
lymphatic

선
seon
gland

신경
singyeong
nerve

비뇨기계
binyogigye
urinary

내분비계
naebunbigye
endocrine

신경계
singyeonggye
nervous

생식계
saengsikgye
reproductive

생식 기관 saengsig gigwan • **reproductive organs**

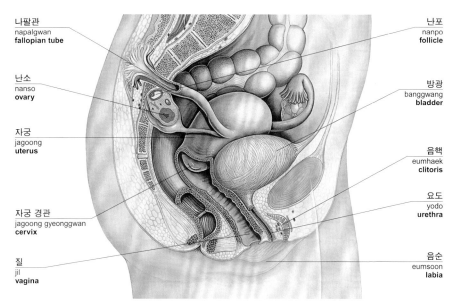

나팔관
napalgwan
fallopian tube

난소
nanso
ovary

자궁
jagoong
uterus

자궁 경관
jagoong gyeonggwan
cervix

질
jil
vagina

난포
nanpo
follicle

방광
banggwang
bladder

음핵
eumhaek
clitoris

요도
yodo
urethra

음순
eumsoon
labia

여성 yeoseong | **female**

생식 saengsik
reproduction

정자°
jeongja
sperm

난자
nanja
egg

수정 sujeong
fertilization

어휘 eohwi • **vocabulary**

가임(의) gaim(ui) **fertile**	월경 wolgyeong **menstruation**	호르몬 horeumon **hormone**
불임(의) bul-im(ui) **infertile**	배란 baeran **ovulation**	발기부전 balgi bujeon **impotent**
성교 seonggyo **intercourse**	임신하다 imsinhada **conceive (v)**	성매개감염병 seongmaegaegamyeombyeong **sexually transmitted infection**

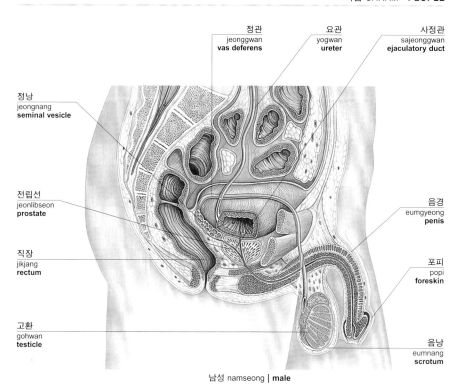

정관
jeonggwan
vas deferens

요관
yogwan
ureter

사정관
sajeonggwan
ejaculatory duct

정낭
jeongnang
seminal vesicle

전립선
jeonlibseon
prostate

직장
jikjang
rectum

고환
gohwan
testicle

음경
eumgyeong
penis

포피
popi
foreskin

음낭
eumnang
scrotum

남성 namseong | **male**

피임 peeim • **contraception**

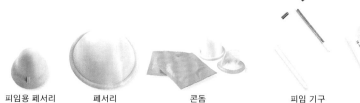

피임용 페서리
peeim-yong
peseori
cervical cap

페서리
peseori
diaphragm

콘돔
kondom
condom

피임 기구
peeim gigu
IUD

피임약
peeimyak
pill

가족 gajok • **family**

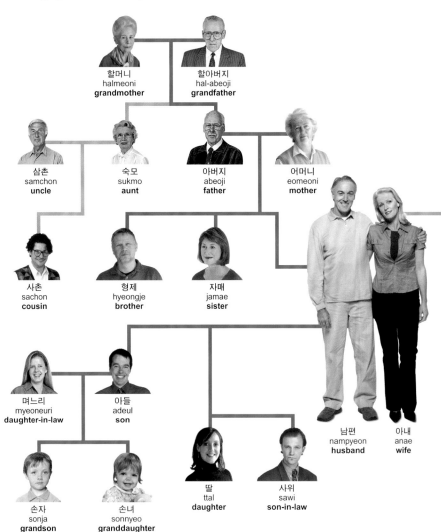

할머니
halmeoni
grandmother

할아버지
hal-abeoji
grandfather

삼촌
samchon
uncle

숙모
sukmo
aunt

아버지
abeoji
father

어머니
eomeoni
mother

사촌
sachon
cousin

형제
hyeongje
brother

자매
jamae
sister

며느리
myeoneuri
daughter-in-law

아들
adeul
son

남편
nampyeon
husband

아내
anae
wife

손자
sonja
grandson

손녀
sonnyeo
granddaughter

딸
ttal
daughter

사위
sawi
son-in-law

어휘 eohwi • **vocabulary**

친척 chincheok **relatives**	부모님 bumonim **parents**	조부모 jobumo **grandparents**	계부 gyebu **stepfather**	의붓아들 uibut-adeul **stepson**	쌍둥이 ssangdungi **twins**
세대 sedae **generation**	자녀 janyeo **children**	손주 sonju **grandchildren**	계모 gyemo **stepmother**	의붓딸 uibuttal **stepdaughter**	동거인 donggeoin **partner**

단계 dangye • **stages**

아기
agi
baby

어린이
eorini
child

배우자의 어머니
baeujaui eomeoni
mother-in-law

배우자의 아버지
baeujaui abeoji
father-in-law

배우자의 남자 형제
baeujaui namja
hyeongje
brother-in-law

배우자의 여자 형제
baeujaui yeoja
hyeongje
sister-in-law

남자아이
namjaai
boy

여자아이
yeojaai
girl

여조카
yeojoka
niece

남조카
namjoka
nephew

(기혼녀) 씨
(gihonnyeo) ssi
Mrs. / Ms.

청소년
cheongsonyeon
teenager

성인
seong-in
adult

호칭 hoching **titles**

(남자) 씨
(namja) ssi
Mr.

(여자) 씨
(yeoja) ssi
Miss

남자
namja
man

여자
yeoja
woman

대인 관계 daein gwangye • **relationships**

상사
sangsa
manager

비서
biseo
assistant

임원
imwon
business partner

직원
jik-won
employee

고용주
goyongju
employer

동료
dongryo
colleague

사무실 samusil | **office**

이웃
iut
neighbor

친구
chingu
friend

지인
jiin
acquaintance

펜팔
penpal
pen pal

남자친구
namjachingu
boyfriend

여자친구
yeojachingu
girlfriend

약혼자
yakhonnam
fiancé

약혼녀
yakhonnyeo
fiancée

커플 keopeul | **couple**

약혼한 커플 yakhonhan keopeul | **engaged couple**

감정 gamjeong · **emotions**

미소
miso
smile

행복한
haengbokhan
happy

슬픈
seulpeun
sad

흥분한
heungboonhan
excited

심심한
simsimhan
bored

놀란
nollan
surprised

겁먹은
geobmeogeun
scared

찌푸림
jjipurim
frown

화난
hwanan
angry

혼란스러운
honlanseureoun
confused

걱정스러운
geogjeongseureoun
worried

초조해하는
chojohaehaneun
nervous

자랑스러운
jarangseureoun
proud

자신만만한
jasinmanmanhan
confident

창피한
changpihan
embarrassed

수줍어하는
sujubeohaneun
shy

어휘 eohwi · **vocabulary**

속상한 soksanghan **upset**	웃다 utda **laugh (v)**	소리 지르다 sori jireuda **shout (v)**	기절하다 gijeolhada **faint (v)**
충격을 받은 chunggyeok- eul bat-eun **shocked**	울다 ulda **cry (v)**	한숨짓다 hansumjitda **sigh (v)**	하품하다 hapumhada **yawn (v)**

인생 중대사 insaeng jungdaesa • **life events**

태어나다
taeeonada
be born (v)

취학하다
chwihakhada
start school (v)

친구를 사귀다
chinguleul sagwida
make friends (v)

졸업하다
jol-eobhada
graduate (v)

취직하다
chwijighada
get a job (v)

사랑에 빠지다
sarang-e ppajida
fall in love (v)

결혼하다
gyeolhonhada
get married (v)

아이를 낳다
aileul natda
have a baby (v)

결혼 gyeolhon | **wedding**

어휘 eohwi • **vocabulary**

결혼 피로연
gyeolhon piroyeon
wedding reception

기념일
ginyeom-il
anniversary

신혼여행
sinhon-yeohaeng
honeymoon

이민 가다
imin gada
emigrate (v)

세례
serye
christening

은퇴하다
euntoehada
retire (v)

출생 증명서
choolsaeng
jeungmyeongseo
birth certificate

유언장을 작성하다
yueonjang-eul
jakseonghada
make a will (v)

바르미츠바 의식
bareumicheuba uisik
bar mitzvah

죽다
jookda
die (v)

이혼
ihon
divorce

장례
janglye
funeral

축하 chukha • **celebrations**

축제 chukje
festivals

카드
kadeu
card

생일 파티
saeng-il pati
birthday party

선물
seonmul
present

생일
saeng-il
birthday

성탄절
seongtanjeol
Christmas

유월절
yuwoljeol
Passover

새해
saehae
New Year

카니발
kanibal
carnival

행진
haengjin
procession

이드
ideu
Eid

리본
libon
ribbon

추수 감사절
chusu gamsajeol
Thanksgiving

부활절
buhwaljeol
Easter

핼러윈
haelleowin
Halloween

디왈리
diwalli
Diwali

외모 waemo
appearance

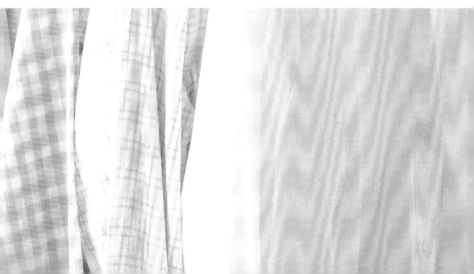

아동복 adongbog · **children's clothing**

아기 agi · **baby**

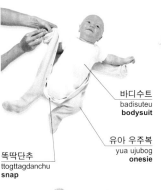

방한복
banghanbok
snowsuit

바디수트
badisuteu
bodysuit

유아 우주복
yua ujubog
onesie

똑딱단추
ttogttagdanchu
snap

잠옷
jam-ot
sleeper

롬퍼
lompeo
romper

턱받이
teokbagee
bib

벙어리장갑
beong-eori janggab
mittens

아기 신발
agi shinbal
booties

천 기저귀
cheon gijeogwi
cloth diaper

일회용 기저귀
ilhoeyong gijeogwi
disposable diaper

방수 팬티
bangsu paenti
plastic pants

유아 yua · **toddler**

챙모자
chaengmoja
sun hat

턱받이
teokbat-i
apron

멜빵바지
melppangbaji
overalls

티셔츠
teesheocheu
T-shirt

반바지
banbaji
shorts

치마
chima
skirt

아동 adong • **child**

원피스
wonpiseu
dress

후드
hoodeu
hood

청바지
cheongbaji
jeans

샌들
saendeul
sandals

배낭
baenang
backpack

토글
togeul
toggle

스카프
seukapeu
scarf

파카
paka
parka

고무장화
gomujanghwa
rain boots

여름
yeoreum
summer

비옷
biot
raincoat

가을
ga-eul
fall

더플 코트
deopeul koteu
duffel coat

겨울
gyeowool
winter

실내 가운
silnae gaun
robe

로고
logo
logo

운동화
undonghwa
**athletic
shoes**

잠옷
jam-ot
nightgown

슬리퍼
seullipeo
slippers

잠옷류
jam-otryu
nightwear

축구복
chookgubog
soccer uniform

운동복
undongbok
tracksuit

레깅스
legingseu
leggings

어휘 eohwi • **vocabulary**

천연 섬유
cheon-yeon seom-yoo
natural fiber

합성
habseong
synthetic

세탁기로 빨 수 있나요?
setakgiro ppal su itnayo?
Is it machine washable?

이 옷이 2살짜리 아이에게 맞을까요?
i osi doosaljjari aiege majeulkkayo?
Will this fit a two-year-old?

옷 ot · **clothes (1)**

칼라
kalla
collar

넥타이
nektai
tie

벨트
belteu
belt

라펠
lapel
lapel

단춧구멍
danchutgumeong
buttonhole

소맷단
somaetdan
cuff

주머니
jumeoni
pocket

재킷
jaekit
jacket

바지
baji
pants

단추
danchu
button

정장
jeongjang
business suit

레인코트
leinkoteu
raincoat

안감
angam
lining

가죽구두
gajookgoodu
**leather
shoes**

어휘 eohwi · **vocabulary**

짧은 jjalbeun **short**	실내 가운 silnae gaun **dressing gown**	코트 koteu **coat**	운동복 undongbok **tracksuit**
긴 gin **long**	속옷 sok-ot **underwear**	카디건 kadigeon **cardigan**	

이 옷 더 큰/더 작은 사이즈가
있어요?
i ot deo keun / deo jageun
saijeuga isseoyo?
**Do you have this in a larger /
smaller size?**

이 옷 입어 봐도 돼요?
i ot ib-eo bwado dwaeyo?
May I try this on?

블레이저
beulleijeo
blazer

스포츠 재킷
seupocheu jaekit
sport coat

조끼
jokki
vest

브이넥
beu-inek
V-neck

라운드넥
laundeunek
crew neck

티셔츠
teesheocheu
T-shirt

파카
paka
parka

운동복 상의
undongbok sang-ui
sweatshirt

셔츠
sheocheu
shirt

청바지
cheongbaji
jeans

스웨터
seuweiteo
sweater

파자마
pajama
pajamas

민소매 셔츠
minsomae sheocheu
undershirt

평상복
pyeongsangbok
casual wear

반바지
banbaji
shorts

팬티
paenti
briefs

사각 팬티
sagak paenti
boxer shorts

양말
yangmal
socks

옷 ot • **clothes (2)**

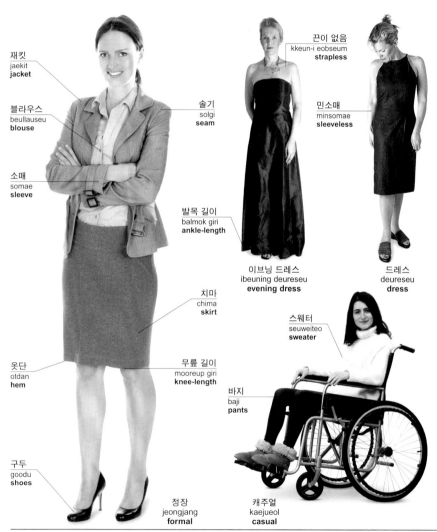

재킷
jaekit
jacket

블라우스
beullauseu
blouse

소매
somae
sleeve

옷단
otdan
hem

구두
goodu
shoes

솔기
solgi
seam

발목 길이
balmok giri
ankle-length

치마
chima
skirt

무릎 길이
mooreup giri
knee-length

정장
jeongjang
formal

끈이 없음
kkeun-i eobseum
strapless

민소매
minsomae
sleeveless

이브닝 드레스
ibeuning deureseu
evening dress

드레스
deureseu
dress

스웨터
seuweiteo
sweater

바지
baji
pants

캐주얼
kaejueol
casual

란제리 lanjeri · **lingerie**

결혼 gyeolhon · **wedding**

실내 가운
silnae gaun
robe

슬립
seullib
slip

끈
kkeun
strap

캐미솔
kaemisol
camisole

부케
buke
bouquet

바스크 속옷
baseukeu sog-ot
bustier

멜빵
melppang
garter straps

스타킹
seutaking
stocking

타이츠
taicheu
panty hose

웨딩 드레스
weding deureseu
wedding dress

어휘 eohwi · **vocabulary**

코르셋 koreuset **corset**	맞춤복 matchumbok **tailored**
가터 gateo **garter**	어깨 패드 eokkae pad **shoulder pad**
레이스 leiseu **lace**	허리 밴드 heori baendeu **waistband**
면사포 myeonsapo **veil**	와이어 보정 waieo bojeong **underwire**
홀터넥 holteonek **halter neck**	스포츠 브라 seupocheu beura **sports bra**

브라
beura
bra

팬티
paenti
panties

나이트 드레스
naiteu deulesseu
nightgown

액세서리 aekseseori · **accessories**

버클
beokeul
buckle

손잡이
sonjabi
handle

캡 모자
kaeb moja
cap

모자
moja
hat

스카프
seukapeu
scarf

벨트
belteu
belt

끝부분
kkeutbubun
tip

손수건
sonsugeon
handkerchief

나비 넥타이
nabi nektai
bow tie

넥타이핀
nektaipin
tiepin

장갑
janggab
gloves

우산
usan
umbrella

보석류 boseok-ryu · **jewelry**

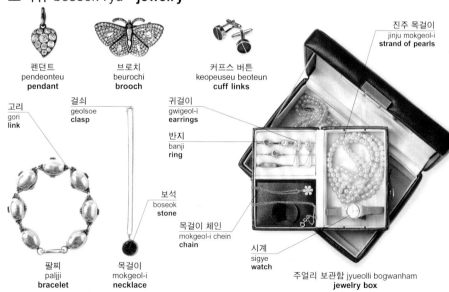

진주 목걸이
jinju mokgeol-i
strand of pearls

펜던트
pendeonteu
pendant

브로치
beurochi
brooch

커프스 버튼
keopeuseu beoteun
cuff links

고리
gori
link

걸쇠
geolsoe
clasp

귀걸이
gwigeol-i
earrings

반지
banji
ring

보석
boseok
stone

목걸이 체인
mokgeol-i chein
chain

시계
sigye
watch

팔찌
paljji
bracelet

목걸이
mokgeol-i
necklace

주얼리 보관함 jyueolli bogwanham
jewelry box

가방류 gabangryu • **bags**

지갑
jigab
wallet

동전 지갑
dongjeon jigab
change purse

숄더백
syoldeobaeg
shoulder bag

잠금 고리
jamgeum gori
clasp

어깨끈
eokkaekkeun
shoulder strap

손잡이
sonjabi
handles

여행용 가방
yeohaeng-yong gabang
duffel bag

서류가방
seoryugabang
briefcase

핸드백
haendeubaeg
handbag

배낭
baenang
backpack

구두 goodu • **shoes**

신발끈 구멍
sinbalkkeun
gumeong
eyelet

신발끈
sinbalkkeun
lace

신발 혀
sinbal hyeo
tongue

신발창
sinbalchang
sole

레이스업 슈즈
leiseu-eob syujeu
lace-up

발뒤꿈치
baldwikkumchi
heel

부츠
bucheu
boot

등산화
deungsanhwa
hiking boot

운동화
undonghwa
sneaker

조리
jori
flip-flop

브로그화
beurogeuhwa
dress shoe

하이힐
haihil
high-heeled shoe

웨지힐
wejihil
wedge

샌들
saendeul
sandal

슬립온
seullip-on
slip-on

펌프스
peompeuseu
flat

머리카락 meorikarak · **hair**

빗
bit
comb

빗다
bitda | **comb (v)**

미용사
miyongsa
hairdresser

세면대
semyeondae
sink

고객
gogaek
client

솔
sol
brush

빗질하다 bitjil-hada
brush (v)

감다 gamda | **wash (v)**

가운
gaun
robe

헹구다
hengguda
rinse (v)

커트하다
keoteuhada
cut (v)

머리를 말리다
meorireul mallida
blow-dry (v)

머리를 세팅하다
meorireul setinghada
set (v)

액세서리 aekseseori · **accessories**

헤어 드라이기
heeo deuraigi
blow-dryer

샴푸
shyampoo
shampoo

컨디셔너
keondishyeoneo
conditioner

젤
jel
gel

헤어스프레이
heeoseupeurei
hairspray

웨이브 고데기
weibeu godegi
curling iron

가위
gawi
scissors

머리띠
meoritti
headband

스트레이트 고데기
seuteureiteu godegi
hair straightener

머리핀
meoripin
bobby pins

스타일 seutail • **styles**

묶은 머리
mook-eun meori
ponytail

땋은 머리
ttah-eun meori
braid

올림머리
ollimmeori
French twist

쪽진 머리
jjogjin meori
bun

갈래머리
gallaemeori
pigtails

단발머리
danbalmeori
bob

크롭컷
keurobkeot
short haircut

곱슬머리
gobseulmeori
curly

파마머리
pamameori
perm

생머리
saengmeori
straight

모근
mogeun
roots

부분 염색
bubun yeomsaek
highlights

대머리
daemeori
bald

가발
gabal
wig

어휘 eohwi • **vocabulary**

두피 dupi **scalp**	이발사 ibalsa **barber**
지성 jiseong **greasy**	머리를 다듬다 meorireul dadeumda **trim (v)**
건성 geonseong **dry**	웨이브를 펴다 weibeureul pyeoda **straighten (v)**
중성 jungseong **normal**	턱수염 teoksuyeom **beard**
비듬 bideum **dandruff**	콧수염 kotsuyeom **mustache**
손상된 머리카락 sonsangdoen meorikarag **split ends**	머리끈 meorikkeun **hairband**

색깔 saegkkal • **colors**

금발
geumbal
blond / blonde

갈색
galsaek
brunette

적갈색
jeoggalsaek
auburn

황갈색
hwang-galsaek
red

검정색
geomjeongsaek
black

회색
hoeisaek
gray

흰색
huinsaek
white

염색
yeomsaeg
dyed

미용 miyong · **beauty**

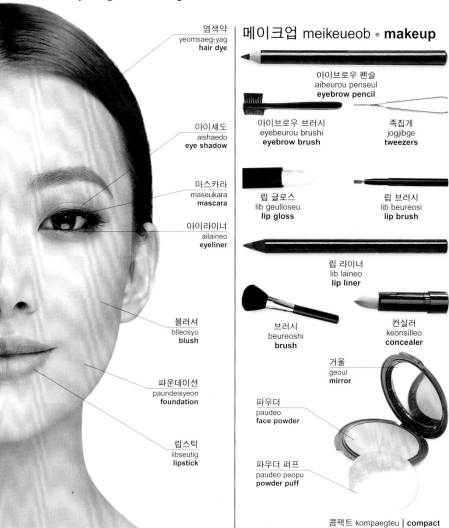

염색약
yeomsaeg-yag
hair dye

아이섀도
aishaedo
eye shadow

마스카라
maseukara
mascara

아이라이너
ailaineo
eyeliner

블러셔
blleosyo
blush

파운데이션
paundeisyeon
foundation

립스틱
libseutig
lipstick

메이크업 meikeueob · **makeup**

아이브로우 펜슬
aibeurou penseul
eyebrow pencil

아이브로우 브러시
eyebeurou brushi
eyebrow brush

족집게
jogjibge
tweezers

립 글로스
lib geulloseu
lip gloss

립 브러시
lib beureosi
lip brush

립 라이너
lib laineo
lip liner

브러시
beureoshi
brush

컨실러
keonsilleo
concealer

거울
geoul
mirror

파우더
paudeo
face powder

파우더 퍼프
paudeo peopu
powder puff

콤팩트 kompaegteu | compact

미용 관리 miyong gwanli
beauty treatments

마스크팩
maseukeupaek
face mask

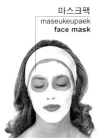

눈썹 정리
nunsseop jeongli
threading

각질을 제거하다
gakjireul jeogeohada
exfoliate (v)

얼굴
eolgul
facial

왁스
wakseu
wax

페디큐어
pedikyueo
pedicure

화장품 hwajangpum • **toiletries**

클렌저
keullenjeo
cleanser

토너
toneo
toner

로션
losyeon
moisturizer

태닝 크림
taening keurim
self-tanning lotion

향수
hyangsu
perfume

오드 뚜왈렛
odeu ttuwallet
eau de toilette

매니큐어 maenikyueo
manicure

매니큐어 제거제
maenikyueo jegeoje
nail polish remover

손톱줄
sontobjul
nail file

매니큐어
maenikyueo
nail polish

손톱가위
sontobgawi
nail scissors

손톱깎이
sontobkkakki
nail clippers

어휘 eohwi • **vocabulary**

안색(피부색)
ansaeg
(pibusaeg)
complexion

흰색 피부
huinsaeg pibu
fair

검은 피부
geom-eun pibu
dark

건성
geonseong
dry

지성
jiseong
oily

저자극성
jeojageukseong
hypoallergenic

민감성
mingamseong
sensitive

음영화장
eumyeonghwajang
shade

그을린 피부
geueullin pibu
tan

문신
munsin
tattoo

주름살 방지
jooreumsal
bangji
antiwrinkle

코코아 버터
kokoa beoteo
cocoa butter

화장솜
hwajangseom
cotton balls

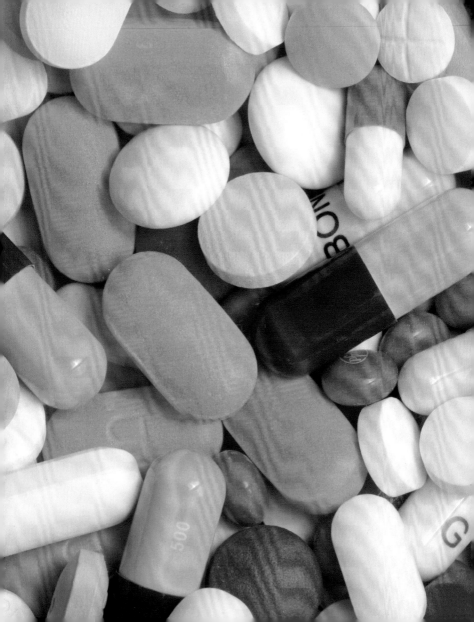

건강 geongang
health

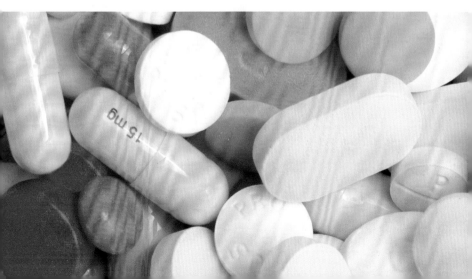

질병 jilbyeong • **illness**

열 yeol | **fever**

두통
dutong
headache

코피
kopi
nosebleed

기침
gichim
cough

재채기
jaechaegi
sneeze

감기
gamgi
cold

독감
dokgam
flu

흡입기
heubipgi
inhaler

천식
cheonsik
asthma

근육 경련
geun-yook gyeonglyeon
cramps

구역질
guyeokjil
nausea

수두
sudu
chicken pox

발진
baljin
rash

어휘 eohwi • **vocabulary**

오한 ohan **chill**	홍역 hong-yeok **measles**	편두통 pyeondutong **migraine**	알레르기 alleleugi **allergy**	심장 마비 simjang mabi **heart attack**	혈압 hyeol-ab **blood pressure**
바이러스 baireoseu **virus**	이하선염 ihaseonyeom **mumps**	복통 boktong **stomachache**	꽃가루 알레르기 kkotgaru allereugi **hay fever**	뇌졸중 neojoljeung **stroke**	기절하다 gijeolhada **faint (v)**
감염 gam-yeom **infection**	습진 seupjin **eczema**	설사 seolsa **diarrhea**	당뇨병 dangnyobyeong **diabetes**	간질 ganjil **epilepsy**	토하다 tohada **vomit (v)**

의사 uisa · **doctor**

상담 sangdam · **consultation**

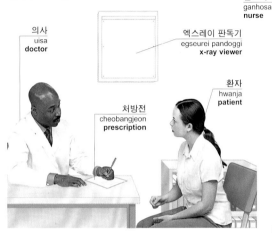

의사
uisa
doctor

엑스레이 판독기
egseurei pandoggi
x-ray viewer

처방전
cheobangjeon
prescription

환자
hwanja
patient

간호사
ganhosa
nurse

체중계
chejung-gye
scale

커프
keopeu
cuff

전자 혈압계
jeonja hyeol-abgye
electric blood pressure monitor

어휘 eohwi · **vocabulary**

수술
soosul
doctor's office

체온계
che-ongye
thermometer

대기실
daegisil
waiting room

보청기
bocheong-gi
hearing aid

예약
yeyak
appointment

예방 접종
yebang jeobjong
vaccination

진찰
jinchal
medical examination

진료를 받고 싶어요.
jinryo-leul batgo sipeoyo
I need to see a doctor.

여기가 아파요.
yeogiga apayo
It hurts here.

부상 busang · **injury**

염좌 yeomjwa | **sprain**

삼각 붕대
samgak
bungdae
sling

목 보조기
mog bojogi
neck brace

골절
goljeol
fracture

목뼈 부상
mogppyeo busang
whiplash

창상
changsang
cut

찰과상
chalgwasang
graze

타박상
tabaksang
bruise

가시
gashi
splinter

일광화상
ilgwanghwasang
sunburn

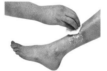

화상
hwasang
burn

교상
gyosang
bite

벌침 쏘임
beolchim ssoim
sting

어휘 eohwi · **vocabulary**

사고 sago **accident**	물집 mooljib **blister**	머리 부상 meori busang **head injury**	그 사람 괜찮을까요? geu saram gwaenchan- eulkkayo? **Will he / she be all right?**
응급 eunggeub **emergency**	부상 busang **wound**	뇌진탕 noejintang **concussion**	어디가 아파요? eodiga apayo? **Where does it hurt?**
출혈 choolhyeol **hemorrhage**	중독 joongdok **poisoning**	감전 gamjeon **electric shock**	구급차를 불러 주세요. gugeubchareul bulleo juseyo **Please call an ambulance.**

응급 처치 eung-geub cheochi · **first aid**

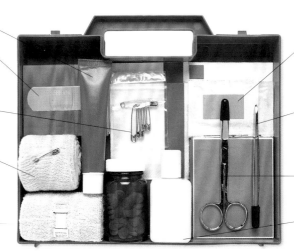

연고
yeongo
ointment

1회용 반창고
ilhoeyong
banchanggo
**adhesive
bandage**

안전핀
anjeonpin
safety pin

붕대
boongdae
bandage

진통제
jintongje
painkillers

항균 물티슈
hanggyun multishyu
antiseptic wipe

족집게
jogjibge
tweezers

가위
gawi
scissors

소독제
sodogje
antiseptic

구급 상자 googeub sangja | **first-aid kit**

거즈
geojeu
gauze

드레싱
deuresing
dressing

부목 boomog | **splint**

반창고
banchang-go
adhesive tape

심폐 소생법
simpye sosaengbeob
resuscitation

어휘 eohwi · **vocabulary**

쇼크 shokeu **shock**	맥박 maegbak **pulse**	질식하다 jilshikhada **choke (v)**
의식 불명 uisik bulmyeong **unconscious**	호흡 hoheub **breathing**	무균 mugyun **sterile**

도와 줄 수 있어요?
dowa jul soo isseoyo?
Can you help me?

응급 처치할 줄 아세요?
eung-geub cheochihal
jul asaeyo?
Do you know first aid?

병원 byeong-won · **hospital**

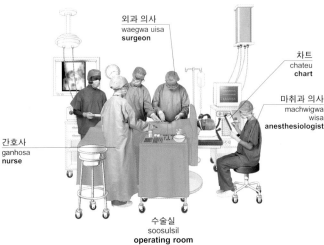

외과 의사
waegwa uisa
surgeon

차트
chateu
chart

마취과 의사
machwigwa
wisa
anesthesiologist

간호사
ganhosa
nurse

수술실
soosulsil
operating room

혈액 검사
hyeol-aeg geomsa
blood test

주사
jusa
injection

엑스레이
ekseurei
x-ray

스캔
seukaen
scan

이동침대
idongchimdae
gurney

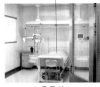

응급실
eunggeubsil
emergency room

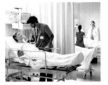

병동
byeongdong
ward

휠체어
hwilcheeo
wheelchair

어휘 eohwi · **vocabulary**

수술 soosul **operation**	입원하다 ibwonhada **admitted**	클리닉 keullinik **clinic**	산부인과 병실 sanbu-ingwa byeongsil **maternity ward**	개인실 gaeinshil **private room**
중환자실 joonghwanjasil **intensive care unit**	퇴원하다 toewonhada **discharged**	면회 시간 myeonhue sigan **visiting hours**	소아과 병실 soagwa byeongsil **children's ward**	외래 환자 waerae hwanja **outpatient**

진료과 jinryogua · **departments**

이비인후과
obimhugwa
ENT

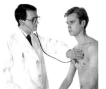

심장내과
simjangnaegwa
cardiology

정형외과
jeonghyeong-waegwa
orthopedics

부인과
buin-gwa
gynecology

물리치료과
mullichiryogwa
physiotherapy

피부과
piboogwa
dermatology

소아과
soagwa
pediatrics

방사선과
bangsaseongwa
radiology

수술
soosul
surgery

산부인과
sanbuin-gwa
maternity

정신과
jeongsin-gwa
psychiatry

안과
an-gwa
ophthalmology

어휘 eohwi · **vocabulary**

신경외과 singyeong-waegwa **neurology**	비뇨기과 binyogigwa **urology**	병리과 byeongree-gwa **pathology**	테스트 teseuteu **test**	의뢰 uiloe **referral**
종양과 jong-yang-gwa **oncology**	내분비과 naebunbigwa **endocrinology**	성형외과 seonghyeong-waegwa **plastic surgery**	결과 gyeolgwa **result**	전문의 jeonmun-ui **specialist**

치과 의사 chigwa uisa · **dentist**

치아 chia · **tooth**

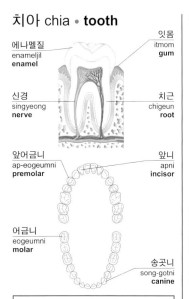

에나멜질
enameljil
enamel

잇몸
itmom
gum

신경
singyeong
nerve

치근
chigeun
root

앞어금니
ap-eogeumni
premolar

앞니
apni
incisor

어금니
eogeumni
molar

송곳니
song-gotni
canine

어휘 eohwi · **vocabulary**

치통 chitong **toothache**	베니어 beni-eo **veneer**
치석 chiseok **plaque**	크라운 keuraun **crown**
충치 choongchi **decay**	드릴 deuril **drill**
필링 pilling **filling**	치간 칫솔 chigan chitsol **interdental brush**
발치 balchi **extraction**	치실 chisil **dental floss**

체크업 chekeueob · **checkup**

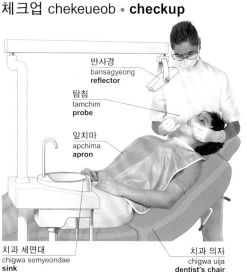

반사경
bansagyeong
reflector

탐침
tamchim
probe

앞치마
apchima
apron

치과 세면대
chigwa semyeondae
sink

치과 의자
chigwa uija
dentist's chair

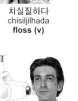

치실질하다
chisiljilhada
floss (v)

양치하다
yangchihada
brush (v)

치아 교정기
chia gyojeong-gi
braces

치과 엑스레이
chigwa ekseurei
dental x-ray

엑스레이 사진
ekseurei sajin
x-ray film

의치
uichi
dentures

안경사 angyeongsa · **optometrist**

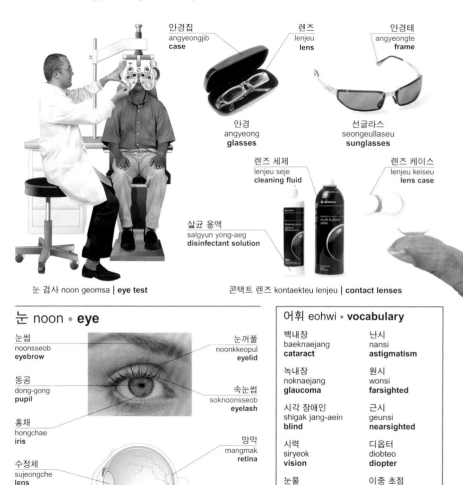

안경집
angyeongjib
case

렌즈
lenjeu
lens

안경테
angyeongte
frame

안경
angyeong
glasses

선글라스
seongeullaseu
sunglasses

렌즈 세제
lenjeu seje
cleaning fluid

렌즈 케이스
lenjeu keiseu
lens case

살균 용액
salgyun yong-aeg
disinfectant solution

눈 검사 noon geomsa | **eye test**

콘택트 렌즈 kontaekteu lenjeu | **contact lenses**

눈 noon · **eye**

눈썹
noonsseob
eyebrow

눈꺼풀
noonkkeopul
eyelid

동공
dong-gong
pupil

속눈썹
soknoonsseob
eyelash

홍채
hongchae
iris

망막
mangmak
retina

수정체
sujeongche
lens

시신경
sisingyeong
optic nerve

각막
gagmak
cornea

어휘 eohwi · **vocabulary**

백내장 baeknaejang **cataract**	난시 nansi **astigmatism**
녹내장 noknaejang **glaucoma**	원시 wonsi **farsighted**
시각 장애인 shigak jang-aein **blind**	근시 geunsi **nearsighted**
시력 siryeok **vision**	디옵터 diobteo **diopter**
눈물 noonmul **tear**	이중 초점 ijung chojeom **bifocal**

임신 imsin · **pregnancy**

스캔
seukaen
scan

임신 테스트
imsin teseuteu
pregnancy test

초음파 cho-eumpa | **ultrasound**

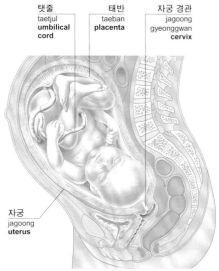

탯줄
taetjul
umbilical cord

태반
taeban
placenta

자궁 경관
jagoong gyeonggwan
cervix

자궁
jagoong
uterus

태아 tae-ah | **fetus**

어휘 eohwi · **vocabulary**

배란
baeran
ovulation

수태
sootae
conception

임신한
imsinhan
pregnant

출산을 앞둔
chulsan-eul apdun
expectant

출산 전
chulsan jeon
prenatal

임신 3개월
imsin sam-gaewol
trimester

배아
bae-ah
embryo

자궁
jagoong
womb

양수
yangsu
amniotic fluid

양수 천자
yangsu cheonja
amniocentesis

진통
jintong
contraction

자궁문이 열림
jagoongmun-i yeollim
dilation

무통주사
mootongjoosa
epidural

분만
bunman
delivery

출생
choolsaeng
birth

유산
yoosan
miscarriage

조산
josan
premature

수유하다
suyuhada
bottle-feed (v)

유아용 유동식
yuayong yudongshik
baby formula

외음 절개술
wae-eum jeolgaesul
episiotomy

봉합
bonghab
stitches

둔위 분만
dun-wi boonman
breech birth

제왕 절개
jewang jeolgae
cesarean section

부인과 의사
buin-gwa uisa
gynecologist

산부인과 의사
sanbuin-gwa uisa
obstetrician

양수가 터졌어요!
yangsuga teojeotseoyo!
My water broke!

출산 chulsan · **childbirth**

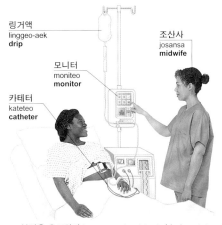

링거액
linggeo-aek
drip

모니터
moniteo
monitor

카테터
kateteo
catheter

조산사
josansa
midwife

분만을 유도하다 bunman-eul yudohada | **induce labor (v)**

인큐베이터 inkyubeiteo | **incubator**

출생 체중 choolsaeng chejoong
birth weight

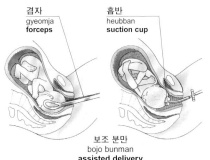

겸자
gyeomja
forceps

흡반
heubban
suction cup

보조 분만
bojo bunman
assisted delivery

식별표
sigbyeolpyo
identity tag

신생아 sinsaeng-ah | **newborn baby**

수유 suyu · **nursing**

유축기
yuchukgi
breast pump

수유 브라
suyu beura
nursing bra

모유 수유하다
moyu suyuhada
breastfeed (v)

수유 패드
suyupaedeu
nursing pads

보완요법 bowan-yobbeop
complementary therapies

요가 자세
yoga jase
yoga pose

마사지
masaji
massage

매트
maeteu
mat

지압 안마
jiab anma
shiatsu

요가 yoga | **yoga**

척추 교정술
cheogchu gyojeongsul
chiropractic

정골요법
jeong-gol-yobeob
osteopathy

반사요법
bansayobeob
reflexology

명상
myeongsang
meditation

상담사
sangdamsa
counselor

집단 치료
jibdan chiryo
group therapy

기 치료
gi chiryo
reiki

침술
chimsul
acupuncture

아유르베다
ayureumeda
ayurveda

최면술
choemyeonsul
hypnotherapy

아로마 오일
aroma oil
essential oils

약초 치료
yakcho chiryo
herbalism

아로마 테라피
aroma taerapi
aromatherapy

동종 요법
dongjong yobeob
homeopathy

지압
jiab
acupressure

테라피스트
terapiseuteu
therapist

심리 치료법
simli chiryobeob
psychotherapy

어휘 eohwi • **vocabulary**

수치료법 suchiryobeob **hydrotherapy**	휴식 hyoosik **relaxation**	한방 hanbang **herbal**	풍수 poongsu **feng shui**
자연 치료법 jayeon chiryobeob **naturopathy**	스트레스 seuteureseu **stress**	영양제 yeong-yangje **supplement**	수정 치료법 sujeong chiryobeob **crystal healing**

가정 gajeong
home

집 jib • **house**

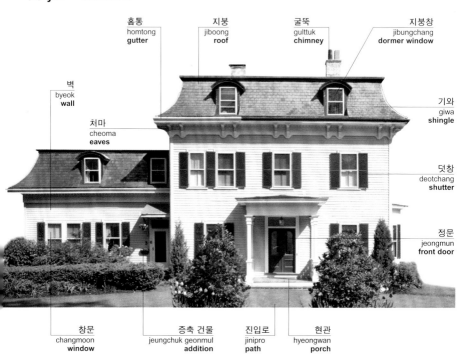

홈통
homtong
gutter

지붕
jiboong
roof

굴뚝
gulttuk
chimney

지붕창
jibungchang
dormer window

벽
byeok
wall

기와
giwa
shingle

처마
cheoma
eaves

덧창
deotchang
shutter

정문
jeongmun
front door

창문
changmoon
window

증축 건물
jeungchuk geonmul
addition

진입로
jinipro
path

현관
hyeongwan
porch

어휘 eohwi • **vocabulary**

타운하우스 taunhauseu **townhouse**	방갈로 bang-gallo **bungalow**	현관등 hyeongwandeung **porch light**	집주인 jibju-in **landlord**	세입자 seibja **tenant**	편지함 pochtoviy pyeonjiham **mailbox**
단독주택 dandogjootaek **single-family**	테라스 주택 teraseu jutaek **row house**	지하실 jihasil **basement**	방 bang **room**	임대료 imdaeryo **rent**	마당 madang **courtyard**
듀플렉스 dyupeullegseu **duplex**	차고 chago **garage**	다락 darak **attic**	층 cheung **floor**	임대하다 imdaehada **rent (v)**	도난 경보기 okhrannaya donan gyeongbogi **burglar alarm**

입구 ibgu • **entrance**

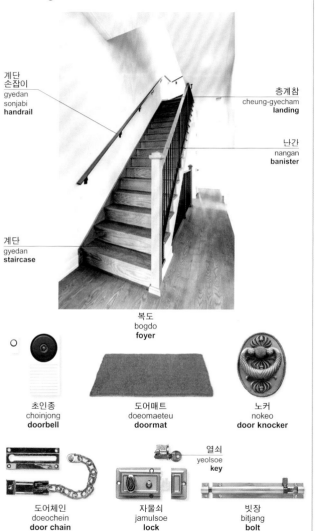

계단
손잡이
gyedan
sonjabi
handrail

층계참
cheung-gyecham
landing

난간
nangan
banister

계단
gyedan
staircase

복도
bogdo
foyer

초인종
choinjong
doorbell

도어매트
doeomaeteu
doormat

노커
nokeo
door knocker

도어체인
doeochein
door chain

자물쇠
jamulsoe
lock

열쇠
yeolsoe
key

빗장
bitjang
bolt

아파트 apateu
apartment

발코니
balkoni
balcony

아파트 건물
apateu geonmul
apartment building

인터콤
inteokom
intercom

엘리베이터
ellibeiteo
elevator

실내 시스템 silnae siseutem
internal systems

날개
nalgae
blade

선풍기
seonpung-gi
fan

라디에이터
ladieiteo
radiator

히터
hiteo
space heater

컨벡션 히터
keonbagsyeon hiteo
convection heater

전기 jeongi • **electricity**

중성선
joongseongseon
neutral

접지 핀
jeopji pin
ground pin

핀
pin
pin

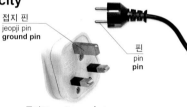

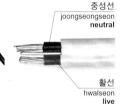

활선
hwalseon
live

절전형 전구
jeoljeonhyeong jeongu
energy-saving bulb

플러그 peulleogeu | **plug**

전선 jeonseon | **wires**

어휘 eohwi • **vocabulary**

전압 jeon-ab **voltage**	퓨즈 pyujeu **fuse**	교류 전류 gyoryu jeonryu **alternating current**	정전 jeongjeon **power outage**	소켓 soket **outlet**
전류 jeonryu **amp**	퓨즈 박스 pyujeu bakseu **fuse box**	직류 전류 jigryu jeonryu **direct current**	발전기 baljeongi **generator**	스위치 seuwichi **switch**
전력 jeonryeok **power**	전력량계 jeonryeokryang-gye **electric meter**	변압기 byeonabgi **transformer**	공급 전원 gong-geup jeon-won **household current**	

배관 baegwan • **plumbing**

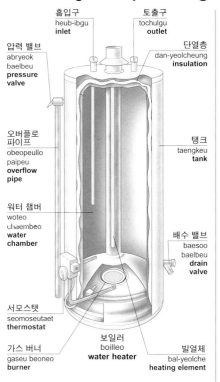

흡입구
heub-ibgu
inlet

토출구
tochulgu
outlet

단열층
dan-yeolcheung
insulation

압력 밸브
abryeok
baelbeu
**pressure
valve**

오버플로
파이프
obeopeullo
paipeu
**overflow
pipe**

탱크
taengkeu
tank

워터 챔버
woteo
chaembeo
**water
chamber**

배수 밸브
baesoo
baelbeu
**drain
valve**

서모스탯
seomoseutaet
thermostat

가스 버너
gaseu beoneo
burner

보일러
boilleo
water heater

발열체
bal-yeolche
heating element

세면대 semyeondae • **sink**

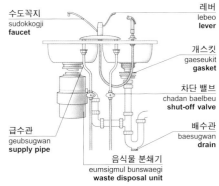

수도꼭지
sudokkogji
faucet

레버
lebeo
lever

개스킷
gaeseukit
gasket

차단 밸브
chadan baelbeu
shut-off valve

배수관
baesugwan
drain

급수관
geubsugwan
supply pipe

음식물 분쇄기
eumsigmul bunswaegi
waste disposal unit

화장실 hwajangsil • **toilet**

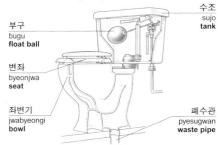

수조
sujo
tank

부구
bugu
float ball

변좌
byeonjwa
seat

좌변기
jwabyeongi
bowl

폐수관
pyesugwan
waste pipe

폐기물 처리 pyegimul cheori • **waste disposal**

병
byeong
bottle

재활용통
jaehwalyongtong
recycling bin

뚜껑
ttukkeong
lid

페달
pedal
pedal

쓰레기통
sseuregitong
trash can

분류 장치
bunryu jangchi
sorting bin

유기성 폐기물
yugiseong pyegimul
organic waste

거실 geosil • **living room**

벽등
byeokdeung
wall light

벽난로
byeoknanlo
fireplace

천장
cheongjang
ceiling

꽃병
kkotbyeong
vase

쿠션
kusyeon
pillow

램프
laempeu
lamp

탁자
takja
coffee table

소파
sopa
sofa

바닥
badak
floor

한국어 hangugeo • **english**

액자
aekja
frame

그림
geurim
picture

커튼
keoteun
curtain

속 커튼
sok keoten
sheer curtain

베니션 블라인드
benisheon beullaindeu
Venetian blind

롤러 블라인드
lolleo beullaindeu
roller blind

몰딩
molding
molding

안락의자
anlak-uija
armchair

책장
chaekjang
bookshelf

소파 베드
sopa bedeu
sofa bed

러그
reogeu
rug

서재 seojae | **study**

다이닝룸 dainingroom · **dining room**

후추
huchu
pepper

소금
sogeum
salt

식탁
siktak
table

식기류
sikgiryu
crockery

커트러리
keoteuleori
cutlery

의자
uija
chair

등받이
deungbat-i
back

앉는 부분
anneon bubun
seat

다리
dari
leg

어휘 eohwi · **vocabulary**

식탁을 차리다
siktak-eul charida
set the table (v)

식탁보
siktakbo
tablecloth

아침
achim
breakfast

배부른
baebureun
full

주인
jooin
host

조금 더 주시겠습니까?
jogeum deo
jusigessseumnikka?
**Can I have some
more, please?**

서빙하다
seobinghada
serve (v)

식탁 매트
siktak maeteu
place mat

점심
jeomsim
lunch

배고픈
baegopeun
hungry

안주인
anjuin
hostess

배부릅니다. 감사합니다.
baebureumnida. gamsahamnida
I've had enough, thank you.

먹다
meokda
eat (v)

식사
siksa
meal

저녁
jeonyeok
dinner

1인분
il-inboon
portion

손님
sonnim
guest

맛있게 먹었어요.
masitge meogeosseoyo
That was delicious.

식기류 sikgiryu · **crockery and cutlery**

머그컵
meogeukeob
mug

커피잔
keopijan
coffee cup

찻잔
chatjan
teacup

티스푼
tiseupun
teaspoon

접시
jeobsi
plate

대접
daejeob
bowl

커피포트
keopipoteu
French press

찻주전자
chatjujeonja
teapot

물병
mulbyeong
pitcher

에그컵
egeukeob
eggcup

와인잔
wainjan
wine glass

텀블러
teombeulleo
tumbler

유리그릇
yoorigeureut
glassware

냅킨링
naebkinling
napkin ring

앞접시
apjeobsi
side plate

대접시
daejeobsi
dinner plate

수프 그릇
supeu geureut
soup bowl

수프 스푼
supeu seupoon
soup spoon

냅킨
naebkin
napkin

포크
pokeu
fork

상차림
sangcharim
place setting

숟가락
sutgarak
spoon

나이프
naipeu
knife

주방 joobang · **kitchen**

선반
seonban
shelf

가림판
garimpan
backsplash

수도꼭지
sudokkogji
faucet

싱크대
singkeudae
sink

서랍
seorab
drawer

환풍기
hwanpung-gi
ventilation hood

전기레인지
jeon-gireinji
ceramic stovetop

조리대
joridae
countertop

오븐
obeun
oven

캐비닛
kaebinit
cabinet

가전품 gajeonpum · **appliances**

전자레인지
jeonjareinji
microwave oven

믹싱볼
miksingbol
mixing bowl

날
nal
blade

뚜껑
ttukkeong
lid

전기 주전자
jeongi jujeonja
electric kettle

토스터
toseuteo
toaster

푸드 프로세서
pudeu peuroseseo
food processor

블렌더
beullendeo
blender

식기 세척기
sikgi secheokgi
dishwasher

제빙기
jebing-gi
ice maker

냉장고
naengjang-go
refrigerator

냉동고
naengdong-go
freezer

채소 보관실
chaeso
bogwansil
crisper

냉장/냉동고 naengjang/naengdong-go
side-by-side refrigerator

어휘 eohwi
vocabulary

식기 건조대
sikgi geonjodae
draining board

찌다
jjida
steam (v)

버너
beoneo
burner

볶다
bokda
sauté (v)

레인지
reinji
stovetop

냉동하다
naengdonghada
freeze (v)

쓰레기통
sseuregitong
garbage can

해동하다
haedonghada
defrost (v)

조리 jori • **cooking**

벗기다
beotgida
peel (v)

얇게 썰다
yalgge sseolda
slice (v)

강판에 갈다
gangpan-e galda
grate (v)

붓다
butda
pour (v)

섞다
seokkda
mix (v)

휘젓다
hwijeotda
whisk (v)

끓이다
kkeulh-ida
boil (v)

튀기다
twigida
fry (v)

밀다
milda
roll (v)

젓다
jeotda
stir (v)

부글부글 끓이다
bugeulbugeul
kkeulh-ida
simmer (v)

졸이다
jol-ida
poach (v)

굽다
gubda
bake (v)

굽다
goobda
roast (v)

석쇠에 굽다
seoksoe-e goobda
broil (v)

주방용품 joobang yongpum • **kitchenware**

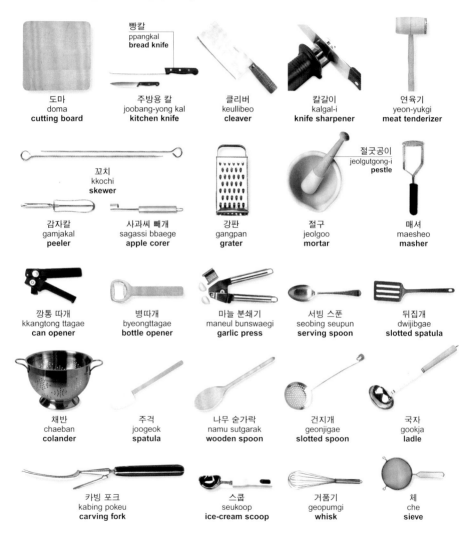

빵칼
ppangkal
bread knife

도마
doma
cutting board

주방용 칼
joobang-yong kal
kitchen knife

클리버
keullibeo
cleaver

칼갈이
kalgal-i
knife sharpener

연육기
yeon-yukgi
meat tenderizer

꼬치
kkochi
skewer

절굿공이
jeolgutgong-i
pestle

감자칼
gamjakal
peeler

사과씨 빼개
sagassi bbaege
apple corer

강판
gangpan
grater

절구
jeolgoo
mortar

매셔
maesheo
masher

깡통 따개
kkangtong ttagae
can opener

병따개
byeongttagae
bottle opener

마늘 분쇄기
maneul bunswaegi
garlic press

서빙 스푼
seobing seupun
serving spoon

뒤집개
dwijibgae
slotted spatula

채반
chaeban
colander

주걱
joogeok
spatula

나무 숟가락
namu sutgarak
wooden spoon

건지개
geonjigae
slotted spoon

국자
gookja
ladle

카빙 포크
kabing pokeu
carving fork

스쿱
seukoop
ice-cream scoop

거품기
geopumgi
whisk

체
che
sieve

뚜껑
ttukkeong
lid

들러붙지 않는
deulleobutji anhneun
nonstick

프라이팬
peuraipaen
frying pan

소스팬
soseupaen
saucepan

그릴팬
geurilpaen
grill pan

웍
wok
wok

타진
tajin
tagine

유리 그릇
yuri geureut
glass

오븐에서 사용 가능
obeun-eseo sayong ganeung
ovenproof

믹싱볼
miksingbol
mixing bowl

수플레 그릇
supeulle geureut
soufflé dish

그라탱 그릇
geurataeng geureut
gratin dish

라미킨
lamikin
ramekin

냄비
naembi
casserole dish

케이크 굽기 keikeu goobgi • **baking cakes**

저울
jeowool
scale

계량컵
gyeryangkeob
measuring cup

케이크 틀
keikeu teul
cake pan

파이 틀
pai teul
pie pan

타르트 틀
tareuteu teul
quiche pan

페이스트리 솔
peiseuteuri sol
pastry brush

밀대 mildae
rolling pin

짤주머니 jjaljoomeoni
piping bag

머핀 트레이
meopin teurei
muffin pan

베이킹 트레이
beiking teurei
cookie sheet

식힘망
sikhim-mang
cooling rack

오븐장갑
obeunjanggab
oven mitt

앞치마
apchima
apron

침실 chimsil · **bedroom**

옷장
otjang
closet

침실등
chimsildeung
bedside lamp

침대 머리판
chimdae meoripan
headboard

침대 협탁
chimdae hyeoptak
nightstand

서랍장
seorabjang
chest of drawers

서랍
seorab
drawer

침대
chimdae
bed

매트리스
maeteuriseu
mattress

침대보
chimdaebo
bedspread

베개
begae
pillow

보온 물주머니
bo-on mooljumeoni
hot-water bottle

라디오 시계
radio sigye
clock radio

자명종 시계
jamyeongjong sigye
alarm clock

각티슈
gaktisyu
box of tissues

옷걸이
otgeori
coat hanger

침구류 chimgooryu • **bed linen**

거울
geoul
mirror

화장대
hwajangdae
dressing table

베갯잇
begaen-nit
pillowcase

시트
siteu
sheet

이불커버
ibulkeobeo
comforter

누비이불
nubi-ibul
quilt

바닥
badak
floor

담요
dam-yo
blanket

어휘 eohwi • **vocabulary**

카펫 kapet **carpet**	싱글 침대 sing-geul chimdae **twin bed**	침대 스프링 chimdae seupeuring **bedspring**	알람을 맞추다 allameul matchuda **set the alarm (v)**	깨어나다 kkae-eo-nada **wake up (v)**
붙박이장 butbak-ijang **closet**	더블 침대 deobeul chimdae **full bed**	불면증 bulmyeonjeung **insomnia**	잠자리에 들다 jamjari-e deulda **go to bed (v)**	일어나다 il-eo-nada **get up (v)**
전기담요 jeonkidam-yo **electric blanket**	발판 balpan **footboard**	코를 골다 koreul golda **snore (v)**	잠자리에 들다 jamjari-e deulda **go to sleep (v)**	잠자리를 정돈하다 jamjarireul jeongdonhada **make the bed (v)**

욕실 yoksil • **bathroom**

수건걸이
sugeongeori
towel rack

샤워실 문
shawosil moon
shower door

찬물 꼭지
chanmul kkogji
cold faucet

온수 꼭지
onsu kkogji
hot faucet

세면대
semyeondae
sink

세면대 팝업
semyeondae
pab-eob
plug

샤워기
shawoe kkogji
shower head

샤워
shawoe
shower

배수구
baesoogoo
drain

변좌
byeonjwa
toilet seat

변기
byeon-gi
toilet

변기솔
byeongisol
toilet brush

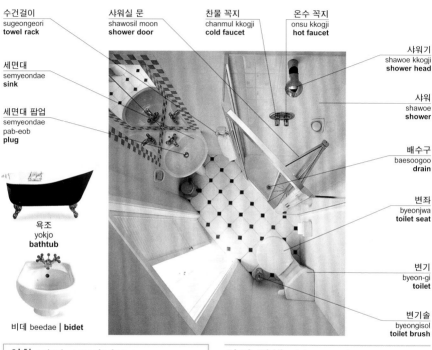

욕조
yokjo
bathtub

비데 beedae | **bidet**

어휘 eohwi • **vocabulary**

욕실용 매트
yojsil-yong maeteu
bath mat

샤워 커튼
shawoe keoteun
shower curtain

샤워하다
shawoehada
take a shower (v)

화장실 수납장
hwajangsil soonabjang
medicine cabinet

화장지
hwajangji
toilet paper

목욕하다
mog-yokhada
take a bath (v)

치과 위생 chigwa wisaeng **dental hygiene**

칫솔
chit-sol
toothbrush

치실
chisil
dental floss

치약
chiyak
toothpaste

구강 청결제
gugang cheong-gyeolje
mouthwash

스펀지
seupeonji
sponge

돌비누
dolbinoo
pumice stone

목욕용 등솔
mog-yok-yong deungsol
back brush

데오도란트
deodoranteu
deodorant

비누 받침
binu batchim
soap dish

사워젤
shawoejel
shower gel

비누
binu
soap

얼굴 크림
eolgul keurim
face cream

거품 목욕제
geopum mog-yokje
bubble bath

핸드타올
haendeutaol
hand towel

목욕 수건
mog-yok
soogeon
bath towel

수건
sugeon
towels

바디 로션
badi loshion
body lotion

베이비 파우더
beibi paudeo
talcum powder

목욕용 가운
mog-yok-yong gaun
bathrobe

면도 myeondo • **shaving**

전기 면도기
jeongi myeondogi
electric razor

쉐이빙 폼
sheibing pom
shaving foam

일회용 면도기
ilhoeyong myeondogi
disposable razor

면도날
myeondonal
razor blade

애프터쉐이브 로션
aepeuteosueibeu loshion
aftershave

어린이집 eorin-i jib • **nursery**

유아 돌보기 yua dolbogi • **baby care**

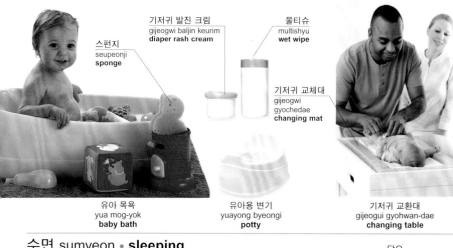

기저귀 발진 크림
gijeogwi baljin keurim
diaper rash cream

물티슈
multishyu
wet wipe

스펀지
seupeonji
sponge

기저귀 교체대
gijeogwi
gyochedae
changing mat

유아 목욕
yua mog-yok
baby bath

유아용 변기
yuayong byeongi
potty

기저귀 교환대
gijeogui gyohwan-dae
changing table

수면 sumyeon • **sleeping**

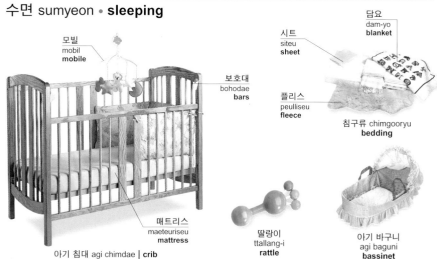

담요
dam-yo
blanket

시트
siteu
sheet

모빌
mobil
mobile

보호대
bohodae
bars

플리스
peulliseu
fleece

침구류 chimgooryu
bedding

매트리스
maeteuriseu
mattress

아기 침대 agi chimdae | **crib**

딸랑이
ttallang-i
rattle

아기 바구니
agi baguni
bassinet

놀이 nol-i • **playing**

인형
inhyeong
doll

봉제완구
bongjewangu
stuffed toy

인형집
inhyeongjib
dollhouse

장난감 집
jangnangam jib
playhouse

곰인형
gom-inhyeong
teddy bear

장난감
jangnangam
toy

장난감 바구니
jangnangam baguni
toy basket

공
gong
ball

아기 놀이 울타리
agi nol-i ultali
playpen

안전 anjeon
safety

차일드 락
chaildeurak
child lock

베이비모니터
beibimoniteo
baby monitor

계단 문
gyedan moon
stair gate

먹기 meokgi
eating

아기의자
agi-uija
high chair

우유병 꼭지
uyubyeong kkogji
nipple

병
byeong
bottle

음료컵
eumryo-keob
sippy cup

외출 waechool • **going out**

유모차
yoomocha
stroller

영아용 유모차
yeong-ayong yoomocha
baby carriage

후드
hoodeu
hood

휴대용 아기 침대
hyudaeyong agi chimdae
carrier

기저귀 가방
gijeogwi gabang
diaper bag

기저귀
gijeogwi
diaper

포대기
podaegi
baby sling

다용도실 dayongdosil · **utility room**

세탁 setak · **laundry**

빨랫감
ppallaetgam
dirty laundry

빨래 바구니
ppallae baguni
laundry basket

세탁기
setakgi
washer

세탁 건조기
setak geonjogi
washer-dryer

회전식 건조기
hoei-jeonsik geonjogi
dryer

빨랫줄
ppallaetjul
clothesline

다리미
darimi
iron

빨래집게
ppallaejibge
clothespin

말리다
mallida
dry (v)

다리미판 darimipan | **ironing board**

어휘 eohwi · **vocabulary**

넣다
neota
load (v)

돌리다
dollida
spin (v)

다림질하다
darimjilhada
iron (v)

헹구다
haeng-gooda
rinse (v)

회전식 건조기
hoei-jeonsik
geonjogi
spin-dryer

섬유 유연제
seom-yu yuyeonje
fabric softener

세탁기를 어떻게 사용해야 합니까?
saetakgireul eotteokke sayonghaeya hamnikka?
How do I operate the washing machine?

색깔이 있는 옷과 흰색 옷을 어떻게 설정해야 합니까?
saegkkal-i itneun otgwa huinsaek ot-eul eotteokke
seoljunghaeya habnikka?
What is the setting for colors / whites?

청소 도구 cheongso dogu · **cleaning equipment**

흡입 호스
heub-ib hoseu
suction hose

솔
sol
brush

쓰레받기
sseurebatgi
dustpan

표백제
pyobaekje
bleach

양동이
yangdong-i
bucket

액체 세제
aegche seje
liquid

가루세제
garooseje
powder

걸레
geolle
dust cloth

진공 청소기
jingong cheongsogi
vacuum cleaner

자루걸레
jarugeolle
mop

세제
seje
detergent

광택제
gwangtaekje
polish

활동 hwaldong · **activities**

청소하다
cheongsohada
clean (v)

씻다
ssitda
wash (v)

닦다
dakda
wipe (v)

문질러 씻다
munjilleo ssitda
scrub (v)

긁어내다
geulgeo-naeda
scrape (v)

빗자루
bitjaru
broom

쓸다
sseulda
sweep (v)

먼지를 털다
meonjileul teolda
dust (v)

광택을 내다
gwangtaek-eul naeda
polish (v)

작업장 jabeobjang · **workshop**

척
cheok
chuck

드릴 비트
deuril biteu
drill bit

직소
jigso
jigsaw

배터리 팩
naeteori paeg
battery pack

무선 드릴
museon deuril
cordless drill

전동 드릴
jeondong deuril
electric drill

글루 건
geulloo geon
glue gun

죔쇠
joemsoe
clamp

날
nal
blade

바이스
baiseu
vise

샌더
saendeo
sander

원형톱
wonhyeong tob
circular saw

작업대
jageobdae
workbench

목공용 접착제
mokgong-yong
jeobchagjae
wood glue

공구 걸이
gong-gu geol-i
tool rack

루터
looteo
router

비트 핸들
biteu haendeul
bit brace

대팻밥
daepaetbab
wood shavings

연장선
yeonjangseon
extension cord

기술 gisool · **techniques**

자르다
jareuda
cut (v)

톱질하다
tobjilhada
saw (v)

구멍을 뚫다
goomung-eul ttoolda
drill (v)

망치로 치다
mangchiro chida
hammer (v)

땜납
ttaemnab
solder

대패질을 하다 daepaejil-eul
hada | **plane (v)**

선반 가공하다 seonban
gagonghada | **turn (v)**

조각하다 jogakhada
carve (v)

납땜하다 nabttaemhada
solder (v)

재료 jaeryo · **materials**

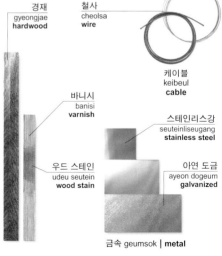

MDF
MDF
MDF

합판
habpan
plywood

칩보드
chipbodeu
**particle
board**

하드보드
hadeubodeu
hardboard

연재
yeonjae
softwood

목재 mokjae | **wood**

경재
gyeongjae
hardwood

바니시
banisi
varnish

우드 스테인
udeu seutein
wood stain

철사
cheolsa
wire

케이블
keibeul
cable

스테인리스강
seuteinliseugang
stainless steel

아연 도금
ayeon dogeum
galvanized

금속 geumsok | **metal**

공구함 gong-gooham · **toolbox**

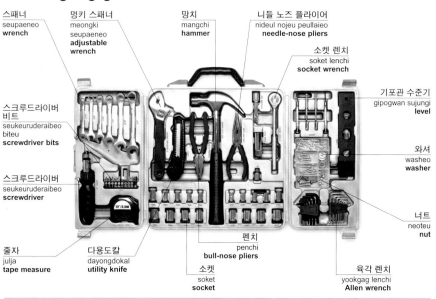

스패너
seupaeneo
wrench

멍키 스패너
meongki
seupaeneo
**adjustable
wrench**

망치
mangchi
hammer

니들 노즈 플라이어
nideul nojeu peullaieo
needle-nose pliers

소켓 렌치
soket lenchi
socket wrench

기포관 수준기
gipogwan sujungi
level

스크루드라이버
비트
seukeuruderaibeo
biteu
screwdriver bits

와셔
washeo
washer

스크루드라이버
seukeuruderaibeo
screwdriver

너트
neoteu
nut

줄자
julja
tape measure

다용도칼
dayongdokal
utility knife

펜치
penchi
bull-nose pliers

소켓
soket
socket

육각 렌치
yookgag lenchi
Allen wrench

드릴 비트 deuril biteu · **drill bits**

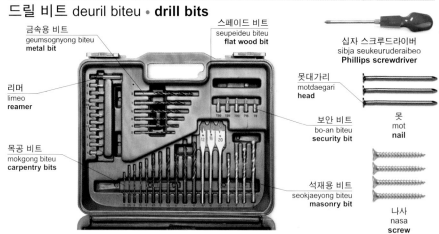

금속용 비트
geumsognyong biteu
metal bit

스페이드 비트
seupeideu biteu
flat wood bit

십자 스크루드라이버
sibja seukeuruderaibeo
Phillips screwdriver

리머
limeo
reamer

못대가리
motdaegari
head

못
mot
nail

보안 비트
bo-an biteu
security bit

목공 비트
mokgong biteu
carpentry bits

석재용 비트
seokjaeyong biteu
masonry bit

나사
nasa
screw

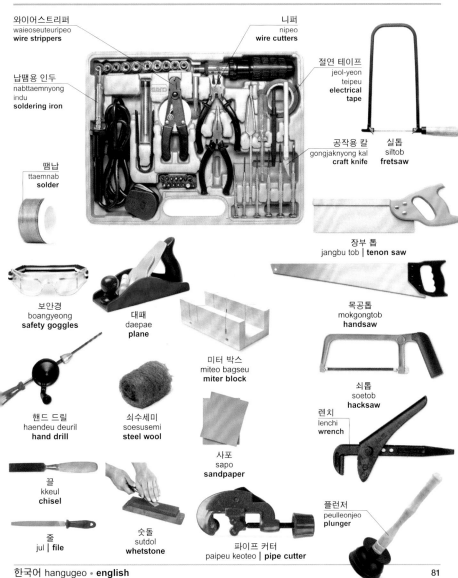

와이어스트리퍼
waieoseuteuripeo
wire strippers

니퍼
nipeo
wire cutters

절연 테이프
jeol-yeon
teipeu
**electrical
tape**

납땜용 인두
nabttaemnyong
indu
soldering iron

공작용 칼
gongjaknyong kal
craft knife

실톱
siltob
fretsaw

땜납
ttaemnab
solder

장부 톱
jangbu tob | **tenon saw**

보안경
boangyeong
safety goggles

대패
daepae
plane

목공톱
mokgongtob
handsaw

미터 박스
miteo bagseu
miter block

쇠톱
soetob
hacksaw

렌치
lenchi
wrench

핸드 드릴
haendeu deuril
hand drill

쇠수세미
soesusemi
steel wool

사포
sapo
sandpaper

끌
kkeul
chisel

플런저
peulleonjeo
plunger

줄
jul | **file**

숫돌
sutdol
whetstone

파이프 커터
paipeu keoteo | **pipe cutter**

장식 jangsik • **decorating**

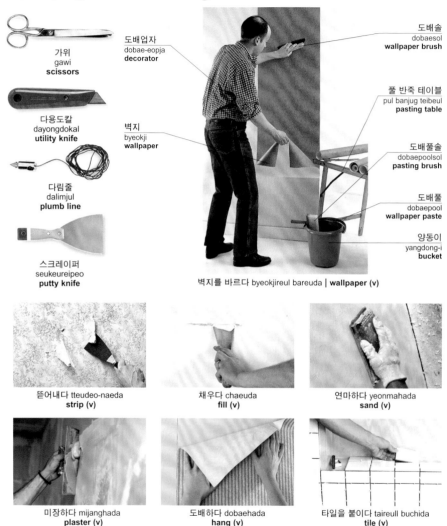

가위
gawi
scissors

도배업자
dobae-eopja
decorator

다용도칼
dayongdokal
utility knife

벽지
byeokji
wallpaper

다림줄
dalimjul
plumb line

스크레이퍼
seukeureipeo
putty knife

도배솔
dobaesol
wallpaper brush

풀 반죽 테이블
pul banjug teibeul
pasting table

도배풀솔
dobaepoolsol
pasting brush

도배풀
dobaepool
wallpaper paste

양동이
yangdong-i
bucket

벽지를 바르다 byeokjireul bareuda | **wallpaper (v)**

뜯어내다 tteudeo-naeda
strip (v)

채우다 chaeuda
fill (v)

연마하다 yeonmahada
sand (v)

미장하다 mijanghada
plaster (v)

도배하다 dobaehada
hang (v)

타일을 붙이다 taireull buchida
tile (v)

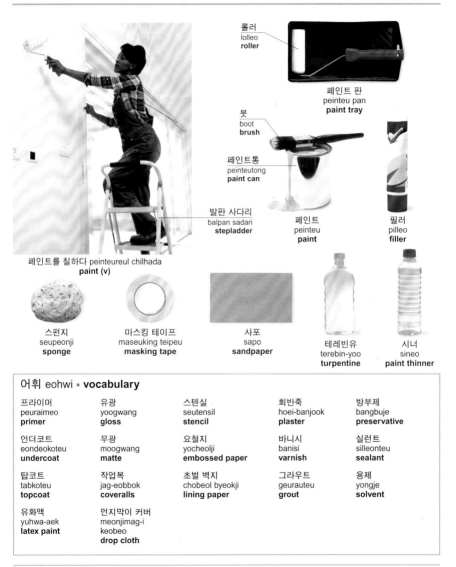

롤러
lolleo
roller

페인트 판
peinteu pan
paint tray

붓
boot
brush

페인트통
peinteutong
paint can

발판 사다리
balpan sadari
stepladder

페인트
peinteu
paint

필러
pilleo
filler

페인트를 칠하다 peinteureul chilhada
paint (v)

스펀지
seupeonji
sponge

마스킹 테이프
maseuking teipeu
masking tape

사포
sapo
sandpaper

테레빈유
terebin-yoo
turpentine

시너
sineo
paint thinner

어휘 eohwi • **vocabulary**

프라이머 peuraimeo **primer**	유광 yoogwang **gloss**	스텐실 seutensil **stencil**	회반죽 hoei-banjook **plaster**	방부제 bangbuje **preservative**
언더코트 eondeokoteu **undercoat**	무광 moogwang **matte**	요철지 yocheolji **embossed paper**	바니시 banisi **varnish**	실런트 silleonteu **sealant**
탑코트 tabkoteu **topcoat**	작업복 jag-eobbok **coveralls**	초벌 벽지 chobeol byeokji **lining paper**	그라우트 geurauteu **grout**	용제 yongje **solvent**
유화액 yuhwa-aek **latex paint**	먼지막이 커버 meonjimag-i keobeo **drop cloth**			

정원 jeong-won • **garden**
정원 양식 jeong-won yangsik • **garden styles**

정원의 특징 jeong-won-ui teukjing **garden features**

파티오 정원 patio jeong-won | **patio garden**

정형식 정원 jeonghyeongsik jeong-won | **formal garden**

시골집 정원
sigoljib jeong-won
cottage garden

허브 정원
heobeu jeong-won
herb garden

옥상 정원
oksang jeong-won
roof garden

바위 정원
bawi jeong-won
rock garden

마당 madang | **courtyard**

수생 식물원
susaeng sikmul-won
water garden

매다는 꽃바구니
maedaneun kkotbaguni
hanging basket

트렐리스 teurelliseu | **trellis**

퍼걸러
peogeolleo
arbor

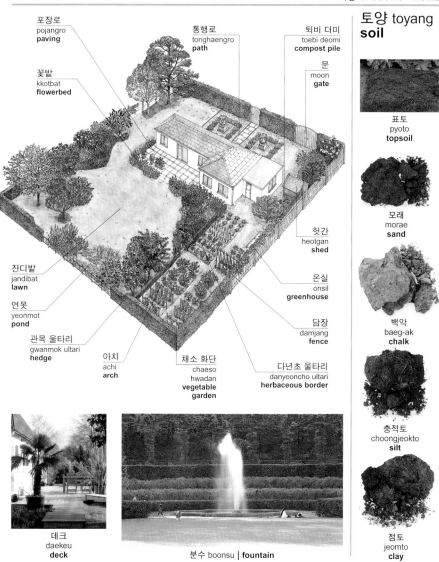

포장로
pojangro
paving

꽃밭
kkotbat
flowerbed

통행로
tonghaengro
path

퇴비 더미
toebi deomi
compost pile

문
moon
gate

헛간
heotgan
shed

온실
onsil
greenhouse

담장
damjang
fence

잔디밭
jandibat
lawn

연못
yeonmot
pond

관목 울타리
gwanmok ultari
hedge

아치
achi
arch

채소 화단
chaeso
hwadan
**vegetable
garden**

다년초 울타리
danyeoncho ultari
herbaceous border

토양 toyang
soil

표토
pyoto
topsoil

모래
morae
sand

백악
baeg-ak
chalk

충적토
choongjeokto
silt

점토
jeomto
clay

데크
daekeu
deck

분수 boonsu | **fountain**

정원수 jeong-wonsu • **garden plants**

식물의 유형 sigmul-ui yuhyeong • **types of plants**

한해살이
hanhaesari
annual

이년생
i-nyeonsaeng
biennial

다년생
danyeonsaeng
perennial

구근
gugeun
bulb

양치식물
yangchisikmul
fern

골풀
golpool
cattail

대나무
daenamu
bamboo

잡초
jabcho
weeds

약초
yakcho
herb

수생 식물
susaeng sigmul
water plant

나무
namu
tree

야자수
yajasoo
palm

침엽수
chimyeobsoo
conifer

상록수
sangroksu
evergreen

낙엽수
nak-yeobsu
deciduous

토피어리
topieori
topiary

고산 식물
gosan sigmul
alpine

다육 식물
dayook sigmul
succulent

선인장
seon-injang
cactus

화분수
hwabunsu
potted plant

녹음수
nog-eumsu
shade plant

덩굴 식물
deong-gul
sigmul
climber

꽃나무
kkotnamu
flowering shrub

지피 식물
jipi sigmul
ground cover

덩굴 식물
deong-gul sigmul
creeper

장식품
jangsikpoom
ornamental

풀
pool
grass

정원 도구 jeong-won dogu · **garden tools**

퇴비
toebi
compost

씨앗
ssiat
seeds

골분
golboon
bone meal

쇠갈퀴
soegalkwi
lawn rake

삽
sab
shovel

쇠스랑
soeseurang
garden fork

원예용 자루 가위
won-yeyong jaru gawi
long-handled shears

갈퀴
galkwi
rake

괭이
gwaeng-i
hoe

자갈
jagal
gravel

잔디 봉투
jandi bongtoo
grass bag

모터
moteo
motor

손잡이
sonjabi
handle

원예용 바구니
won-yeyong baguni
gardening basket

안전판
anjeonpan
shield

예초기
yechogi
trimmer

잔디깍이
jandikkaggi
lawnmower

스탠드
seutaendeu
stand

외바퀴 손수레
waebaqwi sonsoorye
wheelbarrow

소형 갈퀴
sohyeong galqwi
hand fork

전지가위
jeonji gawi
pruners

원예용 장갑
won-yeyong janggab
gardening gloves

모종삽
mojongsab
trowel

날
nal
blade

모종 상자
mojong sangja
seed tray

노끈
nokkeun
twine

표
pyo
labels

작은 철끈
jageun
cheolkkeun
twist ties

링 타이
ling tai
ring ties

막대
makdae
canes

원예용 가위
won-yeyong gawi
shears

살충제
salchoongje
pesticide

체
che
sieve

전지톱
jeonji tob
handsaw

화분
hwaboon
plant pot

고무 장화
gomu janghwa
rubber boots

물주기 muljoogi · watering

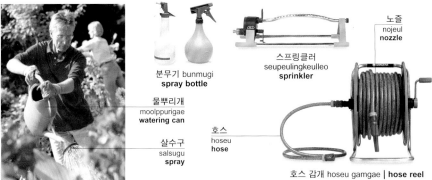

분무기 bunmugi
spray bottle

스프링클러
seupeulingkeulleo
sprinkler

노즐
nojeul
nozzle

물뿌리개
moolppurigae
watering can

살수구
salsugu
spray

호스
hoseu
hose

호스 감개 hoseu gamgae | **hose reel**

원예 won-ye • **gardening**

관목 울타리
gwanmok
ultari
hedge

잔디밭
jandibat
lawn

꽃밭
kkotbat
flowerbed

잔디깎이
jandikkaggi
lawnmower

말뚝
malttug
stake

풀을 베다 pureul baeda | **mow (v)**

잔디를 깔다
jandileul kkalda
sod (v)

말뚝을 박다
malttug-eul bakda
spike (v)

갈퀴질하다
galqwijilhada
rake (v)

다듬다
dadeumda
trim (v)

파다
pada
dig (v)

씨 뿌리다
ssi ppurida
sow (v)

거름 주다
georeum juda
top-dress (v)

물 주다
mool juda
water (v)

막대기
makdaegi
cane

가꾸다
gakkuda
train (v)

시든 꽃을 잘라내다
sideun kkotcheul jallanaeda
deadhead (v)

살포하다
salpohada
spray (v)

접목하다
jeobmokhada
graft (v)

자르기
jareugi
cutting

번식시키다
beonsigsikida
propagate (v)

가지치다
gajichida
prune (v)

말뚝으로 고정하다
malttug-euro gojeonghada
stake (v)

옮겨 심다
omgyeo simda
transplant (v)

잡초를 뽑다
jabchoreul ppobda
weed (v)

뿌리 덮개를 덮어주다
ppuri deopgaereul
deop-eojuda
mulch (v)

수확하다
suhwakhada
harvest (v)

어휘 eohwi · **vocabulary**

경작하다 gyeongjakhada **cultivate (v)**	싹이 트다 ssag-i teuda **pot (v)**	솎아 내다 sokka naeda **pick (v)**	체로 치다 chero chida **sift (v)**	심토 simto **subsoil**	씨 뿌리기 ssi ppurigi **seedling**	비료 biryo **fertilizer**
돌보다 dolboda **tend (v)**	비료를 주다 biryoreul juda **fertilize (v)**	조경하다 jogyeonghada **landscape (v)**	공기가 통하게 하다 gong-giga tonghage hada **aerate (v)**	배수 baesu **drainage**	유기농 yuginong **organic**	제초제 jechoje **weedkiller**

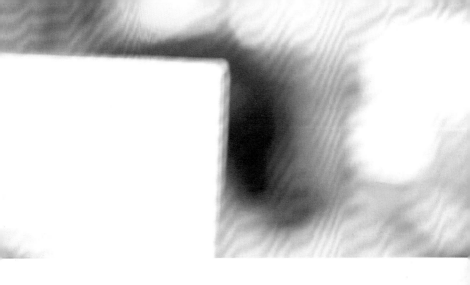

서비스 seobiseu
services

응급 서비스 eung-geub seobiseu • **emergency services**

구급차 gugeubcha • **ambulance**

들것
deulgeot
stretcher

구급차 gugeubcha | **ambulance**

구급대원 gugeubdaewon | **paramedic**

경찰 gyeongchal • **police**

배지
baeji
badge

유니폼
yunipom
uniform

사이렌
sairen
siren

경광등
gyeong-gwangdeung
lights

총
chong
gun

경찰봉
gyeongchalbong
nightstick

경찰차
gyeongchalcha
police car

경찰서
gyeongchalseo
police station

수갑
sugab
handcuffs

경찰관
gyeongchalgwan
police officer

어휘 eohwi • **vocabulary**

범죄 beomjoe **crime**	민원 minwon **complaint**	기소 giso **charge**	경위 gyeong-wi **captain**
폭행 pokhaeng **assault**	조사 josa **investigation**	체포 chepo **arrest**	형사 hyeongsa **detective**
절도 jeoldo **burglary**	지문 jimun **fingerprint**	유치장 yuchijang **cell**	용의자 yong-uija **suspect**

소방대 sobangdae • **fire department**

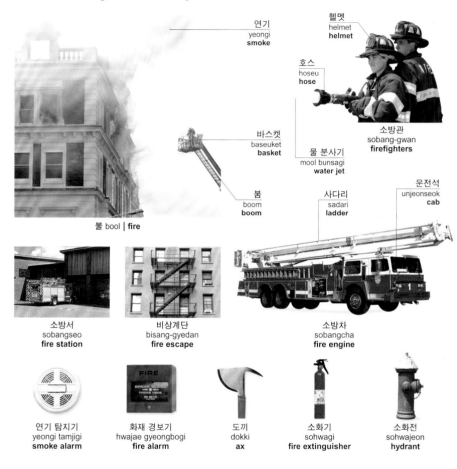

연기
yeongi
smoke

헬멧
helmet
helmet

호스
hoseu
hose

소방관
sobang-gwan
firefighters

바스켓
baseuket
basket

물 분사기
mool bunsagi
water jet

붐
boom
boom

사다리
sadari
ladder

운전석
unjeonseok
cab

불 bool | **fire**

소방서
sobangseo
fire station

비상계단
bisang-gyedan
fire escape

소방차
sobangcha
fire engine

연기 탐지기
yeongi tamjigi
smoke alarm

화재 경보기
hwajae gyeongbogi
fire alarm

도끼
dokki
ax

소화기
sohwagi
fire extinguisher

소화전
sohwajeon
hydrant

경찰 / 소방대 / 구급차 좀 불러주세요.
gyeongchal / sobangdae / gugeubcha jom
bulleojuseyo
**I need the police / the fire department /
an ambulance.**

...에 불이 났습니다.
...e buri natsseumnida
There's a fire at...

사고가 났습니다.
sagoga natsseumnida
**There's been an
accident.**

경찰을
불러주세요!
gyeongchareul
bulleojuseyo!
Call the police!

은행 eunhaeng · **bank**

창문
changmoon
window

텔러
telleo
teller

고객
gogaek
customer

카운터
kaunteo
counter

체크카드
chekeukadeu
debit card

계좌번호
gyejwabeonho
account number

액수
aegsu
amount

신용카드
sin-yongkadeu
credit card

카드 리더기
kadrideogi
card reader

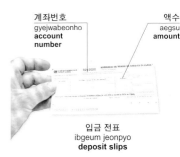

입금 전표
ibgeum jeonpyo
deposit slips

어휘 eohwi · **vocabulary**

세금 segeum **tax**	저축 jeochook **savings**	당좌 예금 dangjwa yegeum **checking account**	은행 수수료 eunhaeng susuryo **bank charge**	은행 송금 eunhaeng song-geum **bank transfer**
대출 daechul **loan**	당좌대월 dangjwadaewol **overdraft**	저축예금 jeochook-yaegeum **savings account**	명세표 myoensepyo **withdrawal slip**	자동 이체 jadong iche **automatic payment**
대출금 daechulgeum **mortgage**	비밀번호 bimilbeonho **PIN**	이자율 ijayool **interest rate**	지불 jibul **payment**	입금하다 ibgeumhada **deposit (v)**

은행 거래 앱
eunhaeng georae aep
banking app

지폐
jipye
bill

동전
dongjeon
coin

온라인 뱅킹
olain baengking
online banking

돈
don
money

화면
hwamyeon
screen

키패드
kipaedeu
keypad

카드 슬롯
kadeu seullot
card reader

현금 자동출납기 hyeon-geum
jadongchoolnabgi | **ATM**

외환 waehwan • **foreign currency**

환전소
hwanjeonso
currency exchange

환율
hwan-yool
exchange rate

금융 geum-yoong • **finance**

재무설계사
jaemooseolgyesa
financial advisor

주가
jootga
share price

증권 브로커
jeung-gwon
beurokeo
stockbroker

증권 거래소 jeung-gwon georaeso
stock exchange

어휘 eohwi • **vocabulary**

투자
tuja
investment

포트폴리오
poteupollio
portfolio

주식
joosik
stocks

지분
jibun
shares

배당금
baedang-geum
dividends

순자산
soonjasan
equity

수수료
susuryo
commission

현금으로 바꾸다
hyeongeum-euro
bakkuda
cash (v)

디지털 통화
dijiteol tong-hwa
digital currency

액면가
aegmyeonga
denomination

회계사
hoeigyesa
accountant

이걸 바꿀 수 있나요?
igeol bakkul su itnayo?
Can I change this, please?

오늘 환율이 어떻게 됩니까?
oneul hwanyuri eotteohge deomnikka?
What's today's exchange rate?

통신 tongsin • **communications**

우체국 직원
uchegook jik-won
postal worker

창문
changmoon
window

저울
jeowool
scale

카운터
kaunteo
counter

우체국 uchegook | **post office**

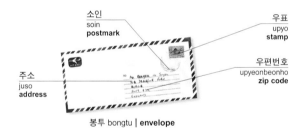

소인
soin
postmark

우표
upyo
stamp

우편번호
upyeonbeonho
zip code

주소
juso
address

봉투 bongtu | **envelope**

우편집배원
upyeonjibaewon
mail carrier

어휘 eohwi • **vocabulary**

편지 pyeonji **letter**	반송처 bansongcheo **return address**	배달 baedal **delivery**	취급 주의 chigeub juui **fragile**
항공 우편 hang-gong upyeon **by airmail**	서명 seomyeong **signature**	수집 soojib **pickup**	이쪽을 위로 ijjog-eul weero **this way up**
등기 우편 deung-gi upyeon **registered mail**	우편요금 upyeon-yogeum **postage**	우편 행낭 upyeon haengnang **mailbag**	접지 마세요 jeobji maseyo **do not bend (v)**

우편함
upyeonham
mailbox

편지함
pyeonjiham
letter slot

소포
sopo
package

택배 회사
taekbae hoeisa
courier

전화 jeonhwa • **telephone**

전화기
jeonhwagi
handset

자동 응답기
jadong eungdabgi
answering machine

전화기 본체
jeonhwagi
bonche
base station

키패드
kipaedeu
keypad

무선 전화기
museon jeonhwagi
cordless phone

앱
aeb
app

스마트폰
seumateupon
smartphone

어휘 eohwi • **vocabulary**

전화를 걸다
jeonhwareul
geolda
dial (v)

응답하다
eungdabhada
answer (v)

통화 중
tonghwa joong
busy

연결 끊김
yeon-gyeol
kkeunkim
disconnected

음성 메시지
eumseong mesiji
voice message

문자(SMS)
munja
(eseu-em-eseu)
text (SMS)

비밀번호
bimilbeonho
passcode

휴대폰
hyudaepon
cell phone

와이파이
waipai
Wi-Fi

모바일 데이터
mobail deiteo
mobile data

데이터 로밍
deiteo roming
data roaming

...전화번호 좀 알려주세요.
...jeonhwabeonho jom
allyeojuseyo
**Can you give me
the number for... ?**

...지역번호가 어떻게 되나요?
...jiyeokbeonhoga
eotteoke doenayo?
What is the area code for... ?

문자하세요!
munjahaseyo!
Text me!

호텔 hotel · **hotel**

로비 lobi · **lobby**

손님
sonnim
guest

키 카드
ki kad
key card

안내 데스크 직원
annae deseukeu
jig-won
receptionist

카운터
kaunteo
counter

안내 데스크 annae deseukeu | **reception**

카트
kateu
cart

짐
jim
luggage

벨보이 belboi | **porter**

엘리베이터 ellibeiteo | **elevator**

객실 번호
gaeksil beonho
room number

객실들 gaeksil · **rooms**

싱글 룸
sing-geul loom
single room

더블 룸
deobeul loom
double room

트윈 룸
teuwin loom
twin room

개별 욕실
gaebyeol yoksil
private bathroom

서비스 seobiseu · **services**

브렉퍼스트 트레이
beuregpeoseuteu teurei
breakfast tray

룸메이드 서비스
lummeideu seobiseu
maid service

세탁 서비스
setak seobiseu
laundry service

룸 서비스 lum seobiseu | **room service**

미니바
miniba
minibar

레스토랑
leseutorang
restaurant

헬스장
helseujang
gym

수영장
sooyeongjang
swimming pool

어휘 eohwi · **vocabulary**

비즈니스 호텔
bijeuniseu hotel
bed and breakfast

1일 3식 제공
il-il samsig jegong
all meals included

1일 2식 제공
il-il i-sig jegong
some meals included

빈 방 있어요?
bin bang isseoyo?
Do you have any vacancies?

예약했습니다.
yeyaghaetsseumnida
I have a reservation.

싱글 룸으로 주세요.
sing-geul loomeuro joosaeyo
I'd like a single room.

3박 투숙할 방이 필요합니다.
sambak tusukhal bang-i piryohamnida
I'd like a room for three nights.

1박에 얼마인가요?
ilbage eolmaingayo?
What is the charge per night?

언제까지 퇴실해야 하나요?
eonjekkaji toesilhaeya hanayo?
When do I have to check out?

쇼핑 shoping
shopping

쇼핑 센터 shoping centeo · **shopping center**

아트리움
ateurium
atrium

3층
samcheung
third floor

2층
i-cheung
second floor

고객
gogaek
customer

1층
ilcheung
ground floor

에스컬레이터
eseukeolleiteo
escalator

어휘 eohwi · **vocabulary**

아동용품 매장
adong-yongpum maejang
children's department

가방 매장
gabang maejang
luggage department

신발 매장
sinbal maejang
shoe department

매장 안내도
maejang annaedo
store directory

판매원
panmaewon
salesclerk

고객 서비스
gogaek seobiseu
customer services

탈의실
tal-uisil
fitting rooms

기저귀 교환실
gijeogwi gyohwansil
baby changing room

화장실
hwajangsil
restroom

이거 얼마예요?
i-geo eolmayeyo?
How much is this?

이거 교환할 수 있어요?
igeo gyohwanhal
sssu isseoyo?
May I exchange this?

백화점 baekhwajeom • **department store**

남성복
namseongbok
menswear

여성복
yeoseongbok
womens wear

란제리
lanjeri
lingerie

향수 가게
hyangsoo gage
perfumes

미용
miyong
cosmetics

침구류
chimgooryu
linens

가정용 가구
gajeong-yong gagu
home furnishings

비닐질 용품
baneujil yongpum
notions

주방용품
joobang-yongpum
kitchenware

자기 그릇
jagi geureut
china

전자 제품
jeonja jepum
electronics

조명
jomyeong
lighting

스포츠
seupocheu
sportswear

완구
wangu
toys

문구
mungu
stationery

식품매장
sikpoom maejang
groceries

슈퍼마켓 shoopeomaket · **supermarket**

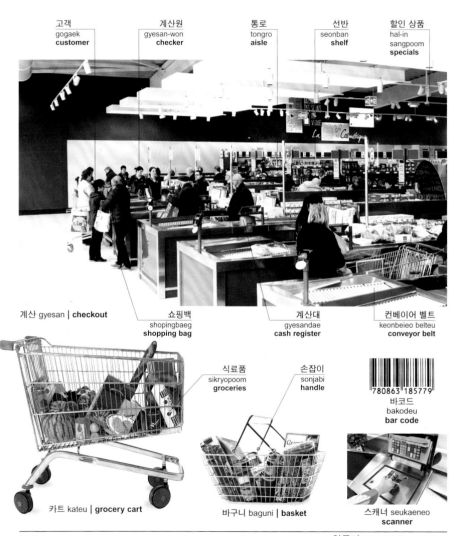

고객
gogaek
customer

계산원
gyesan-won
checker

통로
tongro
aisle

선반
seonban
shelf

할인 상품
hal-in
sangpoom
specials

계산 gyesan | **checkout**

쇼핑백
shopingbaeg
shopping bag

계산대
gyesandae
cash register

컨베이어 벨트
keonbeieo belteu
conveyor belt

식료품
sikryopoom
groceries

손잡이
sonjabi
handle

7 80863 185779

바코드
bakodeu
bar code

카트 kateu | **grocery cart**

바구니 baguni | **basket**

스캐너 seukaeneo
scanner

빵류
ppangryu
bakery

유제품
yujepum
dairy

아침식사용 시리얼
achimsiksayong sirieol
breakfast cereals

통조림
tongjorim
canned food

사탕류
satangryu
candy

채소류
chaesoryu
vegetables

과일류
gwailyu
fruit

육류 및 조류
yukryu mit joryu
meat and poultry

어류
eoryu
fish

델리카트슨
dellikateuseun
dcli

냉동 식품
nengdong sikpoom
frozen food

즉석 식품
jeukseog sikpoom
prepared food

음료
eumryo
drinks

가정용품
gajeong-yongpum
household products

세면용품
semyeon-yongpoom
toiletries

유아용품
yuayongpum
baby products

전자 제품
jeonja jepum
electrical goods

애완동물 사료
aewandongmul saryo
pet food

잡지 jabji | **magazines**

약국 yakgook · **drugstore**

치아 관리용품
chia gwanli-yongpoom
dental care

여성 위생용품
yeoseong wisaeng-yongpoom
feminine hygiene

데오도란트
deodoranteu
deodorants

비타민
bitamin
vitamins

조제실
jojesil
pharmacy

약사
yaksa
pharmacist

기침약
gichim-yak
cough medicine

허브 약품
heobeu yakpoom
herbal remedies

스킨 케어
seukin keeo
skin care

에프터선크림
epeuteoseonkeurim
aftersun lotion

선크림
seonkeurim
sunscreen

자외선 차단제
jaoeseon chadanje
sunblock

벌레 퇴치제
beolle toechije
insect repellent

물티슈
multishyu
wet wipe

티슈
tishu
tissue

생리대
saengridae
sanitary napkin

탐폰
tampon
tampon

팬티 라이너
paenti laineo
panty liner

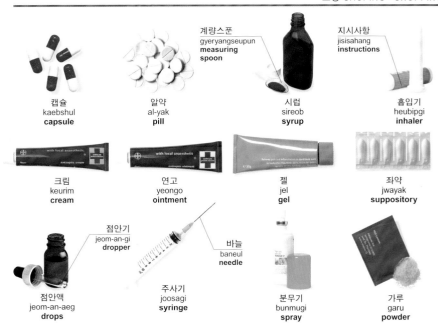

캡슐
kaebshul
capsule

알약
al-yak
pill

계량스푼
gyeryangseupun
measuring spoon

시럽
sireob
syrup

지시사항
jisisahang
instructions

흡입기
heubipgi
inhaler

크림
keurim
cream

연고
yeongo
ointment

젤
jel
gel

좌약
jwayak
suppository

점안기
jeom-an-gi
dropper

바늘
baneul
needle

점안액
jeom-an-aeg
drops

주사기
joosagi
syringe

분무기
bunmugi
spray

가루
garu
powder

어휘 eohwi · **vocabulary**

약물 치료 yagmul chiryo **medication**	철분 cheolbun **iron**	인슐린 inshullin **insulin**	소염제 soyeomje **anti-inflammatory**	목캔디 mogkaendi **throat lozenge**
약 yak **medicine**	칼슘 kalshoom **calcium**	진통제 jintongje **painkiller**	변비약 byeonbiyak **laxative**	일회용 ilhoeyong **disposable**
복용량 bog-yongryang **dosage**	마그네슘 mageuneshoom **magnesium**	진정제 jinjeongje **sedative**	설사약 seolsa yak **diarrhea medication**	유통기한 yutong-gihan **expiration date**
부작용 bujak-yong **side effects**	종합 비타민제 jonghab bitaminje **multivitamins**	수면제 soomyeonje **sleeping pill**	멀미약 meolmiyak **motion-sickness pills**	용해성 yonghaeseong **soluble**
마스크 maseukeu **face mask**				

꽃집 kkotjib · **florist**

꽃
kkot
flowers

백합
baekhab
lily

아카시아
akasia
acacia

화초
hwacho
potted plant

글라디올러스
geulladiolleoseu
gladiolus

아이리스
airiseu
iris

데이지
deiji
daisy

국화
gookhwa
chrysanthemum

안개꽃
angaekkot
baby's breath

카네이션
kaneisheon
carnation

스톡	거베라	군엽	장미	프리지아
stok	geobera	goon-yeob	jangmi	peurijia
stock	**gerbera**	**foliage**	**rose**	**freesia**

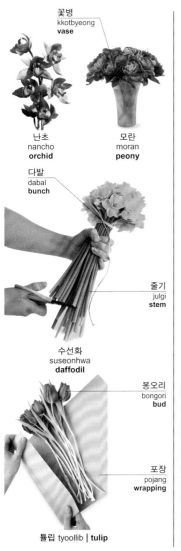

꽃병
kkotbyeong
vase

난초
nancho
orchid

모란
moran
peony

다발
dabal
bunch

줄기
julgi
stem

수선화
suseonhwa
daffodil

봉오리
bongori
bud

포장
pojang
wrapping

튤립 tyoollib | **tulip**

꽃꽂이 kkotkkoji • **arrangements**

리본
libon
ribbon

부케
buke
bouquet

드라이플라워
deuraipeullawoe
dried flowers

포프리 popeuri | **potpourri**

화환 hwahwan
wreath

화관
hwagwan
garland

어휘 eohwi • **vocabulary**

...한 다발 주세요.
...han dabal juseyo
**Can I have a bunch
of... please?**

포장해 드릴까요?
pojanghae deurilkkayo?
Can I have them wrapped?

메시지를 같이 넣어 드릴까요?
mesijireul gachi
neo-eo deurilkkayo?
Can I attach a message?

꽃이 얼마나 오래 갈까요?
kkochi eolmana
orae galkkayo?
How long will these last?

향기가 납니까?
hyang-giga nabnikka?
Are they fragrant?

...(으)로 보내주실 수 있나요?
...(eu)ro bonajoosil
soo itnayo?
Can you send them to... ?

신문 가게 sinmun gage · **newsstand**

담배갑
dambaegab
pack of cigarettes

라이터
laiteo
lighter

재떨이
jaetteol-i
ashtray

우표
upyo
stamps

우편엽서
upyeon-yeopseo
postcard

만화책
manhwachaek
comic book

잡지
jabji
magazine

신문
sinmun
newspaper

흡연 heub-yeon · **smoking**

잎담배
ipdambae
tobacco

시가
siga
cigar

전자담배
jeonjadambae
vape

전자담배 액상
joenjadambae aeksang
vape liquid

과자점 gwajajeom • **candy store**

초콜릿 박스
chokollit bakseu
box of chocolates

에너지 바
ae-neoji ba
snack bar

칩스 과자류
chipseu
gwajaryu
potato chips

어휘 eohwi • **vocabulary**

밀크 초콜릿
milkeu chokollit
milk chocolate

카라멜
karamel
caramel

플레인 초콜릿
peullein chokollit
dark chocolate

트러플
teureopeul
truffle

화이트 초콜릿
hwaiteu chokollit
white chocolate

비스킷
biseukit
cookie

골라 담기
golla damgi
pick and mix

사탕류 satangryu • **confectionery**

초콜릿
chokollit
chocolate

초콜릿 바
chokollit ba
chocolate bar

사탕
satang
hard candy

막대 사탕
makdae satang
lollipop

토피 사탕 topi satang
toffee

누가 nuga
nougat

마시멜로
masimello
marshmallow

민트
minteu
mint

껌
kkeom
chewing gum

젤리빈
jellibin
jellybean

과일껌
gwailkkeom
gumdrop

감초 사탕
gamcho satang
licorice

기타 상점 gita sangjeom · **other stores**

제과점
jegwajeom
bakery

케이크 가게
keikeu gage
pastry shop

정육점
jeong-yookjeom
butcher shop

생선 가게
sangseon gage
fish counter

청과물 가게
cheong-gwamul gage
produce stand

식료품점
sigryopumjeom
grocery store

신발 가게
shinbal gage
shoe store

철물점
cheolmuljeom
hardware store

골동품점
goldongpumjeom
antiques store

선물 가게
seonmul gage
gift shop

여행사
yeohaengsa
travel agency

보석상
boseoksang
jewelry store

서점
seojeom
bookstore

주류 판매점
juryu panmaejeom
liquor store

애완동물 가게
aewandongmul gage
pet supplies store

가구점
gagujeom
furniture store

양장점
yangjangjeom
boutique

어휘 eohwi • **vocabulary**

원예용품점
won-yeyongpumjeom
garden center

빨래방
bballaebang
laundromat

세탁소
saetakso
dry cleaner

열쇠 가게
yeolsoe gage
locksmith

부동산 중개소
budongsan jung-gaeso
real estate office

건강식품점
geongang sikpoomjeom
health food store

미술용품점
misulyongpoomjeom
art supply store

중고용품 가게
joong-goyongpoom gage
secondhand store

델리카트슨
dellikateuseun
deli

양복점
yangbokjeom
tailor shop

미용실
miyongsil
salon

휴대폰 샵
hiudaepon shap
phone store

신발 수선
shinbal suseon
shoe repairs

시장 sijang | **market**

식품 sikpoom
food

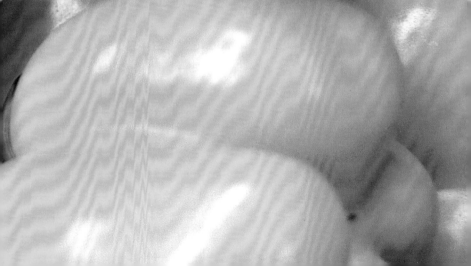

육류 yukryu • **meat**

양고기
yang-gogi
lamb

정육점 주인
jeongyukjeom
jooin
butcher

고기용 갈고리
gogiyong galgori
meat hook

저울
jeowool
scale

칼갈이
kalgal-i
knife sharpener

베이컨
beikeon
bacon

소시지
sosiji
sausages

간
gan
liver

어휘 eohwi • **vocabulary**

돼지고기 dwaejigogi **pork**	토끼고기 tokkigogi **rabbit**	혀 hyeo **tongue**	유기농 yuginong **organic**	흰살 고기 huinsal gogi **white meat**
소고기 sogogi **beef**	사슴고기 saseumgogi **venison**	내장 naejang **variety meat**	방목 bangmok **free range**	붉은 고기 bulgeun gogi **red meat**
송아지 고기 song-aji gogi **veal**	사냥감 sanang-gam **game**	코셔 kosheo **kosher**	염장 yeomjang **cured**	살코기 salkogi **lean meat**
염소 yeomso **goat**		할랄 halal **halal**	훈제 hoonje **smoked**	익힌 고기 ikhin gogi **cooked meat**

고기 커팅 방식 gogi keoting bangsik • **cuts**

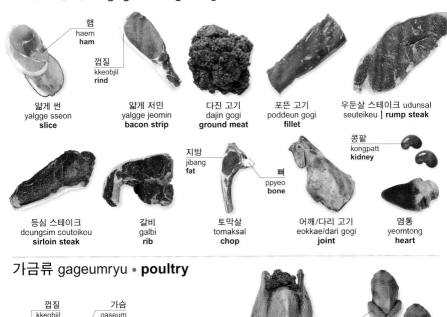

얇게 썬
yalgge sseon
slice

햄
haem
ham

껍질
kkeobjil
rind

얇게 저민
yalgge jeomin
bacon strip

다진 고기
dajin gogi
ground meat

포뜬 고기
poddeun gogi
fillet

우둔살 스테이크 udunsal
seuteikeu | **rump steak**

등심 스테이크
dcungsim scutcikou
sirloin steak

갈비
galbi
rib

지방
jibang
fat

뼈
ppyeo
bone

토막살
tomaksal
chop

콩팥
kongpatt
kidney

어깨/다리 고기
eokkae/dari gogi
joint

염통
yeomtong
heart

가금류 gageumryu • **poultry**

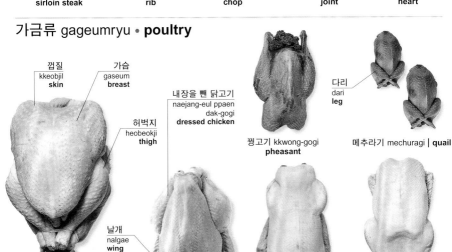

껍질
kkeobjil
skin

가슴
gaseum
breast

내장을 뺀 닭고기
naejang-eul ppaen
dak-gogi
dressed chicken

다리
dari
leg

허벅지
heobeokji
thigh

꿩고기 kkwong-gogi
pheasant

메추라기 mechuragi | **quail**

날개
nalgae
wing

칠면조
chilmyeonjo
turkey

닭고기 dak-gogi
chicken

오리고기 origogi
duck

거위고기
geowigogi | **goose**

어류 eoryu · **fish**

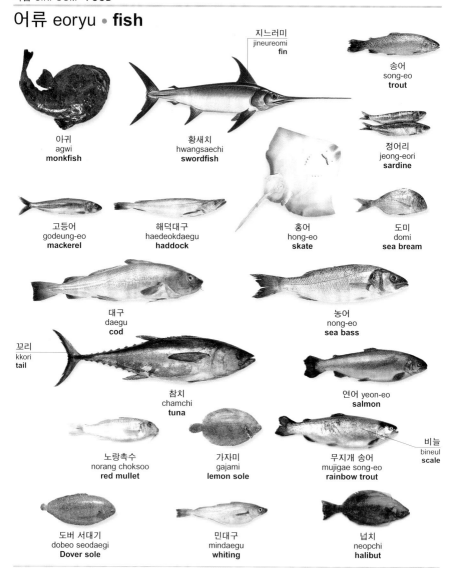

지느러미
jineureomi
fin

송어
song-eo
trout

아귀
agwi
monkfish

황새치
hwangsaechi
swordfish

정어리
jeong-eori
sardine

고등어
godeung-eo
mackerel

해덕대구
haedeokdaegu
haddock

홍어
hong-eo
skate

도미
domi
sea bream

대구
daegu
cod

농어
nong-eo
sea bass

꼬리
kkori
tail

참치
chamchi
tuna

연어 yeon-eo
salmon

노랑촉수
norang choksoo
red mullet

가자미
gajami
lemon sole

무지개 송어
mujigae song-eo
rainbow trout

비늘
bineul
scale

도버 서대기
dobeo seodaegi
Dover sole

민대구
mindaegu
whiting

넙치
neopchi
halibut

해산물 haesanmul • seafood

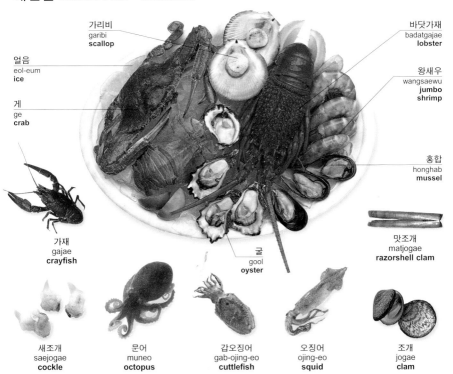

가리비
garibi
scallop

바닷가재
badatgajae
lobster

얼음
eol-eum
ice

왕새우
wangsaewu
jumbo shrimp

게
ge
crab

홍합
honghab
mussel

가재
gajae
crayfish

맛조개
matjogae
razorshell clam

굴
gool
oyster

새조개
saejogae
cockle

문어
muneo
octopus

갑오징어
gab-ojing-eo
cuttlefish

오징어
ojing-eo
squid

조개
jogae
clam

어휘 eohwi • vocabulary

신선한 sinseonhan **fresh**	소금 뿌린 sogeum bburin **salted**	비늘을 벗겨낸 bineul-eul beotgyeonaen **scaled**	손질한 sonjilhan **cleaned**	포를 뜬 poreul ddeun **filleted**	새우 saewu **shrimp**	몸통살 momtongsal **loin**
냉동 naengdong **frozen**	훈제 hoonje **smoked**	뼈를 발라낸 ppyeoreul ballanaen **boned**	껍질 벗긴 kkeobjil beotgin **skinned**	포뜬 고기 poddeun gogi **fillet**	스테이크 seuteikeu **steak**	뼈 ppyeo **bone**

손질해 주시겠어요?
sonjilhe joosigesseoyo?
Will you clean it for me?

채소류 chaesoryu • **vegetables (1)**

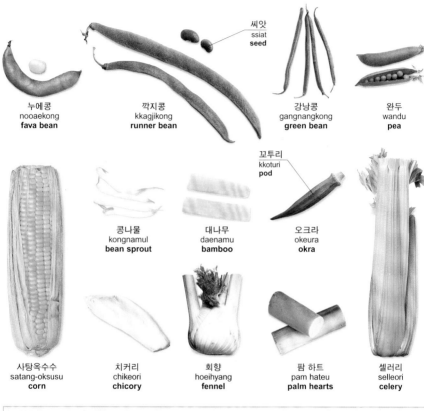

씨앗
ssiat
seed

누에콩
nooaekong
fava bean

깍지콩
kkagjikong
runner bean

강낭콩
gangnangkong
green bean

완두
wandu
pea

꼬투리
kkoturi
pod

콩나물
kongnamul
bean sprout

대나무
daenamu
bamboo

오크라
okeura
okra

사탕옥수수
satang-oksusu
corn

치커리
chikeori
chicory

회향
hoeihyang
fennel

팜 하트
pam hateu
palm hearts

셀러리
selleori
celery

어휘 eohwi • **vocabulary**

잎 ip **leaf**	꽃 부분 kkot bubun **floret**	끝부분 kkeutbubun **tip**	유기농 yuginong **organic**	유기농 채소가 있나요? yuginong chaesoga itnayo? **Do you sell organic vegetables?**
줄기 julgi **stalk**	알맹이 almaeng-i **kernel**	심장 simjang **heart**	비닐 봉지 binil bongji **plastic bag**	이 지역산입니까? i jiyeoksan-imnikka? **Are these grown locally?**

루콜라
rukolla
arugula

물냉이
mulnaeng-i
watercress

레드 치커리
laedue chikeori
radicchio

방울 양배추
bang-ul yangbaechu
Brussels sprout

근대
geundae
Swiss chard

케일
keil
kale

수영
sooyeong
sorrel

꽃상추
kkotsangchu
endive

민들레
mindeulle
dandelion

시금치
sigeumchi
spinach

콜라비
kollabi
kohlrabi

청경채
cheong-gyeongchae
bok choy

양상추
yangsangchoo
lettuce

브로콜리
beurokolli
broccoli

양배추
yangbaechu
cabbage

어린 양배추 잎
eorin yangbaechut nip
spring greens

채소류 chaesoryu • **vegetables (2)**

순무
soonmu
turnip

아티초크
atichokeu
artichoke

콜리플라워
kollipeullawoe
cauliflower

무
mu
radish

아스파라거스
aseuparageoseu
asparagus

감자
gamja
potato

늙은
주키니 호박
neulgeun
jookini hobak
squash

양파
yangpa
onion

후추
hoochu
bell pepper

고추
gochu
chili pepper

사탕옥수수
satang-oksusu
sweetcorn

어휘 eohwi • **vocabulary**

방울 토마토 bang-ul tomato **cherry tomato**	셀러리악 selleoriak **celeriac**	냉동 naengdong **frozen**	쓴 sseun **bitter**	감자 1킬로 주세요. gamja il-killo jooseyo **A kilo of potatoes, please.**
당근 dang-geun **carrot**	타로토란 tarotoran **taro root**	날것의 nalgeot-ui **raw**	단단한 dandanhan **firm**	1킬로에 얼만가요? ilkilloae eolmangayo? **What's the price per kilo?**
빵나무 열매 ppangnamu yeolmae **breadfruit**	카사바 kasaba **cassava**	매운 maeun **hot (spicy)**	과육 gwayuk **flesh**	이건 이름이 뭔가요? i-geon i-reum-i mwongayo? **What are those called?**
햇감자 haetgamja **new potato**	마름 mareum **water chestnut**	달콤한 dalkomhan **sweet**	뿌리 ppuri **root**	

고구마
goguma
sweet potato

참마
chamma
yam

비트 뿌리
biteu ppuri
beet

스웨덴 순무
seuweden soonmu
rutabaga

돼지감자
dwaejigamja
Jerusalem artichoke

양고추냉이
yang-gochu-nang-i
horseradish

파스닙
paseu-nib
parsnip

생강
saeng-gang
ginger

가지
gaji
eggplant

토마토
tomato
tomato

파
pa
scallion

서양 대파
seoyang daepa
leek

샬롯
shallot
shallot

정향
jeonghyang
clove

마늘
maneul
garlic

송로
songlo
truffle

버섯
beoseot
mushroom

오이
oi
cucumber

주키니 호박
jookini hobak
zucchini

땅콩 호박
ddangkong hobak
butternut squash

도토리 호박
dotori hobak
acorn squash

호박
hobag
pumpkin

과일류 gwailyu • **fruit (1)**

감귤류 gamgyulyu • **citrus fruit**

오렌지
orenji
orange

귤
gyul
clementine

속
sok
pith

자메이카 귤
jameika gyul
ugli fruit

자몽
jamong
grapefruit

귤 한 쪽
gyul han jjok
segment

온주귤
onjoogyul
satsuma

편귤
pyeon-gyul
tangerine

껍질
kkeobjil
zest

라임
la-im
lime

레몬
lemon
lemon

금귤
geumgyul
kumquat

핵과 haekgwa • **stone fruit**

복숭아
boksoonga
peach

천도 복숭아
cheondo boksoonga
nectarine

살구
salgu
apricot

자두
jadu
plum

체리
cheri
cherry

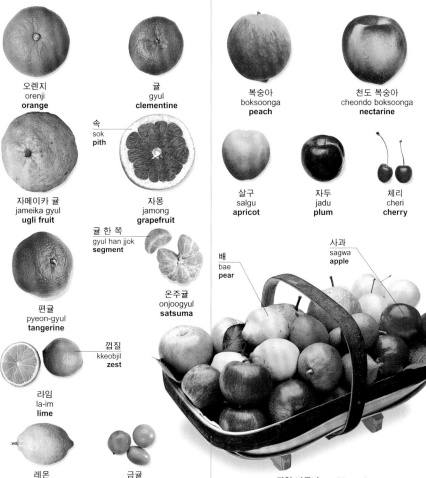

배
bae
pear

사과
sagwa
apple

과일 바구니 gwail baguni
basket of fruit

장과류 및 멜론류 jang-gwaryu mit mellonryu
berries and melons

딸기
ttalgi
strawberry

라즈베리
lajeuberi
raspberry

멜론
mellon
melon

포도
podo
grapes

블랙베리
beullaekberi
blackberry

레드커런트
ledeu keoreonteu
red currant

크랜베리
keuraenberi
cranberry

블랙커런트
beullaegkeoreonteu
black currant

껍질
kkeobjil
rind

씨
ssi
seed

과육
gwayuk
flesh

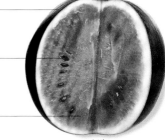

수박
subak
watermelon

블루베리
beulluberi
blueberry

화이트커런트
hwaiteukeoreonteu
white currant

로건베리
logeonberi
loganberry

구스베리
guseumeri
gooseberry

어휘 eohwi · **vocabulary**

달콤한 dalkomhan **sweet**	신선한 sinseonhan **fresh**	즙이 많은 jeub-i man-eun **juicy**	이거 잘 익었나요? i-geo jal ik-eotnayo? **Are they ripe?**
신 sin **sour**	썩은 sseok-eun **rotten**	아삭아삭한 asak-asakhan **crisp**	먹어봐도 돼요? meog-eobwado dwaeyo? **Can I try one?**
섬유질 seom-yujil **fiber**	주스 jooseu **juice**	루바브 lubabeu **rhubarb**	얼마동안 신선도를 유지합니까? eolmadong-an sinseondoreul yujihamnikka? **How long will they keep?**
과육 gwayuk **pulp**	속 sok **core**	씨없는 ssieomneun **seedless**	

과일류 gwailyu • **fruit (2)**

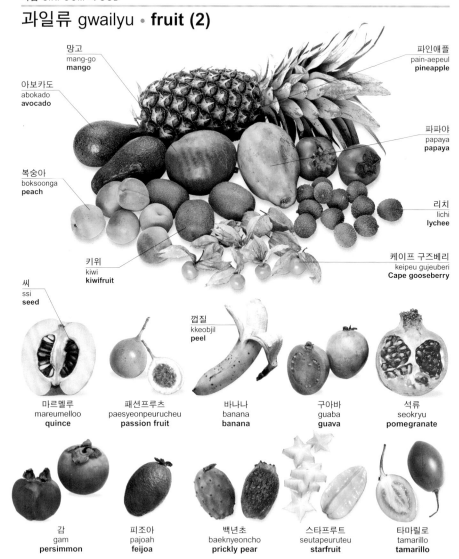

망고
mang-go
mango

파인애플
pain-aepeul
pineapple

아보카도
abokado
avocado

파파야
papaya
papaya

복숭아
boksoonga
peach

리치
lichi
lychee

케이프 구즈베리
keipeu gujeuberi
Cape gooseberry

키위
kiwi
kiwifruit

씨
ssi
seed

껍질
kkeobjil
peel

마르멜루
mareumelloo
quince

패션프루츠
paesyeonpeurucheu
passion fruit

바나나
banana
banana

구아바
guaba
guava

석류
seokryu
pomegranate

감
gam
persimmon

피조아
pajoah
feijoa

백년초
baeknyeoncho
prickly pear

스타프루트
seutapeuruteu
starfruit

타마릴로
tamarillo
tamarillo

견과류 및 말린 과일 gyeongwaryu mit mallin gwail
nuts and dried fruit

잣
jat
pine nut

피스타치오
piseutachio
pistachio

캐슈넛
kaeshooneot
cashew

땅콩
ttangkong
peanut

헤이즐넛
heijeulneot
hazelnut

브라질넛
beurajilneot
brazil nut

피칸
pikan
pecan

아몬드
amondeu
almond

호두
hodu
walnut

밤
bam
chestnut

마카다미아
makadamia
macadamia

무화과
muhwagwa
fig

대추
daechu
date

말린 자두
mallin jadu
prune

껍질
kkeobjil
shell

과육
gwayuk
flesh

술타나 건포도
sool tana geonpodo
sultana

건포도
geonpodo
raisin

커런트
keoreonteu
currant

코코넛
kokoneot
coconut

어휘 eohwi · vocabulary

딱딱한	날것의	전체	볶은	알맹이	제철	설탕 조림 과일
ttakttakhan	nalgeot-ui	jeonche	bok-eun	almaeng-i	jaecheol	seoltang jorim gwail
hard	**raw**	**whole**	**roasted**	**kernel**	**seasonal**	**candied fruit**
부드러운	익은	껍질을 벗긴	소금을 첨가한	건조한	덜 익은	열대 과일
budeureoun	ik-eun	kkeobjil-eul beotgin	sogeum cheomgahan	geonjohan	deol ik-eun	yeoldae gwa-il
soft	**ripe**	**shelled**	**salted**	**desiccated**	**green**	**tropical fruit**
						잭푸르트
						jacpureuteu
						jackfruit

곡물 및 콩류 gogmul mit kongryu · **grains and legumes**

곡물 gogmul · **grains**

밀
mil
wheat

귀리
gwiri
oats

보리
bori
barley

수수
susu
millet

옥수수
oksusu
corn

퀴노아
kwinoa
quinoa

쌀 ssal · **rice**

백미
baekmi
white rice

현미
hyeonmi
brown rice

야생쌀
yasaengssal
wild rice

푸딩용 쌀
puding-yong ssal
arborio rice

가공 곡물 gagong gogmul
processed grains

쿠스쿠스
kuseukuseu
couscous

빻은 밀
ppah-eun mil
cracked wheat

세몰리나
semollina
semolina

속겨
sokgyeo
bran

콩류 kongryu · **legumes**

리마콩
limakong
butter beans

풋강낭콩
putgangnangkong
haricot beans

강낭콩
gangnangkong
red kidney beans

팥
pat
adzuki beans

누에콩
nooaekong
fava beans

대두
daedu
soybeans

동부콩
dongbukong
black-eyed peas

핀토빈
pintobin
pinto beans

녹두
nokdu
mung beans

플라졸레콩
peullajollaekong
flageolet beans

갈색 렌틸콩
galsaeg lentilkong
brown lentils

적색 렌틸콩
jeoksaeg lentilkong
red lentils

초록 렌틸콩
chorog lentilkong
green peas

병아리콩
byeong-arikong
chickpeas

완두 짜개
wandoo jjagae
split peas

씨앗 ssiat · **seeds**

호박씨
hobagssi
pumpkin seed

겨자씨
gyeojassi
mustard seed

캐러웨이 씨드
kaereowei ssideu
caraway seed

참깨
chamkkae
sesame seed

해바라기씨
haebaragissi
sunflower seed

허브 및 향신료 heobeu mit hyangsinryo
herbs and spices

향신료 hyangsinryo · **spices**

바닐라 banilla
vanilla

육두구
yookdugu
nutmeg

육두구 껍질
yookdugoo kkeobjil
mace

강황
ganghwang
turmeric

커민
keomin
cumin

부케가르니
bookaegareuni
bouquet garni

올스파이스
olseupaiseu
allspice

통후추
tonghuchu
peppercorn

호로파
horopa
fenugreek

고추
gochu
chili powder

통째로
tongjjaero
whole

으깬
eukkaen
crushed

사프란
sapeuran
saffron

카다몬
kadamon
cardamom

카레 가루
kare garu
curry powder

갈아 놓은
gara noh-eun
ground

파프리카
papeurika
paprika

박편
bakpyeon
flakes

마늘
maneul
garlic

허브 heobeu · **herbs**

막대기
makdaegi
sticks

계피
gyepi
cinnamon

회향씨
hoeihyangssi
fennel seeds

월계수잎
wolgyesu-ip
bay leaf

파슬리
paseulli
parsley

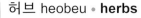

회향
hoeihyang
fennel

레몬그라스
lemongeuraseu
lemongrass

정향
jeonghyang
cloves

골파
golpa
chives

민트
minteu
mint

백리향
baeglihyang
thyme

세이지
seiji
sage

팔각
palgag
star anise

타라곤
taragon
tarragon

마저럼
majeoreom
marjoram

바질
bajil
basil

생강
saeng-gang
ginger

오레가노
oregano
oregano

코리안더
koriandeo
cilantro

딜
dil
dill

로즈마리
lojeumari
rosemary

병조림 byeongjorim · **bottled foods**

코르크
koreukeu
cork

해바라기유
haebaragiyu
sunflower oil

호두유
hoduyu
walnut oil

포도씨유
podossiyu
grapeseed oil

아몬드유
amondeuyu
almond oil

참기름
chamgireum
**sesame
seed oil**

헤이즐넛유
heijeulneot-yu
hazelnut oil

올리브유
ollibeuyu
olive oil

허브
heobeu
herbs

맛을 첨가한 기름
maseul cheomgahan
gireum
flavored oil

기름
gireum
oils

스위트 스프레드 seuwiteu seupeuredeu
sweet spreads

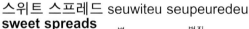

병
byeong
jar

벌집
beoljib
honeycomb

생꿀
saengkkul
raw honey

레몬 커드
lemon keodeu
lemon curd

라즈베리 잼
lajeubaeri jaem
raspberry jam

마멀레이드
mameolleideu
marmalade

정제꿀
jeongjekkul
clear honey

메이플 시럽
meipeul sireob
maple syrup

소스 및 양념 soseu mit yangnyeom
sauces and condiments

병
byeong
bottle

사과 식초
sagwa sikcho
cider vinegar

발사믹 식초
balsamig sikcho
balsamic vinegar

마요네즈
mayonejeu
mayonnaise

케첩
kecheob
ketchup

잉글리쉬 머스타드
ing-geulliswi meoseutadeu
English mustard

프렌치 머스타드
peurenchi meoseutadeu
Dijon mustard

처트니
cheoteuni
chutney

맥아 식초
maeg-a sikcho
malt vinegar

와인 식초
wa-in sikcho
wine vinegar

소스
soseu
sauce

홀그레인 머스타드
holgeurein meoseutadeu
whole-grain mustard

식초
sikcho
vinegar

절임용 유리용기
jeol-im-yong yooriyong-gi
canning jar

땅콩 버터
ttangkong beoteo
peanut butter

초콜릿 스프레드
chokollit seupeuredeu
chocolate spread

절인 과일
jeorin gwail
preserved fruit

어휘 eohwi • vocabulary

옥수수기름
oksusugireum
corn oil

유채씨유
yuchaessiyu
canola oil

식용유
sig-yong-yu
vegetable oil

냉압착유
naeng-abchak-yu
cold-pressed oil

땅콩유
ttangkong-yu
peanut oil

간장
ganjang
soy sauce

유제품 yujepum · **dairy products**

치즈 chijeu · **cheese**

껍질
kkeobjil
rind

반경질 치즈
bangyeongjil chijeu
semi-hard cheese

가루 치즈
garoo chijeu
grated cheese

경질 치즈
gyeongjil chijeu
hard cheese

반연질 치즈
ban-yeonjil chijeu
semi-soft cheese

코티지 치즈
kotiji chijeu
cottage cheese

크림 치즈
keurim chijeu
cream cheese

블루 치즈
beullu chijeu
blue cheese

연질 치즈
yeonjil chijeu
soft cheese

신선한 치즈 sinseonhan chijeu | **fresh cheese**

우유 uyoo · **milk**

전유
jeonyoo
whole milk

저지방 우유
jeojibang uyoo
reduced-fat milk

무지방 우유
mujibang uyoo
skim milk

우유팩
uyoopaek
milk carton

염소젖
yeomso jeot
goat's milk

연유
yeon-yoo
condensed milk

우유 uyoo | **cow's milk**

버터
beoteo
butter

마가린
magarin
margarine

크림
keurim
cream

싱글 크림
sing-geul keurim
half-and-half

더블 크림
deobeul keurim
heavy cream

휘핑 크림
hwiping keurim
whipped cream

사워 크림
sawo keurim
sour cream

요거트
yogeoteu
yogurt

아이스크림
aiseu keurim
ice cream

달걀 dalgyal · **eggs**

노른자
noreunja
egg yolk

흰자
huinja
egg white

껍질
kkeobjil
shell

에그컵
egeukeob
eggcup

삶은 달걀 salmeun dalgyal
soft-boiled egg

거위알
geowial
goose egg

메추리알
mechurial
quail egg

달걀
dalgyal
hen's egg

오리알
orial
duck egg

어휘 eohwi · **vocabulary**

밀크쉐이크
milkeusheikeu
milk shake

소금에 절인
sogeum-e jeorin
salted

무지방
mujibang
fat-free

무살균
musalgyun
unpasteurized

귀리 우유
guiri wuyu
oat milk

분유
bun-yoo
powdered milk

냉동 요거트
naengdong yogeoteu
frozen yogurt

무염
muyeom
unsalted

유당
yoodang
lactose

살균
salgyun
pasteurized

아몬드 우유
amondeu wuyu
almond milk

버터밀크
beoteomilkeu
buttermilk

빵과 밀가루 ppang-gwa milgaru · **breads and flours**

빵 한 덩이
ppang han deong-i
loaf

바게트
bageteu
baguette

치아바타
chiabata
ciabatta

호밀빵
homilppang
rye bread

크루아상
keuruasang
croissant

빵류 ppangryu | **bakery**

빵 만들기 ppang mandeulgi · **making bread**

흰 밀가루
huin milgaru
white flour

갈색 밀가루
galsaek milgaru
brown flour

통밀가루
tongmilgaru
whole-wheat flour

이스트
iseuteu
yeast

체로 치다 chida
sift (v)

섞다 seokkda
mix (v)

반죽
banjook
dough

반죽하다 banjookhada
knead (v)

굽다 goobda
bake (v)

빵 껍질
ppang
kkeobjil
crust

흰 빵
huin ppang
white bread

흑빵
heukppang
brown bread

통밀빵
tongmilppang
whole-wheat bread

얇게 썬
yalgge sseon
slice

그라나리 빵
geuranari ppang
multigrain bread

옥수수빵
oksusuppang
corn bread

소다빵
sodappang
soda bread

사워도우 빵
sawodou ppang
sourdough bread

플랫브레드
peullaet beuraedeu
flat bread

베이글
beigeul
bagel

납작하고 둥근 빵 nabjakhago
doong-geun ppang | **bun**

롤
lol | **roll**

과일빵
gwailppang
fruit bread

씨앗빵
ssiatppang
seeded bread

난
nan
naan bread

피타 브레드
pita beuredeu
pita bread

크네케브뢰드
keunaekaebeuroedue
crispbread

어휘 eohwi • **vocabulary**

강력분 gangryeokbun **bread flour**	중력분 joongryeogboon **all-purpose flour**	부풀다 bupulda **rise (v)**	슬라이서 seullaiseo **slicer**	빵가루 ppang-garu **breadcrumbs**
팽창제 혼합 밀가루 paengchangje honhap milgaroo **self-rising flour**	글루텐 무함유 geuluten muhamyu **gluten-free**	부풀리다 bupullida **prove (v)**	가늘고 긴 프랑스 빵 ganeulgo gin peurangseu ppang **flute**	제빵사 jeppangsa **baker**

케이크 및 디저트 keikeu mit dijeoteu
cakes and desserts

에클레르
ekeullereu
éclair

크림
keurim
cream

필링
pilling
filling

슈 페이스트리
syoo peiseuteuri
choux pastry

퍼프 페이스트리
peopeu peiseuteuri
puff pastry

필로 페이스트리
pillo peiseuteuri
phyllo dough

과일 케이크
gwail keikeu
fruitcake

과일 타르트
gwail tareuteu
fruit tart

머랭
meoraeng
meringue

초콜릿 케이크
chokollit keikeu
chocolate-covered

머핀
meopin
muffin

스펀지 케이크
seuponji keikeu
sponge cake

케이크 keikeu | **cakes**

어휘 eohwi · **vocabulary**

커스터드 크림
keoseuteodeu keurim
crème pâtissière

초콜릿 케이크
chokollit keikeu
chocolate cake

번
beon
bun

페이스트리
peiseuteuri
pastry

커스타드
keoseutadeu
custard

라이스 푸딩
laiseu puding
rice pudding

조각
jogak
slice

축하
chukha
celebration

한 조각만 주세요.
han jogakman
juseyo
**May I have a
slice, please?**

초콜릿 칩
chokollit chib
chocolate chip

레이디 핑거
leidi ping-geo
ladyfinger

트라이플
teuraipeul
trifle

플로랑탱
peullorangtaeng
Florentine

비스킷 biseukit | **cookies**

무스
mooseu
mousse

셔벗
syeobeot
sherbet

크림 파이
keurim pai
cream pie

카라멜 크림
karamel keurim
crème caramel

축하 케이크 chukha keikeu · **celebration cakes**

가장 윗 단
gajang wit dan
top tier

리본
libon
ribbon

아랫단
alaetdan
bottom tier

아이싱
aissing
frosting

마지팬
majipaen
marzipan

웨딩 케이크 weding keikeu | **wedding cake**

장식
jangsik
decoration

생일 촛불
saeng-il chotbul
birthday candles

불어서 끄다
bul-eoseo
kkeuda
blow out (v)

생일 케이크 saeng-il keikeu
birthday cake

델리카트슨 dellikateuseun • **delicatessen**

매운 소시지
maeun sosiji
spicy sausage

오일
oil
oil

식초
sikcho
vinegar

타르트
tareuteu
quiche

날고기
nalgogi
uncooked meat

카운터
kaunteo
counter

살라미
sallami
salami

페퍼로니
paepaeroni
pepperoni

파테
pate
pâté

모차렐라
mocharella
mozzarella

브리
beuri
Brie

염소 치즈
yeomso chijeu
goat cheese

체다
chaeda
cheddar

파르메산
pareumaesan
Parmesan

카망베르
kamangbereu
Camembert

껍질
kkeobjil
rind

에담
aedam
Edam

만체고
manchego
Manchego

고기 파이
gogi pai
meat pies

블랙 올리브
beullaek ollibeu
black olive

칠리
chilli
chili pepper

소스
soseu
sauce

롤빵
lolppang
bread roll

익힌 고기
ikhin gogi
cooked meat

그린 올리브
grin ollibeu
green olive

샌드위치 판매대 saendeuwichi panmaedae
sandwich counter

햄
haem
ham

훈제 생선
hoonje saengseon
smoked fish

케이퍼
keipeo
capers

어휘 eohwi • **vocabulary**

소금물에 절인
sogeummul-e
jeorin
in brine

양념에 재운
yangnyeomae
jaeun
marinated

훈제
hoonje
smoked

기름에 보관한
gireumae
bogwanhan
in oil

소금에 절인
sogeum-e jeorin
salted

염장한
yeomjanghan
cured

번호표를 뽑으세요.
beonhopyoreul ppobeusaeyo
Take a number, please.

저것 조금만 먹어봐도 돼요?
jeogeot jogeumman meok-eobwado dwaeyo?
Can I try some of that, please?

저거 여섯 조각만 주세요.
jeogeo yeoseot jogakman jooseyo
May I have six slices of that, please?

프로슈토
peuroshooto
prosciutto

초리조
chorijo
chorizo

속을 채운 올리브
sok-eul chaeun ollibeu
stuffed olive

음료 eumryo • **drinks**

물 mool • **water**

병에 든 생수
byeong-e deun saengsu
bottled water

탄산수
tansansoo
sparkling

탄산이 없는 생수
tansan-i eobneun
saengsoo
still

생수
saengsoo | **mineral water**

수돗물
sudotmool
tap water

토닉 워터
tonig woteo
tonic water

소다 워터
soda woteo
soda water

뜨거운 음료 tteugeoun eumryo • **hot drinks**

티백
tibaeg
teabag

잎차
ipcha
loose-leaf tea

차
cha
tea

원두
wondu
beans

분쇄 커피
boonswae keopi
ground coffee

커피
keopi
coffee

핫 초콜릿
hat chokollit
hot chocolate

맥아 음료
maeg-a eumryo
malted milk

소프트 드링크 sopeuteu deuringkeu • **soft drinks**

빨대
ppaldae
straw

토마토 주스
tomato juseu
tomato juice

과일 주스
gwail juseu
fruit juice

레모네이드
lemo-neideu
lemonade

오렌지에이드
oraenjieideu
orangeade

콜라
kolla
cola

주류 jooryu • **alcoholic drinks**

진
jin | **gin**

캔
kaen
can

맥주
maekju
beer

사과술
sagwasool
hard cider

비터
biteo
amber ale

스타우트
seutauteu
stout

보드카
bodeuka | **vodka**

위스키 wiseuki
whiskey

럼
leom
rum

브랜디
beuraendi
brandy

포트와인
poteuwain
port

드라이
deurai
dry

세리주
sheriju
sherry

사케
sake
saké

로제
loje
rosé

화이트
hwaiteu
white

레드
ledeu
red

리큐어
likyu-eo
liqueur

테킬라
tekilla
tequila

샴페인
syampein
champagne

와인 wain | **wine**

외식 waesik
eating out

카페 kape • **café**

파라솔
parasol
umbrella

차양막
chayangmak
awning

테라스 카페
teraseu kape
patio café

메뉴
menyu
menu

커피 머신
keopi meosin
coffee machine

식탁
siktak
table

노상 카페 nosang kape | **sidewalk café**

간이 음식점 gan-i eumsikjeom
snack bar

커피 keopi • **coffee**

밀크 커피
milkeu keopi
coffee with milk

블랙 커피
beullaek keopi
black coffee

코코아 가루
kokoa garu
cocoa powder

거품
geopum
froth

필터 커피
pilteo keopi
filter coffee

에스프레소
eseupeureso
espresso

카푸치노
kapuchino
cappuccino

아이스 커피
aiseu keopi
iced coffee

차 cha • **tea**

허브티
heobeuti
herbal tea

카모마일티 kamomailti
chamomile tea

녹차
nokcha
green tea

밀크티
milkeuti
tea with milk

홍차
hongcha
black tea

레몬티
lemonti
tea with lemon

민트티
minteuti
mint tea

아이스티
aiseuti
iced tea

주스 및 밀크쉐이크 juseu mit milkeusheikeu
juices and milkshakes

초콜릿 밀크쉐이크
chokollit milkeusheikeu
chocolate milkshake

딸기 밀크쉐이크
ttalgi milkeusheikeu
strawberry milkshake

오렌지 주스
orenji juseu
orange juice

사과 주스
sagwa juseu
apple juice

파인애플 주스
pain-aepeul juseu
pineapple juice

토마토 주스
tomato juseu
tomato juice

커피 밀크쉐이크
keopi milkeusheikeu
coffee milkshake

식품 sikpoom • **food**

흑빵
heukppang
whole-wheat bread

스쿠프
seukupeu
scoop

토스트 샌드위치
toseuteu saendeuwichi
toasted sandwich

샐러드
saelleodeu
salad

아이스크림
aiseu keurim
ice cream

페이스트리
peiseuteuri
pastry

바 ba • **bar**

커피 머신
keopi meosin
coffee machine

맥주탭
maegjutaeb
beer tap

바텐더
batendeo
bartender

금전 출납기
geumjeon chulnabgi
cash register

바 카운터
ba kaunteo
bar counter

컵받침
keobbadchim
coaster

병따개
byeongttagae
bottle opener

집게
jibge
tongs

바 스푼
ba seupoon
stirrer

레버
lebeo
lever

계량컵
gyeryangkeob
measure

코르크 따개 corku ddagae
corkscrew

칵테일 셰이커 kakteil sheikeo
cocktail shaker

어휘 eohwi
vocabulary

주류 디스펜서
jooryu diseupaenseo
dispenser

얼음통
eol-eumtong
ice bucket

재떨이
jaetteol-i
ashtray

바 스툴
ba seutul
bar stool

피처
picheo
pitcher

각얼음
gag-eol-eum
ice cube

진토닉
jintonik
gin and tonic

물 탄 스카치 위스키
mool tan seukachi wiseuki
scotch and water

럼앤콕
leomaenkog
rum and cola

보드카 오렌지
bodeuka orenji
screwdriver

마티니
matlni
martini

칵테일
kakteil
cocktail

와인
wain
wine

맥주
maekju
beer

싱글
sing-geul
single

더블
deobeul
double

얼음과 레몬
eol-eumgwa lemon
ice and lemon

샷
shat
shot

분량
boonryang
measure

얼음 없이
eol-eum eobsi
without ice

얼음을 넣은
eol-eum-eul neoh-eun
with ice

안주류 anjooryu • **bar snacks**

캐슈넛
kaeshooneot
cashews

아몬드
amondeu
almonds

땅콩
ttangkong
peanuts

감자칩 gamjachip | **potato chips**

견과류 gyeongwaryu | **nuts**

올리브 ollibeu | **olives**

레스토랑 leseutorang • **restaurant**

테이블 셋팅
teibeul seting
table setting

보조 셰프
bojo shepeu
sous chef

셰프
shepeu
chef

주방 joobang | **kitchen**

잔
jan
glass

쟁반
jaengban
tray

웨이터 / 웨이트리스
weiteo m / weiteuriseu f
server

어휘 eohwi • **vocabulary**

저녁 메뉴 jeonyeok menyu **dinner menu**	특별 메뉴 teukbyeol maenyu **specials**	뷔페 bwipae **buffet**	가격 gagyeok **price**	팁 tib **tip**	봉사료 포함 bongsaryo poham **service charge included**
점심 메뉴 jeomsim menyu **lunch menu**	와인 목록 wain moglok **wine list**	바 ba **bar**	계산서 gyesanseo **check**	소금 sogeum **salt**	봉사료 제외 bongsaryo jae-oe **service charge not included**
일품 요리 ilpoom yori **à la carte**	후식 카트 husig kateu **dessert cart**	고객 gogaek **customer**	영수증 yeongsujeung **receipt**	후추 huchu **pepper**	

메뉴
menyu
menu

키즈밀
kijeumil
child's meal

주문하다 joomunhada
order (v)

지불하다 jibulhada | **pay (v)**

코스 koseu · **courses**

식전 술
sigjeon sool
apéritif

전채 요리
jeonchae yori
appetizer

수프
supeu
soup

메인 코스
maein koseu
entrée

사이드 디시
saideu dissi
side dish

디저트 dijeoteu
dessert

커피 keopi
coffee

2인용 테이블로 부탁해요.
i-in-yong teibeullo butakhaeyo
A table for two, please.

메뉴/와인 목록을 볼 수 있을까요?
menyu / wain moglog-eul bol
su isseulkkayo?
**Can I see the menu / wine
list, please?**

가격이 정해진 식사 메뉴도 있나요?
gagyeog-i jeonghaejin siksa
maenyudo itnayo?
Is there a fixed-price menu?

채식주의자용 메뉴도 있나요?
chaesikjooeuijayong maenudo itnayo?
Do you have any vegetarian dishes?

계산서/영수증을 주시겠어요?
gyesanseo / yeongsujeung-eul
jusigesseoyo?
**Could I have the check /
a receipt, please?**

각자 계산하겠습니다.
gakja gyesanhagessseumnida
Can we pay separately?

화장실이 어디입니까?
hwajangsil-i eodipnikka?
Where is the restroom, please?

패스트푸드 paeseuteupudeu • **fast food**

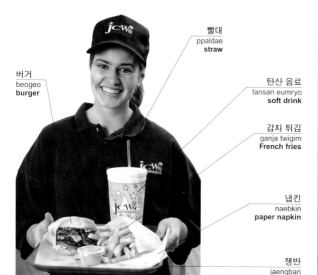

버거
beogeo
burger

빨대
ppaldae
straw

탄산 음료
tansan eumryo
soft drink

감자 튀김
ganja twigim
French fries

냅킨
naebkin
paper napkin

쟁반
jaengban
tray

버거 세트 beogeo seteu | **burger meal**

어휘 eohwi
vocabulary

피자 가게
pija gage
pizzeria

햄버거 가게
hambeogeo gage
burger bar

메뉴
menyu
menu

가게 안에서 먹기
gage an-aeseo meokgi
eat in

테이크아웃
teikeuaut
to go

재가열하다
jaegayeolhada
reheat (v)

케챱
kachap
ketchup

이거 가져가도 되나요?
i-geo gajyeogado doenayo?
**Can I have that
to go, please?**

배달 되나요?
baedal doenayo?
Do you deliver?

캔 음료
kaen eumryo
canned drink

가격 목록
gagyeok
moglog
price list

가정 배달 gajeong baedal
home delivery

거리 가판대 geori gapandae
street vendor

번
beon
bun

머스타드
meoseu-tadeu
mustard

소시지
sosiji
sausage

햄버거
haembeogeo
hamburger

치킨 버거
chikin beogeo
chicken sandwich

야채 버거
yachae beogeo
veggie burger

핫도그 hatdogeu | **hot dog**

필링
pilling
filling

샌드위치
saendeuwichi
sandwich

클럽 샌드위치
keulleob saendeuwichi
club sandwich

오픈 샌드위치
opeun saendeuwichi
open-faced sandwich

랩 샌드위치
laeb saendeuwichi
wrap

소스
soseu
sauce

짭짤한
jjabjjalhan
savory

달콤한
dalkomhan
sweet

케밥
kebab
kebab

치킨 너겟
chikin neoget
chicken nuggets

크레페 keurepe | **crepes**

토핑
toping
topping

피시 앤 칩스
pisi aen chipseu
fish and chips

갈비
galbi
ribs

프라이드 치킨
peuraideu chikin
fried chicken

피자
pija
pizza

아침식사 achimsigsa • **breakfast**

우유
uyoo
milk

시리얼
sirieol
cereal

설탕
seoltang
sugar

말린 과일
mallin gwail
dried fruit

햄
haem
ham

치즈
chijeu
cheese

크네케브뢰드
keunaekae-
beuroedue
crispbread

아침 뷔페
achim bwipe
breakfast buffet

마멀레이드
mameolleideu
marmalade

잼
jaem
jam

파테
pate
pâté

버터
beoteo
butter

과일 주스
gwail juseu
fruit juice

커피
keopi
coffee

핫 초콜릿
hat chokollit
hot chocolate

크루아상
keuruasang
croissant

차
cha
tea

아침 테이블 achim teibeul | **breakfast table**

음료 eumryo | **drinks**

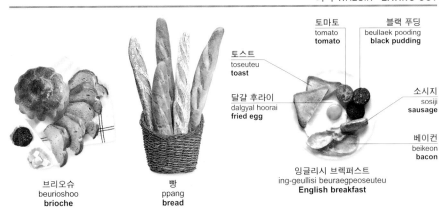

토마토
tomato
tomato

블랙 푸딩
beullaek pooding
black pudding

토스트
toseuteu
toast

달걀 후라이
dalgyal hoorai
fried egg

소시지
sosiji
sausage

베이컨
beikeon
bacon

잉글리시 브렉퍼스트
ing-geullisi beuraegpeoseuteu
English breakfast

브리오슈
beurioshoo
brioche

빵
ppang
bread

노른자
noreunja
egg yolk

흰자
huinja
egg white

훈제 청어
hunje cheong-eo
kippers

프렌치 토스트
peurenchi toseuteu
French toast

삶은 달걀
salmeun dalgyal
soft-boiled egg

스크램블 에그
seukeuraembeul egeu
scrambled eggs

크림
keurim
whipped cream

과일 요거트
gwail yogeoteu
fruit yogurt

팬케이크
paenkeikeu
crepes

와플
wapeul
waffles

죽
joog
oatmeal

신선한 과일
sinseonhan gwail
fresh fruit

저녁식사 jeonyeoksigsa • **dinner**

수프 supeu | **soup**

국 gook | **broth**

스튜 seutyu | **stew**

카레 kare | **curry**

구이 요리 gu-i yori | **roast**

파이 pai | **pie**

수플레 supeulle | **soufflé**

케밥 kebab | **kebab**

면 요리
myeon yori
noodles

젓가락
jeotgarak
chopsticks

미트볼 miteubol
meatballs

오믈렛 omeullet
omelet

볶음 요리 bokk-eum yori
stir-fry

파스타 paseuta
pasta

밥 bab
rice

모둠 샐러드 modeum
saelleodeu | **tossed salad**

채소 샐러드 chaeso
saelleodeu | **green salad**

드레싱 deuresing
dressing

조리 방법 jori bangbeob • **techniques**

속을 채운 sog-eul chaeun
stuffed

소스가 있는 soseuga itneun
in sauce

구운 goo-un
grilled

양념에 재운 yangnyeomae
jaeun | **marinated**

수란 sooran
poached

으깬 eukkaen
mashed

구운 goo-un
baked

프라이팬에 볶은
peuraipaen-ae bogeun
pan-fried

튀긴 twigin
fried

식초에 절인
sikcho-e jeorin | **pickled**

훈제 hoonje
smoked

담가 튀긴 damga twigin
deep-fried

당절임
dangjeolim
in syrup

드레싱을 한
deuresing-eul han
dressed

찐
jjin
steamed

염장한
yeomjanghan
cured

학업 hageop
study

학교 hakgyo • **school**

화이트보드
hwaiteubodeu
whiteboard

선생님
seonsaengnim
teacher

책가방
chaekgabang
school backpack

책상
chaeksang
desk

교실 gyosil | **classroom**

학생
haksaeng
student

어휘 eohwi • **vocabulary**

역사 yeoksa **history**	미술 misool **art**	물리 moolli **physics**
지리 jiri **geography**	음악 eum-ak **music**	화학 hwahak **chemistry**
문학 munhak **literature**	수학 soohak **math**	생물 saengmul **biology**
언어 eon-eo **languages**	과학 gwahak **science**	체육 cheyook **physical education**

활동 hwaldong • **activities**

읽다 ilgda | **read (v)**

쓰다 sseuda | **write (v)**

철자를 쓰다 cheoljareul sseuda | **spell (v)**

그리다 geurida
draw (v)

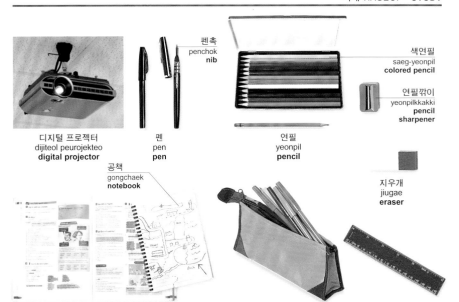

펜촉
penchok
nib

색연필
saeg-yeonpil
colored pencil

연필깎이
yeonpilkkakki
**pencil
sharpener**

디지털 프로젝터
dijiteol peurojekteo
digital projector

펜
pen
pen

연필
yeonpil
pencil

공책
gongchaek
notebook

지우개
jiugae
eraser

교과서 gyogwaseo | **textbook**

필통 piltong | **pencil case**

자 ja | **ruler**

질문하다 jilmunhada
question (v)

응답하다 eungdabhada
answer (v)

토론하다 toronhada
discuss (v)

배우다 baeuda
learn (v)

어휘 eohwi · **vocabulary**

질문 jilmun **question**	사전 sajeon **dictionary**	수업 sueob **lesson**
해답 haedab **answer**	백과사전 baekgwasajeon **encyclopedia**	숙제 sookje **homework**
시험 siheom **test**	성적 seongjeok **grade**	메모하다 memohada **take notes (v)**
작문 jakmoon **essay**	연도 yeondo **year**	교장 선생님 gyojang seonsaengnim **principal**

수학 soohak · **math**

모양 moyang · **shapes**

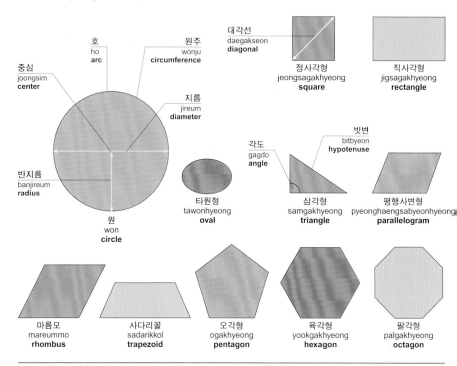

중심
joongsim
center

호
ho
arc

원주
wonju
circumference

지름
jireum
diameter

반지름
banjireum
radius

원
won
circle

타원형
tawonhyeong
oval

대각선
daegakseon
diagonal

정사각형
jeongsagakhyeong
square

직사각형
jigsagakhyeong
rectangle

각도
gagdo
angle

빗변
bitbyeon
hypotenuse

삼각형
samgakhyeong
triangle

평행사변형
pyeonghaengsabyeonhyeong
parallelogram

마름모
mareummo
rhombus

사다리꼴
sadarikkol
trapezoid

오각형
ogakhyeong
pentagon

육각형
yookgakhyeong
hexagon

팔각형
palgakhyeong
octagon

입체형 ibchehyeong · **solids**

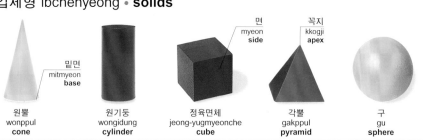

밑면
mitmyeon
base

면
myeon
side

꼭지
kkogji
apex

원뿔
wonppul
cone

원기둥
wongidung
cylinder

정육면체
jeong-yugmyeonche
cube

각뿔
gakppul
pyramid

구
gu
sphere

선 seon • **lines**

직선
jigseon
straight

평행선
pyeonghaengseon
parallel

직각
jiggag
perpendicular

곡선
gogseon
curved

측량 cheugryang • **measurements**

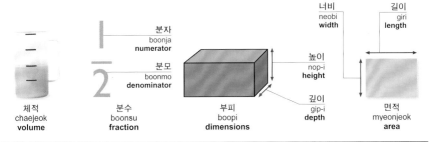

분자
boonja
numerator

분모
boonmo
denominator

너비
neobi
width

길이
giri
length

높이
nop-i
height

깊이
gip-i
depth

체적
chaejeok
volume

분수
boonsu
fraction

부피
boopi
dimensions

면적
myeonjeok
area

도구 dogu • **equipment**

삼각자
samgagja
triangle

각도기
gagdogi
protractor

자
ja
ruler

컴퍼스
keompeoseu
compass

계산기
gyesangi
calculator

어휘 eohwi • **vocabulary**

기하학 gihahag **geometry**	더하기 deohagi **plus**	곱하기 gob-hagi **times**	같음 gateum **equals**	더하다 deohada **add (v)**	곱하다 gobhada **multiply (v)**	방정식 bangjeongsig **equation**
산수 sansoo **arithmetic**	빼기 ppaegi **minus**	나누기 nanugi **divided by**	세다 seda **count (v)**	빼다 ppaeda **subtract (v)**	나누다 nanuda **divide (v)**	비율 biyool **percentage**

과학 gwahak · **science**

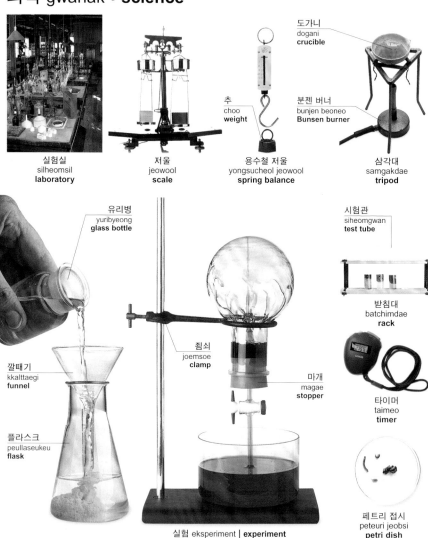

실험실
silheomsil
laboratory

저울
jeowool
scale

추
choo
weight

용수철 저울
yongsucheol jeowool
spring balance

도가니
dogani
crucible

분젠 버너
bunjen beoneo
Bunsen burner

삼각대
samgakdae
tripod

유리병
yuribyeong
glass bottle

깔때기
kkalttaegi
funnel

플라스크
peullaseukeu
flask

죔쇠
joemsoe
clamp

마개
magae
stopper

시험관
siheomgwan
test tube

받침대
batchimdae
rack

타이머
taimeo
timer

페트리 접시
peteuri jeobsi
petri dish

실험 eksperiment | **experiment**

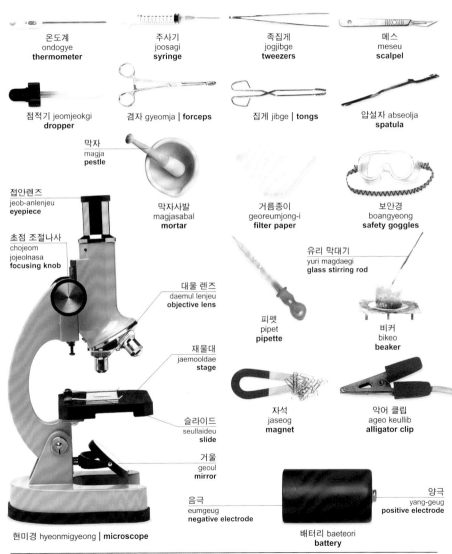

온도계
ondogye
thermometer

주사기
joosagi
syringe

족집게
jogjibge
tweezers

메스
meseu
scalpel

점적기 jeomjeokgi
dropper

겸자 gyeomja | **forceps**

집게 jibge | **tongs**

압설자 abseolja
spatula

막자
magja
pestle

막자사발
magjasabal
mortar

거름종이
georeumjong-i
filter paper

보안경
boangyeong
safety goggles

접안렌즈
jeob-anlenjeu
eyepiece

초점 조절나사
chojeom
jojeolnasa
focusing knob

대물 렌즈
daemul lenjeu
objective lens

유리 막대기
yuri magdaegi
glass stirring rod

재물대
jaemooldae
stage

피펫
pipet
pipette

비커
bikeo
beaker

슬라이드
seullaideu
slide

자석
jaseog
magnet

악어 클립
ageo keullib
alligator clip

거울
geoul
mirror

음극
eumgeug
negative electrode

양극
yang-geug
positive electrode

현미경 hyeonmigyeong | **microscope**

배터리 baeteori
battery

대학 daehak · **college**

운동장
undongjang
playing field

식당
sigdang
cafeteria

헬스클럽
helseukeulleob
health center

기숙사
gisugsa
residence hall

입학처
ibhakcheo
admissions office

캠퍼스 kaempeoseu | **campus**

어휘 eohwi · **vocabulary**

책
chaek
book

제목
jemok
title

통로
tongro
aisle

대출
daechul
loan

대출 예약하다
daechul yeyakhada
reserve (v)

빌리다
billida
borrow (v)

갱신하다
gaengsinhada
renew (v)

도서관 카드
doseo-gwan kadeu
library card

문의처
mun-uicheo
help desk

반납일
bannab-il
due date

독서실
dogseosil
reading room

추천 도서
chucheon doseo
reading list

사서
saseo
librarian

대출대
daechuldae
circulation desk

책꽂이
chaegkkoji
bookshelf

정기 간행물
jeong-gi ganhaengmul
periodical

신문
sinmun
journal

도서관 doseogwan | **library**

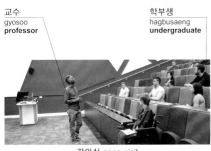

교수
gyosoo
professor

학부생
hagbusaeng
undergraduate

강의실 gang-uisil
lecture hall

졸업생
joreobsaeng
graduate

가운
gaun
gown

졸업식 jol-eobsik
graduation ceremony

단과대학 dan-gwadaehak • **schools**

모델
model
model

예술대학 yesuldaehak
art school

음악대학 eum-agdaehak
music school

무용대학 mooyongdaehak
dance school

어휘 eohwi • **vocabulary**

수료증 suryojeung **diploma**	연구 yeongu **research**	학과 hakgwa **department**	수의학 suuihak **zoology**	정치학 jeongchihak **political science**
학위 hag-wi **degree**	학사 및 석사 논문 haksa mit seoksa nonmun **dissertation**	법학 beob-hak **law**	물리학 mullihak **physics**	철학 cheol-hak **philosophy**
석사학위 seoksahag-ui **master's**	박사 논문 baksa nonmun **thesis**	공학 gonghak **engineering**	문학 munhak **literature**	경제학 gyeongjehak **economics**
박사학위 baksahak-wi **doctorate**	대학원생 daehak-wonsaeng **postgraduate**	의학 uihak **medicine**	예술사 yesulsa **art history**	장학금 janghakgeum **scholarship**

업무 eobmu
work

사무실 samusil · **office (1)**

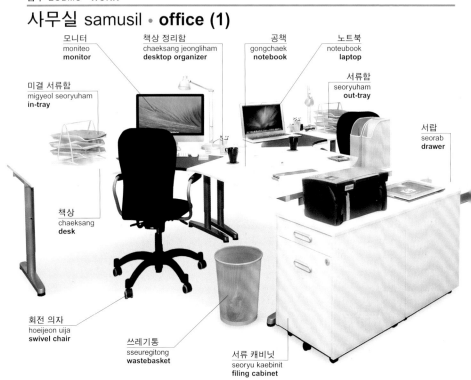

모니터
moniteo
monitor

책상 정리함
chaeksang jeongliham
desktop organizer

공책
gongchaek
notebook

노트북
noteubook
laptop

미결 서류함
migyeol seoryuham
in-tray

서류함
seoryuham
out-tray

서랍
seorab
drawer

책상
chaeksang
desk

회전 의자
hoeijeon uija
swivel chair

쓰레기통
sseuregitong
wastebasket

서류 캐비닛
seoryu kaebinit
filing cabinet

사무실 비품 samusil bipum
office equipment

용지함
yongjiham
paper tray

프린터 peurinteo | **printer**

파쇄기 paswaegi | **shredder**

어휘 eohwi · **vocabulary**

인쇄하다
inswaehada
print (v)

확대하다
hwagdaehada
enlarge (v)

복사하다
bogsahada
copy (v)

축소하다
chooksohada
reduce (v)

복사할 게 있습니다.
bogsahal ge itseumnida.
I need to make some copies.

사무용 소모품 samuyong somopum · **office supplies**

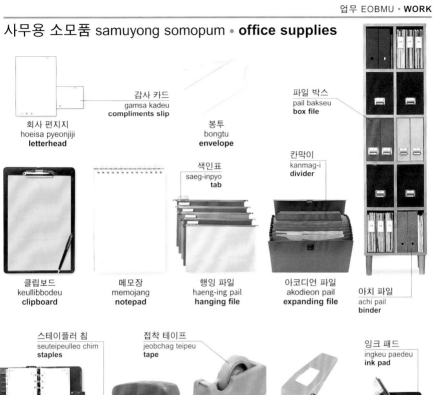

회사 편지지
hoeisa pyeonjiji
letterhead

감사 카드
gamsa kadeu
compliments slip

봉투
bongtu
envelope

파일 박스
pail bakseu
box file

색인표
saeg-inpyo
tab

칸막이
kanmag-i
divider

클립보드
keullibbodeu
clipboard

메모장
memojang
notepad

행잉 파일
haeng-ing pail
hanging file

아코디언 파일
akodieon pail
expanding file

아치 파일
achi pail
binder

스테이플러 침
seuteipeulleo chim
staples

접착 테이프
jeobchag teipeu
tape

잉크 패드
ingkeu paedeu
ink pad

수첩
sucheob
personal organizer

스테이플러
seuteipeulleo
stapler

테이프 디스펜서
teipeu diseupenseo
tape dispenser

펀치
peonchi
hole punch

고무 도장
gomu dojang
rubber stamp

고무줄
gomujul
rubber band

집게
jibge
bulldog clip

종이 클립
jong-i keullip
paper clip

압정
abjeong
thumbtack

게시판 gesipan | **bulletin board**

사무실 samusil · **office (2)**

플립 차트
peullib chateu
flip chart

받침대
batchimdae
easel

회의록
hoei-ui-log
minutes

보고서
bogoseo
report

제안서
jeanseo
proposal

사장
sajang
manager

임원
imwon
executive

회의 hoei-ui | **meeting**

어휘 eohwi · **vocabulary**

회의실
hoei-uisil
meeting room

의제
uije
agenda

참여하다
cham-yeohada
attend (v)

회의의 사회를 맡다
hoeiuiui sahoereul matda
chair (v)

회의가 몇 시에 있어요?
hoei-uiga myeot sie isseoyo?
What time is the meeting?

근무 시간이 어떻게 됩니까?
geunmu sigan-i eotteokke deomnikka?
What are your office hours?

발표자
balpyoja
speaker

발표 prezentatsiya | **presentation**

비즈니스 bijeuniseu • **business**

비즈니스맨
bijeuniseumaen
**businessman /
businessperson**

비즈니스우먼
bijeuniseu-umeon
**businesswoman /
businessperson**

업무상 점심식사 eobmusang jeomsimsigsa
business lunch

출장 chuljang | **business trip**

약속
yagsok
appointment

고객
gogaek
client

대표이사
daepyo-i-sa
CEO

디지털 달력 dijiteol dalyeok
digital calendar

비즈니스 거래 bijeuniseu georae
business deal

어휘 eohwi • **vocabulary**

회사 hoeisa **company**	사원 sawon **staff**	회계 부서 hoeigye buseo **accounting department**	법무 부서 beobmu buseo **legal department**
본사 bonsa **head office**	급여 geub-yeo **salary**	마케팅 부서 maketing buseo **marketing department**	고객 서비스 부서 gogaek seobiseu buseo **customer service department**
지사 jisa **regional office**	급여 대상자 명단 geub-yeo daesangja myeongdan **payroll**	영업부 yeong-eobbu **sales department**	인사부 insabu **human resources department**

컴퓨터 keompyuteo · **computer**

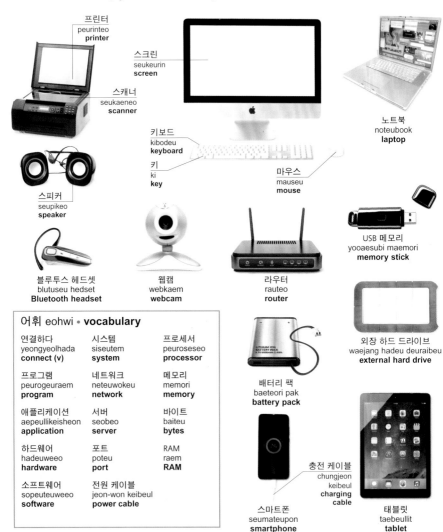

프린터
peurinteo
printer

스크린
seukeurin
screen

스캐너
seukaeneo
scanner

노트북
noteubook
laptop

키보드
kibodeu
keyboard

키
ki
key

마우스
mauseu
mouse

스피커
seupikeo
speaker

블루투스 헤드셋
blutuseu hedset
Bluetooth headset

웹캠
webkaem
webcam

라우터
rauteo
router

USB 메모리
yooaesubi maemori
memory stick

외장 하드 드라이브
waejang hadeu deuraibeu
external hard drive

배터리 팩
baeteori pak
battery pack

충전 케이블
chungjeon
keibeul
**charging
cable**

스마트폰
seumateupon
smartphone

태블릿
taebeullit
tablet

어휘 eohwi · **vocabulary**

연결하다 yeongyeolhada **connect (v)**	시스템 siseutem **system**	프로세서 peuroseseo **processor**
프로그램 peurogeuraem **program**	네트워크 neteuwokeu **network**	메모리 memori **memory**
애플리케이션 aepeullikeisheon **application**	서버 seobeo **server**	바이트 baiteu **bytes**
하드웨어 hadeuweeo **hardware**	포트 poteu **port**	RAM raem **RAM**
소프트웨어 sopeuteuweeo **software**	전원 케이블 jeon-won keibeul **power cable**	

데스크톱 deseukeutob · **desktop**

메뉴 모음
maenyu moeum
menu bar

글꼴
geulkkol
font

도구 모음
dogu moeum
toolbar

아이콘
aikon
icon

창
chang
window

파일
pail
file

폴더
poldeo
folder

휴지통
hyujitong
trash

인터넷 inteo-net · **internet**

웹사이트
websaiteu
website

브라우저
beuraujeo
browser

탐색하다 tamsaekhada | **browse (v)**

이메일 i-meil · **email**

받은 편지함
badeun
pyeonjiham
inbox

이메일 주소
i-meil juso
email address

어휘 eohwi · **vocabulary**

서비스 제공자 seobiseu jegongja **service provider**	온라인 ollain **online**	비밀번호 bimilbeonho **password**	다운로드하다 daunlodeuhada **download (v)**	보내다 bonaeda **send (v)**	저장하다 jeojanghada **save (v)**
클라우드 저장소 klaudeu jeojangso **cloud storage**	첨부 파일 cheombu pail **attachment**	설치하다 seolchihada **install (v)**	로그인하다 logeu-inhada **log on (v)**	수신하다 soosinhada **receive (v)**	검색하다 geomsaekhada **search (v)**

미디어 midieo · **media**

텔레비전 스튜디오 tellebijeon seutyudio · **television studio**

세트
seteu
set

진행자
jinhaengja
host

조명
jomyeong
light

카메라
kamera
camera

카메라 크레인
kamera keurein
camera crane

촬영 감독
chwaryeong gamdok
camera operator

어휘 eohwi · **vocabulary**

채널 chaeneol **channel**	뉴스 nyuseu **news**	언론 eonlon **press**	연속극 yeonsokgeug **soap opera**	만화 manhwa **cartoon**	생방송 saengbangsong **live**
프로그래밍 peurogeuraeming **programming**	다큐멘터리 dakyumenteori **documentary**	텔레비전 시리즈 tellebijeon sirijeu **television series**	예능 프로그램 yaeneung peurogeuraem **game show**	방송하다 bangsonghada **broadcast (v)**	녹화방송 nokhwabangsong **prerecorded**

인터뷰 진행자 inteobyu
jinhaengja | **interviewer**

리포터 lipoteo
reporter

텔레프롬프터
taellaepeuromteo
teleprompter

뉴스 앵커 nyuseu
aengkeo | **anchor**

배우
baewoo
actors

붐 마이크
boom maikeu
sound boom

클래퍼 보드
keullaepeo bodeu
clapper board

영화 세트장
yeonghwa seteujang
movie set

라디오 ladio · **radio**

어휘 eohwi · **vocabulary**

라디오 방송국
ladio bangsong-gook
radio station

아날로그
analogeu
analog

방송
bangsong
broadcast

디지털
dijiteol
digital

파장
pajang
wavelength

음량
eumryang
volume

주파수
joopasoo
frequency

DJ
deejaei
DJ

주파수를 맞추다
jupasureul matchuda
tune (v)

음향 기사
eumhyang gisa
sound technician

믹싱 데스크
miksing deseukeu
mixing desk

마이크
maikeu
microphone

녹음실 nogeumsil | **recording studio**

법 beob · **law**

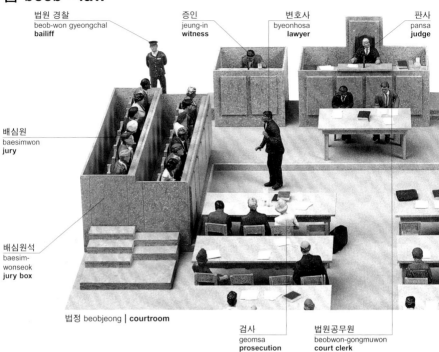

법원 경찰
beob-won gyeongchal
bailiff

증인
jeung-in
witness

변호사
byeonhosa
lawyer

판사
pansa
judge

배심원
baesimwon
jury

배심원석
baesim-
wonseok
jury box

법정 beobjeong | **courtroom**

검사
geomsa
prosecution

법원공무원
beobwon-gongmuwon
court clerk

어휘 eohwi · **vocabulary**

변호사 사무소 byeonhosa samuso **lawyer's office**	영장 yeongjang **warrant**	진술 jinsool **statement**	소환장 sohwanjang **summons**
법률 상담 beobryul sangdam **legal advice**	기소 giso **charge**	진술 jinsool **plea**	소송 사건 sosong sageon **court case**
고객 gogaek **client**	피고인 pigoin **accused**	영장 yeongjang **writ**	재판일 jaepan-il **court date**

속기사
sokgisa
stenographer

용의자
yong-uija
suspect

변호인
byeonhoin
defense

피고
pigo
defendant

범죄자
beomjoeja
criminal

몽타주 mongtajoo
composite sketch

전과
jeongwa
criminal record

교도관
gyodogwan | **prison guard**

감방 gambang | **cell**

감옥 gam-ok | **prison**

어휘 eohwi · **vocabulary**

유죄
yujoe
guilty

무죄
mujoe
innocent

무죄선고
mujoeseon-go
acquitted

증거
jeung-geo
evidence

판결
pangyeol
verdict

선고
seongo
sentence

항소
hangso
appeal

보석
boseok
bail

가석방
gaseokbang
parole

변호를 받고 싶습니다.
byeonhoreul batgo
sipseumnida
I want to see a lawyer.

법원이 어디에 있습니까?
beob-won-i eodie
isseumnikka?
Where is the courthouse?

보석금을 낼 수 있습니까?
boseokgeum-eul nael
su isseumnikka?
Can I post bail?

농장 nongjang · **farm (1)**

가축
gachook
livestock

사일로
saillo
silo

목초지
mogchoji
pasture

밭
bat
field

농부
nongbu
farmer

별채
byeolchae
outbuilding

농가
nong-ga
farmhouse

채소밭
chaesobat
vegetable garden

담장
damjang
fence

곳간
gotgan
barn

농장 안마당
nongjang anmadang
farmyard

문
moon
gate

트랙터 teuraegteo | **tractor**

콤바인 kombain | **combine**

농장의 유형 nongjang-ui yuhyeong · **types of farms**

농작물
nongjakmul
crop

경작 농장
gyeongjak nongjang
crop farm

낙농장
naknongjang
dairy farm

양 목장
yang mokjang
sheep farm

가축떼
gachooktte
flock

양계장 yang-gyejang
poultry farm

양돈장
yangdonjang
pig farm

양식장
yangsikjang
fish farm

과수원
gwasoowon
fruit farm

포도나무
podonamoo
vine

포도 과수원
podo gwasoowon
vineyard

활동 hwaldong · **actions**

고랑
gorang
furrow

쟁기질하다
jaeng-gijilhada
plow (v)

씨 뿌리다
ssi ppurida
sow (v)

우유를 짜다
uyooreul jjada
milk (v)

먹이를 주다
meog-i-leul juda
feed (v)

물 주다 mool juda
water (v)

수확하다 suhwakhada
harvest (v)

어휘 eohwi · **vocabulary**

제초제 jechoje **herbicide**	떼 tte **herd**	관목 울타리 gwanmok ultari **hedge**
살충제 salchoongje **pesticide**	구유 gooyu **trough**	심다 simda **plant (v)**

농장 nongjang • **farm (2)**

농작물 nongjakmul • **crops**

밀
mil
wheat

옥수수
oksusu
corn

보리
bori
barley

유채씨
yuchaessi
rapeseed

해바라기
haebaragi
sunflower

더미
deomi
bale

건초
geoncho
hay

알팔파
alpalpa
alfalfa

담배
dambae
tobacco

쌀
ssal
rice

차
cha
tea

커피
keopi
coffee

아마
ah-ma
flax

사탕수수
satangsusu
sugarcane

목화
mokhwa
cotton

허수아비
heosuabi
scarecrow

가축 gachook · **livestock**

새끼 돼지
saekki dwaeji
piglet

돼지
dwaeji
pig

송아지
song-aji
calf

소
so
cow

황소
hwangso
bull

양
yang
sheep

새끼양
saekkiyang
lamb

새끼 염소
saekki yeomso
kid

염소
yeomso
goat

망아지
mang-aji
foal

말
mal
horse

당나귀
dangnagwi
donkey

병아리
byeong-ari
chick

닭
dak
chicken

어린 수탉
eorin sutak
rooster

칠면조
chilmyeonjo
turkey

새끼 오리
saekki ori
duckling

오리
ori
duck

헛간
heotgan
stable

우리
uri
pen

닭장
dakjang
chicken coop

양돈장
yangdonjang
pigsty

건설 geonseol
construction

팔레트
palleteu
pallet

벽
byeok
wall

서까래
seo-kkarae
rafter

비계
bigyae
scaffolding

기둥
gidung
beam

건축부지 geonchookbuji | **construction site**

창문
changmoon
window

사다리
sadari
ladder

대들보
daedeulbo
girder

안전모
anjeonmo
hard hat

공구벨트
gong-gubelteu
toolbelt

시멘트
simenteu
cement

건설하다
geonseolhada
build (v)

건축업자
geonchookeobja
construction worker

콘크리트 혼합기
konkeuriteu honhabgi
cement mixer

재료 jaeryo • **materials**

벽돌
byeokdol
brick

목재
mokjae
lumber

기와
giwa
roof tile

경량 블록
gyeongryang beullog
cinder block

공구 gong-gu • **tools**

모르타르
moreutareu
mortar

흙손
heukson
trowel

기포관 수준기
gipogwan sujungi
level

손잡이
sonjabi
handle

양손 망치
yangson mangchi
sledgehammer

곡괭이
goggwaeng-i
pickax

삽
sab
shovel

기계류 gigyeryu **machinery**

로드 롤러
lodeu lolleo
road roller

덤프트럭
deompeuteureok
dump truck

지지대
jijidae
support

고리
gori
hook

크레인 keurein | **crane**

도로 공사 doro gongsa **roadwork**

포장도로
pojangdoro
asphalt

로드콘
rodeukon
cone

공압 드릴
gong-ab deuril
jackhammer

재포장
jaepojang
resurfacing

굴착기
goolchaggi
excavator

직업 jig-eob · **occupations (1)**

목수
mogsu
carpenter

전기공
jeon-gigong
electrician

배관공
baegwangong
plumber

건축업자
geonchookeobja
construction worker

기계공
gigyegong
mechanic

정육점 주인
jeongyukjeom jooin
butcher

어부
eo-boo
fisherman / fisherwoman

플로리스트
peulloriseuteu
florist

보석상
boseoksang
jeweler

정원사
jeong-wonsa
gardener

미용사
miyongsa
hairdresser

이발사
ibalsa
barber

상점 점원
sangjeom jeom-won
salesperson

운전 교습 강사
unjeon gyoseup gangsa
driving instructor

진공 청소기
jingong
cheongsogi
**vacuum
cleaner**

청소부
cheongsobu
cleaner

측량사
cheukriangsa
surveyor

약사
yaksa
pharmacist

안경사
angyeongsa
optometrist

마스크
maseukeu
mask

치과 의사
chigwa uisa
dentist

의사
uisa
doctor

간호사
ganhosa
nurse

수의사
soo-uisa
veterinarian

물리 치료사
muli chiriosa
physical therapist

수방관
sobang-gwan
firefighter

유니폼
yunipom
uniform

군인
goon-in
soldier

경찰관
gyeongchalgwan
police officer

신분 증명
배지
sinbun
jeungmyeong
baeji
badge

경비원
gyeongbiwon
security guard

선원
seon-won
sailor

어휘 eohwi · **vocabulary**

마케팅 이사
maketing isa
marketing executive

기업가
gi-eopga
entrepreneur

앱 개발자
aep gaebalja
app developer

웹 디자이너
wep dijaineo
web designer

통역사
tong-yeoksa
interpreter

개인 비서
gaein biseo
personal assistant (PA)

홍보 이사
hongbo isa
**public relations
(PR) executive**

직업 jig-eob • **occupations (2)**

변호사
byeonhosa
lawyer

회계사
hoeigyesa
accountant

모형
mohyeong
model

건축가
geonchukga
architect

데이터 분석가
deiteo bunseokga
data analyst

과학자
gwahakja
scientist

교사
gyosa
teacher

부동산 중개업자
budongsan joong-gae-eobja
real estate agent

접수원
jeobsuwon
receptionist

우편 행낭
upyeon
haengnang
mailbag

우편집배원
upyeonjibaewon
mail carrier

버스 운전사
beoseu unjeonsa
bus driver

트럭 운전사
teureok unjeonsa
truck driver

택시 운전사
taeksi unjeonsa
taxi driver

조종사
jojongsa
pilot

항공 승무원
hang-gong seungmuwon
flight attendant

여행사 직원
yeohaengsa jig-won
travel agent

세프 모자
shepeu moja
chef's hat

셰프
shepeu
chef

음악가
eum-akga
musician

튀튀
twitwi
tutu

무용가
muyong-ga
dancer

배우 / 여배우
baewoo *m* / yeobaewoo *f*
actor

가수
gasoo
singer

웨이터 / 웨이트리스
weiteo *m* / weiteuriseu *f*
server

바텐더
batendeo
bartender

개인 트레이너
gaein teureineo
personal trainer

조각가
jogakga
sculptor

화가
hwaga
painter

사진 작가
sajin jakga
photographer

뉴스 앵커
nyuseu aengkeo
anchor

메모
memo
notes

기자
gija
journalist

편집자
pyeonjibja
editor

디자이너
dijaineo
designer

재봉사
jaebongsa
dressmaker

재단사
jaedansa
tailor

수송 susong
transportation

도로 doro · **roads**

지하도
jihado
underpass

도로 표시
doro pyosi
road markings

출구 도로
choolgoo doro
off-ramp

중앙 분리대
joong-ang
bunridae
**median
strip**

갓길
gatgil
shoulder

교통
gyotong
traffic

바깥쪽 차선
baggatjjok
chaseon
driving lane

가운데 차선
gaunde
chaseon
middle lane

진출입로
jinchul-ibro
on-ramp

입체 교차로
ibche gyocharo
overpass

안쪽 차선
anjjok chaseon
passing lane

고속도로
gosokdoro
freeway

교통신호등
gyotongsinhodeung
traffic light

횡단보도
hoengdanbodo
crosswalk

트럭
teureok
truck

교차로
gyocharo
interchange

응급전화기
eung-geubjeonhwagi
emergency phone

장애인 주차구역
jang-aein
joochagooyeok
disabled parking

교통 체증
gyotong chejeung
traffic jam

어휘 eohwi • **vocabulary**

주차하다 juchahada **park (v)**	우회 uhoe **detour**	중앙 분리 고속도로 jung-ang bunli gosokdoro **divided highway**
운전하다 unjeonhada **drive (v)**	도로 공사 doro gongsa **roadwork**	일방 통행로 ilbang tonghaengro **one-way street**
추월하다 choowolhada **pass (v)**	가드레일 gadeureil **guardrail**	
후진하다 hujinhada **reverse (v)**	로터리 loteori **roundabout**	이 길이... (으)로 가는 길인가요? i giri... (eu)ro ganeun girin-gayo? **Is this the road to... ?**
견인하다 gyeon-inhada **tow away (v)**	도로 요금소 doro yogeumso **tollbooth**	주차할 수 있는 곳이 어딘가요? joochahal soo itneun gosi eodingayo? **Where can I park?**

주차 미터
joocha miteo
parking meter

교통경찰
gyotong-gyeongchal
traffic police officer

도로 표지판 doro pyojipan • **road signs**

진입 금지
jin-ib geumji
do not enter

속도 제한
sogdo jehan
speed limit

위험
wiheom
hazard

정차 금지
jeongcha geumji
no stopping

우회전 금지
uhoejeon geumji
no right turn

버스 beoseu · **bus**

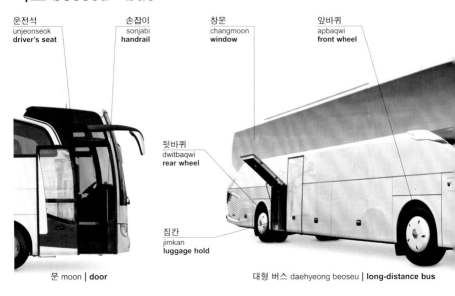

운전석
unjeonseok
driver's seat

손잡이
sonjabi
handrail

창문
changmoon
window

앞바퀴
apbaqwi
front wheel

뒷바퀴
dwitbaqwi
rear wheel

짐칸
jimkan
luggage hold

문 moon | **door**

대형 버스 daehyeong beoseu | **long-distance bus**

버스 종류 beoseu jongryu · **types of buses**

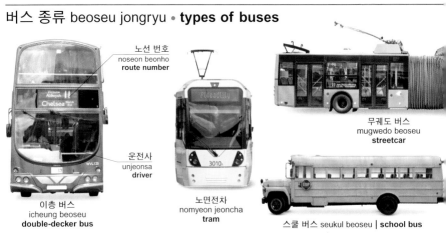

노선 번호
noseon beonho
route number

운전사
unjeonsa
driver

이층 버스
icheung beoseu
double-decker bus

노면전차
nomyeon jeoncha
tram

무궤도 버스
mugwedo beoseu
streetcar

스쿨 버스 seukul beoseu | **school bus**

자동문
jadongmoon
automatic door

하차 버튼
hacha beoton
stop button

버스표
beoseupyo
bus ticket

벨
bel
bell

버스 터미널
beoseu teomi-neol
bus station

버스 정류장
beoseu
jeongryujang
bus stop

어휘 eohwi · **vocabulary**

요금	(지붕이 있는) 버스 정류소
yogeum	(jiboong-i itneun) beoseu jeongryuso
fare	**bus shelter**
시간표	휠체어 탑승 가능
siganpyo	hwilcheeo tabseung ganeung
schedule	**wheelchair access**

...에 가나요?	어느 버스가... 에 가나요?
...e ga-nayo?	eo-neu beoseuga... ae ganayo?
Do you stop at... ?	**Which bus goes to... ?**

미니버스
minibeoseu
minibus

관광 버스 gwangwang beoseu | **tour bus**

셔틀 버스
syeoteul beoseu | **shuttle bus**

자동차 jadongcha · **car (1)**

외관 wae-gwan · **exterior**

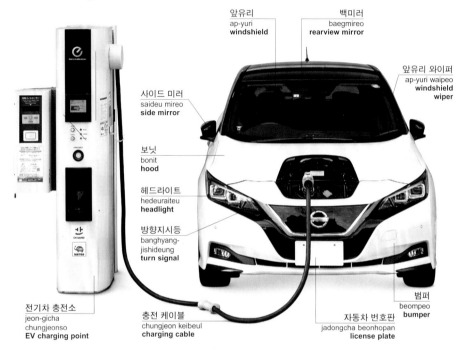

앞유리
ap-yuri
windshield

백미러
baegmireo
rearview mirror

앞유리 와이퍼
ap-yuri waipeo
windshield wiper

사이드 미러
saideu mireo
side mirror

보닛
bonit
hood

헤드라이트
hedeuraiteu
headlight

방향지시등
banghyang-
jishideung
turn signal

전기차 충전소
jeon-gicha
chungjeonso
EV charging point

충전 케이블
chungjeon keibeul
charging cable

자동차 번호판
jadongcha beonhopan
license plate

범퍼
beompeo
bumper

짐
jim
luggage

루프랙
roopeuraek
roof rack

트렁크
teureongkeu
trunk

안전 벨트
anjeon belteu
seat belt

카시트
kasiteu
car seat

유형 yuhyeong • **types**

전기자동차
jeongijadongcha
electric car

해치백
haechibaeg
hatchback

문
moon
door

세단
saedan
sedan

휠
hwil
wheel

스테이션 웨건
seuteisheon wegeon
station wagon

컨버터블
keonbeoteobeul
convertible

스포츠카
seupocheuka
sports car

승합차
seunghabcha
minivan

4륜 구동
sa-ryoon gudong
four-wheel drive

타이어
taleo
tire

빈티지
bintiji
vintage

리무진
limoojin
limousine

주유소 juyuso • **gas station**

가격
gagyeok
price

주유 펌프
juyu peompeu
gas pump

주유소 마당
juyuso madang
entryway

어휘 eohwi • **vocabulary**

휘발유 hwibal-yoo **gasoline**	유연 yuyeon **leaded**	차고 chago **garage**
디젤 dijel **diesel**	무연 moo-yeon **unleaded**	세차장 saechajang **car wash**
오일 oil **oil**	부동액 budong-aek **antifreeze**	워셔액 woesheo-aek **windshield washer fluid**

가득 채워 주세요.
gadeuk chaewoe joosaeyo
Fill it up, please.

자동차 jadongcha · **car (2)**

내부 naebu · **interior**

뒷좌석
dwitjwaseok
backseat

팔걸이
palgeol-i
armrest

헤드레스트
haedeuraeseuteu
headrest

도어 로크
do-eo lokeu
door lock

손잡이
sonjabi
handle

어휘 eohwi · **vocabulary**

2 도어 차량 too do-eo charyang **two-door**	4 도어 차량 peo do-eo charyang **four-door**	수동 sudong **manual**	브레이크 beureikeu **brake**	점화 jeomhwa **ignition**
3 도어 차량 seuri do-eo charyang **hatchback**	에어컨 ae-eokon **air-conditioning**	자동 jadong **automatic**	클러치 keulleochi **clutch**	가속 페달 gasog pedal **accelerator**

...에 어떻게 가요?
...e eotteoke gayo?
Can you tell me the way to... ?

주차장이 어디입니까?
juchajang-i eodimnikka?
Where is the parking lot?

여기에 주차할 수 있습니까?
yeogi-e juchahal su isseumnikka?
Can I park here?

컨트롤 keonteurol • **controls**

핸들
haendeul
**steering
wheel**

경적
gyeongjeok
horn

계기판
gyegipan
dashboard

위성 내비게이션
uiseong
naebeegeesyeon
GPS

고장 경고 표시등
gojang gyeong-go
pyosideung
hazard lights

핸들이 왼쪽에 있는 차 haendeul-i oenjjog-e itneun cha | **left-hand drive**

연료계
yeonlyogye
fuel gauge

타코미터
takomiteo
tachometer

속도계
sokdogye
speedometer

카 오디오
ka odio
car stereo

조명 스위치
jomyeong seuwichi
light switch

온도 게이지
ondo geiji
temperature gauge

히터 컨트롤
hiteo keonteurol
heater controls

주행 기록계
joohaeng girokgye
odometer

기어스틱
gieoseutik
gearshift

에어백
e-eo-baeg
air bag

오른쪽 운전석
oreunjjog unjeonseok | **right-hand drive**

자동차 jadongcha · **car (3)**

정비공 jeongbigong · **mechanics**

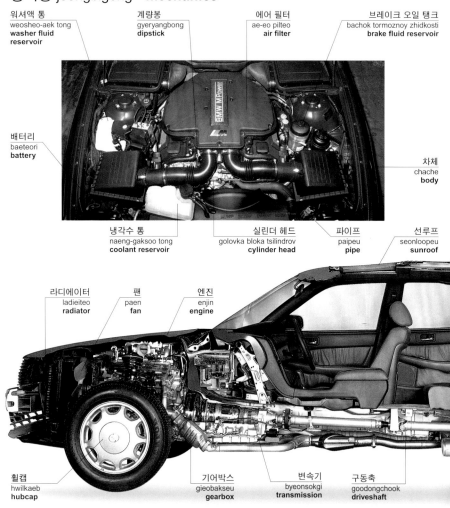

워셔액 통
weosheo-aek tong
**washer fluid
reservoir**

계량봉
gyeryangbong
dipstick

에어 필터
ae-eo pilteo
air filter

브레이크 오일 탱크
bachok tormoznoy zhidkosti
brake fluid reservoir

배터리
baeteori
battery

차체
chache
body

냉각수 통
naeng-gaksoo tong
coolant reservoir

실린더 헤드
golovka bloka tsilindrov
cylinder head

파이프
paipeu
pipe

선루프
seonloopeu
sunroof

라디에이터
ladieiteo
radiator

팬
paen
fan

엔진
enjin
engine

휠캡
hwilkaeb
hubcap

기어박스
gieobakseu
gearbox

변속기
byeonsokgi
transmission

구동축
goodongchook
driveshaft

펑크 peongkeu • **flat tire**

스페어 타이어
seupae-eo taieo
spare tire

렌치
lenchi
tire iron

휠 너트
hwil neoteu
lug nuts

잭
jaek
jack

바퀴를 갈다
bakwireul galda
change a tire (v)

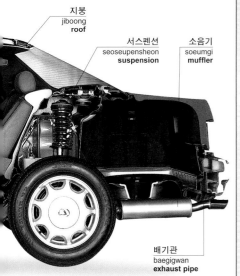

지붕
jiboong
roof

서스펜션
seoseupensheon
suspension

소음기
soeumgi
muffler

배기관
baegigwan
exhaust pipe

어휘 eohwi • **vocabulary**

자동차 사고
jadongcha sago
car accident

고장
gojang
breakdown

보험
boheom
insurance

견인차
gyeon-incha
tow truck

타이어 압력
taieo abryeok
tire pressure

퓨즈 박스
pyujeu bakseu
fuse box

점화 플러그
jeomhwa peulleogeu
spark plug

팬 벨트
paen belteu
fan belt

배전기
baejeongi
distributor

타이밍
taiming
timing

캠 벨트
kaem belteu
timing belt

연료 탱크
yeongryo taengkeu
gas tank

터보차저
teobochajeo
turbocharger

핸드 브레이크
haendeu beureikeu
parking brake

섀시
shaeshi
chassis

교류 발전기
gyoryu baljeongi
alternator

정비공
jeongbigong
mechanic

차가 고장났어요.
chaga gojangnasseoyo
My car has broken down.

차가 시동이 안 걸려요.
chaga sidong-i
an geollyeoyo
My car won't start.

오토바이 otobai • **motorcycle**

헬멧
helmet
helmet

방향지시등
banghyangjishideung
turn signal

속도계
sokdogye
speedometer

브레이크
beureikeu
brake

클러치
keulleochi
clutch

경적
gyeongjeok
horn

스로틀
seuroteul
throttle

컨트롤
keonteurol
controls

캐리어
kaerieo
carrier

반사경
bansagyeong
reflector

뒷자리
dwitjari
passenger seat

좌석
jwaseok
seat

엔진
enjin
engine

연료 탱크
yeonlo taengkeu
fuel tank

미등
mideung
taillight

배기관
baegigwan
exhaust pipe

소음기
soeumgi
muffler

오일 탱크
oil taengkeu
oil tank

기어박스
gieobakseu
gearbox

에어 필터
ae-eo pilteo
air filter

바이저
baijeo
visor

가죽 의류
gajook uiryu
leathers

반사띠
bansatti
reflector strap

무릎 보호대
mooreup bohodae
knee pad

복장 bogjang
clothing

헤드라이트
hedeuraiteu
headlight

서스펜션
seoseupensheon
suspension

흙받이
heukbat-i
fender

브레이크 페달
beureikeu pedal
brake pedal

차축
chachook
axle

타이어
taieo
tire

유형 yuhyeong • **types**

경주용 오토바이
gyeongjuyong otobai | **racing bike**

윈드스크린
windeuseukeurin
windshield

투어링 오토바이
tueoring otobai | **tourer**

산악용 오토바이
san-ak-yong otobai | **dirt bike**

스탠드
seutaendeu
stand

스쿠터 seu-kuteo | **scooter**

자전거 jajeongeo · **bicycle**

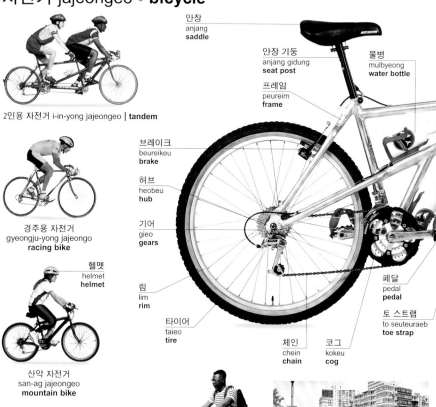

2인용 자전거 i-in-yong jajeongeo | **tandem**

경주용 자전거
gyeongju-yong jajeongo
racing bike

산악 자전거
san-ag jajeongeo
mountain bike

안장
anjang
saddle

안장 기둥
anjang gidung
seat post

물병
mulbyeong
water bottle

프레임
peureim
frame

브레이크
beureikeu
brake

허브
heobeu
hub

기어
gieo
gears

림
lim
rim

타이어
taieo
tire

헬멧
helmet
helmet

페달
pedal
pedal

토 스트랩
to seuteuraeb
toe strap

체인
chein
chain

코그
kokeu
cog

패러사이클
paereo-saikeul
paracycle

접이식 자전거
jeobishik jajeon-geo
folding bike

자전거 도로
jajeongeo doro | **bike lane**

크로스바
keuroseuba
crossbar

핸들바
haendeulba
handlebar

변속 레버
byeonsog lebeo
gear lever

타이어 레버
taieo lebeo
tire lever

패치
paechi
patch

제동 레버
jedong lebeo
brake lever

수리 도구
suri dogu | **repair kit**

포크
pokeu
fork

열쇠
yeolsoe
key

바큇살
bakwitsal
spoke

펌프
peompeu
pump

자물쇠
jamulsoe
lock

휠
hwil
wheel

밸브
baelbeu
valve

트레드
teuraedeu
tread

튜브
tyubeu
inner tube

카시트
kasiteu
child seat

어휘 eohwi · **vocabulary**

램프 laempeu **headlight**	바구니 baguni **basket**	토클립 tokeullib **toe clip**	펑크 peongkeu **flat tire**	케이블 keibeul **cable**	브레이크를 잡다 beurae-i-keureul jabda **brake (v)**
미등 mideung **rear light**	킥스탠드 kikseutaendeu **kickstand**	스프로킷 seupeurokit **sprocket**	브레이크 블록 beurae-i-keu beullog **brake block**	자전거 거치대 jajeongeo geochidae **bike rack**	기어를 바꾸다 gieoreul bakkuda **change gears (v)**
반사경 bansagyeong **reflector**	보조바퀴 bojobakwi **training wheels**	다이너모 daineomo **dynamo**	전기 자전거 jeon-gi jajeon-geo **electric bike**	자전거 타다 jajeongeo tada **cycle (v)**	페달을 밟다 pedal-eul balbda **pedal (v)**

기차 gicha · **train**

플랫폼 번호
peullaetpom
beonho
**platform
number**

플랫폼
peullaetpom
platform

객차
gaekcha
railcar

선로
seonlo
track

통근자
tong-geunja
commuter

기차역 gichayeok | train station

기차의 유형 gicha-ui yuhyeong · **types of train**

엔진
enjin
engine

조종실
jojongsil
engineer's cab

레일
leil
rail

증기 기관차
jeung-gi gigwancha
steam train

디젤 기관차 dijel gigwancha | diesel train

전기 열차
jeongi yeolcha
electric train

고속 열차
gosok yeolcha
high-speed train

모노레일
monorael
monorail

지하철
jihacheol
subway

노면전차
nomyeon jeoncha
tram

화물 열차
hwamul yeolcha
freight train

짐 선반
jim seonban
luggage rack

창문
changmoon
window

개찰구 gaechalgu | **ticket gates**

문 　　좌석
moon 　jwaseok
door 　**seat**

객실 gaeksil | **compartment**

안내방송 설비
an-naebangsong seolbi
public address system

시간표
siganpyo
schedule

표
pyo
ticket

식당차
sigdangcha | **dining car**

대합실 daehabsil | **concourse**

침대칸
chimdaekan
sleeping compartment

어휘 eohwi • **vocabulary**

철도망
cheoldomang
railroad network

러시아워
reosiawo
rush hour

요금
yogeum
fare

신호
shinho
signal

도시간 열차
dosigan yeolcha
express train

연착
yeonchak
delay

매표소
maepyoso
ticket office

비상 레버
bisang lebeo
emergency lever

통전 선로
tongjeon seonro
live rail

지하철 노선도
jihacheol noseondo
subway map

검표원
geompyowon
ticket inspector

환승하다
hwanseunghada
transfer (v)

비행기 bihaeng-gi • **aircraft**

항공사 hang-gongsa • **airliner**

항공기 앞부분
hang-gong-gi
apboobun
nose

조종실
jojongsil
cockpit

엔진
enjin
engine

동체
dongche
fuselage

날개
nalgae
wing

수직 안정판
soojig
anjeongpan
fin

방향타
banghyangta
rudder

출입구
chool-ipgu
exit

앞바퀴
apbaqwi
nosewheel

착륙 장치
chakryoog jangchi
landing gear

꼬리
kkori
tail

꼬리날개
kkorinalgae
tailplane

객실 gaeksil • **cabin**

승무원
seungmuwon
flight attendant

좌석 위 선반
jwaseok wi seonban
overhead bin

통풍구
tongpoong-goo
air vent

창문
changmoon
window

독서등
dokseodeung
reading light

좌석열
jwaseog-yeol
row

좌석
jwaseok
seat

테이블
teibeul
tray table

통로
tongro
aisle

팔걸이
palgeol-i
armrest

좌석 등받이
jwaseok deungbaji
seat back

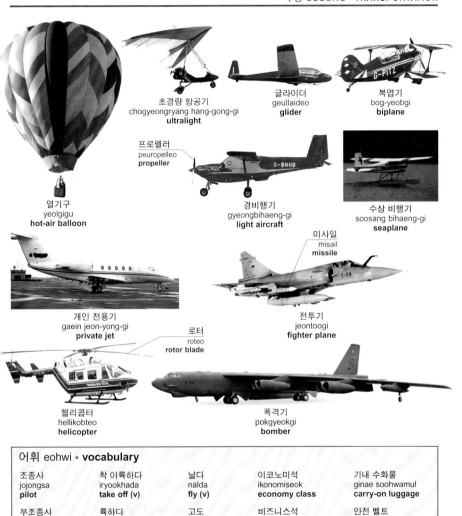

초경량 항공기
chogyeongryang hang-gong-gi
ultralight

글라이더
geullaideo
glider

복엽기
bog-yeobgi
biplane

프로펠러
peuropelleo
propeller

열기구
yeolgigu
hot-air balloon

경비행기
gyeongbihaeng-gi
light aircraft

수상 비행기
soosang bihaeng-gi
seaplane

미사일
misail
missile

개인 전용기
gaein jeon-yong-gi
private jet

전투기
jeontoogi
fighter plane

로터
roteo
rotor blade

헬리콥터
hellikobteo
helicopter

폭격기
pokgyeokgi
bomber

어휘 eohwi • vocabulary

조종사 jojongsa **pilot**	착 이륙하다 iryookhada **take off (v)**	날다 nalda **fly (v)**	이코노미석 ikonomiseok **economy class**	기내 수화물 ginae soohwamul **carry-on luggage**
부조종사 bujojongsa **copilot**	륙하다 chagryukhada **land (v)**	고도 godo **altitude**	비즈니스석 bijeuniseuseok **business class**	안전 벨트 anjeon belteu **seat belt**

공항 gonghang • **airport**

에이프런
apron
apron

수화물 트레일러
soohwamul teureilleo
baggage trailer

제트웨이
jeteuwei
jetway

서비스 차량
seobiseu charyang
service vehicle

항공사 hang-gongsa | airliner

어휘 eohwi • **vocabulary**

관제탑
gwanjetab
control tower

활주로
hwaljuro
runway

국제선
gookjeseon
international flight

국내선
gooknaeseon
domestic flight

연결
yeon-gyeol
connection

터미널
teomineol
terminal

비행 번호
bihaeng beonho
flight number

체크인하다
chekeu-inhada
check in (v)

세관
segwan
customs

이민
i-min
immigration

백드랍
bakdrap
baggage drop

추가 수화물
chooga soohwamul
excess baggage

X-레이 기계
ekseu-lei gigye
x-ray machine

수화물 컨베이어 벨트
soohwamul
keonbeieo belteu
baggage carousel

보안
boan
security

휴가 안내 책자
hyooga annae
chaekja
travel brochure

항공권을 예약하다
hang-gong-gwoneul
yaeyakhada
book a flight (v)

휴가
hyooga
vacation

기내 수화물
ginae soohwamul
carry-on luggage

카트
kateu
cart

짐
jim
luggage

비자
bija
visa

여권 yeogwon | **passport**

체크인 데스크
chekeu-in deseukeu
check-in desk

여권 심사
yeogwon simsa
passport control

탑승권
tabseung-gwon
boarding pass

탑승구 번호
tabseung-gu
beonho
gate number

출발 라운지
choolbal launji
departure lounge

출발
choolbal
departures

도착
dochak
arrivals

목적지
mokjeogji
destination

정보 화면
jeongbo hwa-myeon
information screen

자동 출입국 시스템
jadong churipguk sistem
eGate

면세점
myeonsejeom
duty-free shop

수화물 찾는 곳
soohwamul chatneun got
baggage claim

택시 승차장
taeksi seungchajang
taxi stand

랜터카
laenteoka
car rental

배 bae · **ship**

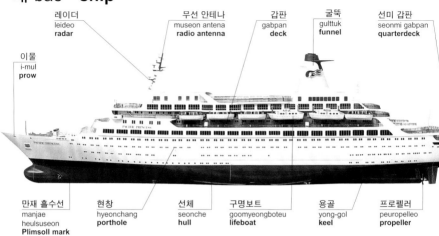

레이더
leideo
radar

무선 안테나
museon antena
radio antenna

갑판
gabban
deck

굴뚝
gulttuk
funnel

선미 갑판
seonmi gabban
quarterdeck

이물
i-mul
prow

만재 흘수선
manjae
heulsuseon
Plimsoll mark

현창
hyeonchang
porthole

선체
seonche
hull

구명보트
goomyeongboteu
lifeboat

용골
yong-gol
keel

프로펠러
peuropelleo
propeller

원양 정기선 won-yang jeong-giseon | **ocean liner**

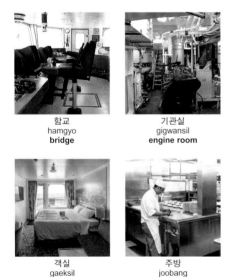

함교
hamgyo
bridge

기관실
gigwansil
engine room

객실
gaeksil
cabin

주방
joobang
galley

어휘 eohwi · **vocabulary**

항구
hang-goo
port

부두
boodu
dock

닻
dat
anchor

연결도교
yeon-gyeoldogyo
gangway

차량 진입
방지 말뚝
charyang jin-ib
bangji malttuk
bollard

원치
winchi
windlass

쾌속정
kwaesogjeong
speedboat

노젓는 배
nojeotneun bae
rowboat

카누
kanu
canoe

선장
seonjang
captain

기타 보트 gita boteu • **other boats**

페리
paeri
ferry

선외 모터
seon-wae moteo
outboard motor

고무 보트
gomoo boteu
inflatable dinghy

수중익선
soojung-ikseon
hydrofoil

요트
yoteu
yacht

쌍동선
ssangdongseon
catamaran

예인선
yeinseon
tugboat

호버크라프트
hobeokeurapeuteu
hovercraft

컨테이너선
keonteineoseon
container ship

항해
hanghae
sail

범선
beomseon
sailboat

화물창
hwamulchang
hold

화물선
hwamulseon
freighter

유조선
yoojoseon
oil tanker

항공모함
hang-gongmoham
aircraft carrier

전함
jeonham
battleship

함교탑
hamgyotap
conning tower

잠수함
jamsooham
submarine

항구 hang-goo • **port**

화물
hwa-mool
cargo

창고
chang-go
warehouse

크레인
keuraein
crane

선창
seonchang
quay

세관 사무소
saegwan samuso
customs house

컨테이너
keonteineo
container

지게차
jigecha
forklift

부두
boodu
dock

페리
paeri
ferry

매표소
maepyoso
ticket office

승객
seung-gaek
passenger

페리 터미널
paeri teomineol
ferry terminal

컨네이너항 keonteineohang | **container port**

여객선 항구
yeogaekseon hang-gu | **passenger port**

그물
geumul
net

어선
eoseon
fishing boat

계류용 밧줄
gyeryuyong batjul
mooring

정박지
jeongbagji | **marina**

어항 eohang | **fishing port**

항만 hangman | **harbor**

부두 boodu | **pier**

방파제 bangpaje | **jetty**

조선소 joseonso | **shipyard**

램프
laempeu
lamp

등대
deungdae
lighthouse

부표
boopyo
buoy

어휘 eohwi • vocabulary

드라이 독
deurai dog
dry dock

해안경비대
hae-an gyeongbidae
coast guard

항만 관리소장
hangman gwanrisojang
harbor master

닻을 내리다
dacheul naerida
drop anchor (v)

계류하다
gyeryuhada
moor (v)

부두에 대다
boodu-e daeda
dock (v)

내리다
naerida
disembark (v)

배에 타다
bae-e tada
board (v)

출범하다
chulbeomhada
set sail (v)

스포츠 seupocheu
sports

미식축구 misigchookgu • **football**

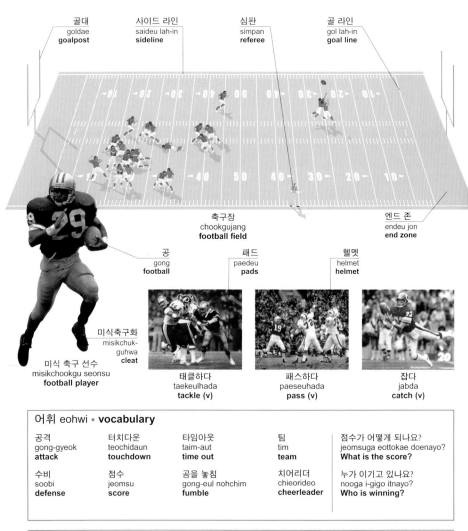

골대
goldae
goalpost

사이드 라인
saideu lah-in
sideline

심판
simpan
referee

골 라인
gol lah-in
goal line

축구장
chookgujang
football field

엔드 존
endeu jon
end zone

공
gong
football

패드
paedeu
pads

헬멧
helmet
helmet

미식축구화
misikchuk-guhwa
cleat

미식 축구 선수
misikchookgu seonsu
football player

태클하다
taekeulhada
tackle (v)

패스하다
paeseuhada
pass (v)

잡다
jabda
catch (v)

어휘 eohwi • **vocabulary**

공격 gong-gyeok **attack**	터치다운 teochidaun **touchdown**	타임아웃 taim-aut **time out**	팀 tim **team**	점수가 어떻게 되나요? jeomsuga eottokae doenayo? **What is the score?**
수비 soobi **defense**	점수 jeomsu **score**	공을 놓침 gong-eul nohchim **fumble**	치어리더 chieorideo **cheerleader**	누가 이기고 있나요? nooga i-gigo itnayo? **Who is winning?**

럭비 leogbi · **rugby**

득점 지역
deugjeom jiyeok
in-goal area

터치 라인
teochi lah-in
touchline

깃발
gitbal
flag

데드볼 라인
dedeubol lah-in
dead-ball line

골
gol
goal

럭비 경기장 leogbi gyeong-gijang | **rugby field**

공
gong
ball

던지다
deonjida
throw (v)

럭비 유니폼
leogbi yoonipom
rugby uniform

차다
chada
kick (v)

패스하다
paeseuhada
pass (v)

공을 뺏다
gong-eul ppaetda
tackle (v)

트라이
teurai
try

선수
seonsu
player

럭 leok | **ruck**

스크럼 seukeureom | **scrum**

축구 chookgu • **soccer**

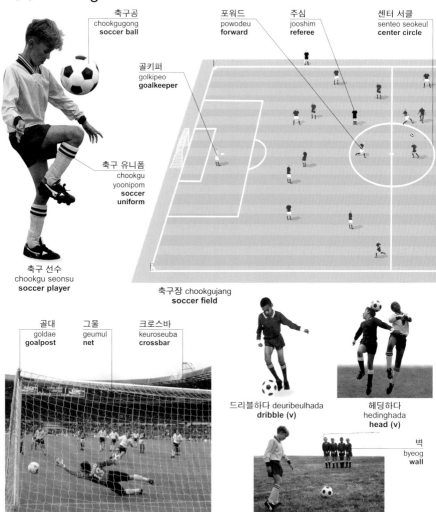

축구공
chookgugong
soccer ball

포워드
powodeu
forward

주심
jooshim
referee

센터 서클
senteo seokeul
center circle

골키퍼
golkipeo
goalkeeper

축구 유니폼
chookgu
yoonipom
**soccer
uniform**

축구 선수
chookgu seonsu
soccer player

축구장 chookgujang
soccer field

골대
goldae
goalpost

그물
geumul
net

크로스바
keuroseuba
crossbar

드리블하다 deuribeulhada
dribble (v)

헤딩하다
hedinghada
head (v)

벽
byeog
wall

골 gol | **goal**

프리킥
peurikik | **free kick**

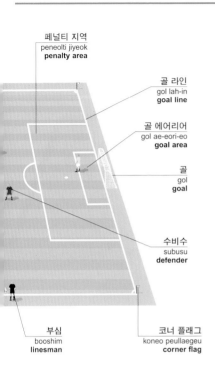

페널티 지역
peneolti jiyeok
penalty area

골 라인
gol lah-in
goal line

골 에어리어
gol ae-eori-eo
goal area

골
gol
goal

수비수
subusu
defender

부심
booshim
linesman

코너 플래그
koneo peullaegeu
corner flag

스로인 seuroin
throw-in

차다 chada
kick (v)

부츠
bucheu
cleat

패스하다
passhahda
pass (v)

숫을 하다
shooseul hada
shoot (v)

태클하다
taekeulhada
tackle (v)

막다
jeojanghada
save (v)

어휘 eohwi · **vocabulary**

경기장 gyeong-gijang **stadium**	페널티 peneolti **penalty**	퇴장 toejang **send off**	무승부 mooseungbu **tie**	리그 ligeu **league**
득점하다 deugjeomhada **score a goal (v)**	반칙 banchik **foul**	옐로카드 yaellokadeu **yellow card**	연장전 yeonjangjeon **extra time**	교체 gyoche **substitution**
코너 koneo **corner**	오프사이드 opeusaideu **offside**	레드카드 ledeukadeu **red card**	하프타임 hapeutaim **half-time**	교체 선수 gyoche seonsu **substitute**

하키 haki • **hockey**

아이스 하키 aiseu haki • **ice hockey**

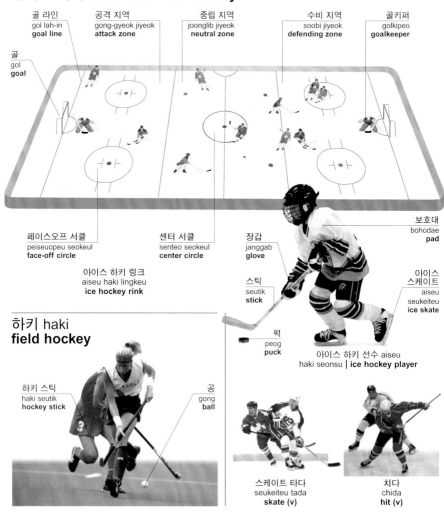

골 라인
gol lah-in
goal line

공격 지역
gong-gyeok jiyeok
attack zone

중립 지역
joonglib jiyeok
neutral zone

수비 지역
soobi jiyeok
defending zone

골키퍼
golkipeo
goalkeeper

골
gol
goal

보호대
bohodae
pad

페이스오프 서클
peiseuopeu seokeul
face-off circle

센터 서클
senteo seokeul
center circle

장갑
janggab
glove

아이스
스케이트
aiseu
seukeiteu
ice skate

아이스 하키 링크
aiseu haki lingkeu
ice hockey rink

스틱
seutik
stick

퍽
peog
puck

아이스 하키 선수 aiseu
haki seonsu | **ice hockey player**

하키 haki
field hockey

하키 스틱
haki seutik
hockey stick

공
gong
ball

스케이트 타다
seukeiteu tada
skate (v)

치다
chida
hit (v)

크리켓 keuriket • **cricket**

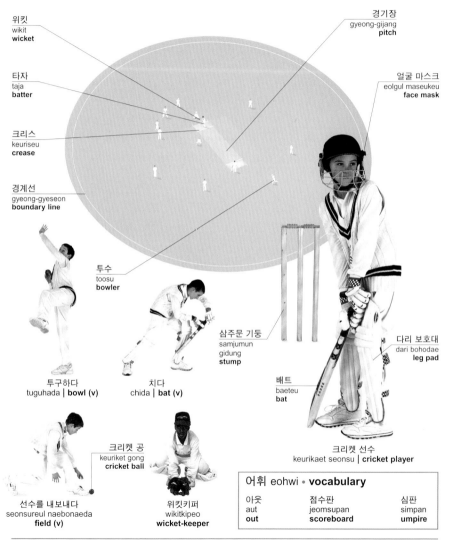

위킷
wikit
wicket

타자
taja
batter

크리스
keuriseu
crease

경계선
gyeong-gyeseon
boundary line

경기장
gyeong-gijang
pitch

얼굴 마스크
eolgul maseukeu
face mask

투수
toosu
bowler

삼주문 기둥
samjumun
gidung
stump

다리 보호대
dari bohodae
leg pad

배트
baeteu
bat

투구하다
tuguhada | **bowl (v)**

치다
chida | **bat (v)**

크리켓 선수
keurikaet seonsu | **cricket player**

크리켓 공
keuriket gong
cricket ball

선수를 내보내다
seonsureul naebonaeda
field (v)

위킷키퍼
wikitkipeo
wicket-keeper

어휘 eohwi • **vocabulary**

아웃	점수판	심판
aut	jeomsupan	simpan
out	**scoreboard**	**umpire**

농구 nong-gu · **basketball**

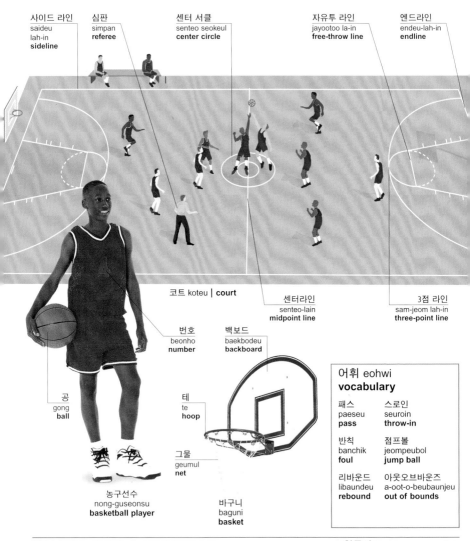

사이드 라인
saideu
lah-in
sideline

심판
simpan
referee

센터 서클
senteo seokeul
center circle

자유투 라인
jayootoo la-in
free-throw line

엔드라인
endeu-lah-in
endline

코트 koteu | **court**

센터라인
senteo-lain
midpoint line

3점 라인
sam-jeom lah-in
three-point line

번호
beonho
number

백보드
baekbodeu
backboard

공
gong
ball

테
te
hoop

그물
geumul
net

농구선수
nong-guseonsu
basketball player

바구니
baguni
basket

어휘 eohwi
vocabulary

패스	스로인
paeseu	seuroin
pass	**throw-in**
반칙	점프볼
banchik	jeompeubol
foul	**jump ball**
리바운드	아웃오브바운즈
libaundeu	a-oot-o-beubaunjeu
rebound	**out of bounds**

동작 dongjak • **actions**

던지다
deonjida
throw (v)

잡다
jabda
catch (v)

숫을 하다
shooseul hada
shoot (v)

점프하다
jeompeuhada
jump (v)

마크하다
makeuhada
mark (v)

블로킹하다
beullokinghada
block (v)

공을 튀기다
gong-eul tuigida
dribble (v)

덩크 숫하다
deongkeu shoothada
dunk (v)

배구 baegu • **volleyball**

차단하다
chadanhada
block (v)

그물
geumul
net

받아내다
badanaeda
dig (v)

심판
simpan
referee

무릎 보호대
mooreup
bohodae
knee support

코트 koteu | **court**

야구 yagu · **baseball**

필드 pildeu · **field**

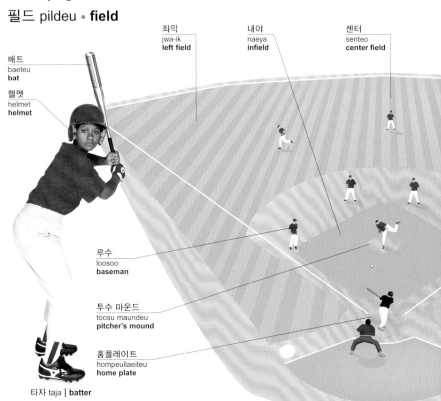

좌익
jwa-ik
left field

내야
naeya
infield

센터
senteo
center field

배트
baeteu
bat

헬멧
helmet
helmet

루수
loosoo
baseman

투수 마운드
toosu maundeu
pitcher's mound

홈플레이트
hompeullaeiteu
home plate

타자 taja | **batter**

어휘 eohwi · **vocabulary**

이닝 i-ning **inning**	세이프 seipeu **safe**	파울 볼 paul bol **foul ball**
득점 deukjeom **run**	아웃 aut **out**	스트라이크 seuteuraikeu **strike**

공
gong
ball

글러브
geulleobeu
glove

마스크
maseukeu
mask

동작 dongjak • **actions**

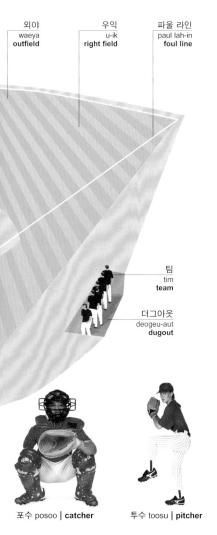

외야
waeya
outfield

우익
u-ik
right field

파울 라인
paul lah-in
foul line

팀
tim
team

더그아웃
deogeu-aut
dugout

포수 posoo | **catcher**

투수 toosu | **pitcher**

던지다 deonjida | **throw (v)**

잡다 jabda | **catch (v)**

달리다
dallida
run (v)

수비하다 subihada
field (v)

슬라이드하다
seulaideuhada
slide (v)

태그하다
taegeuhada
tag (v)

던지다
deonjida
pitch (v)

치다
chida
bat (v)

심판
simpan
umpire

시합하다 sihabhada | **play (v)**

테니스 teniseu · **tennis**

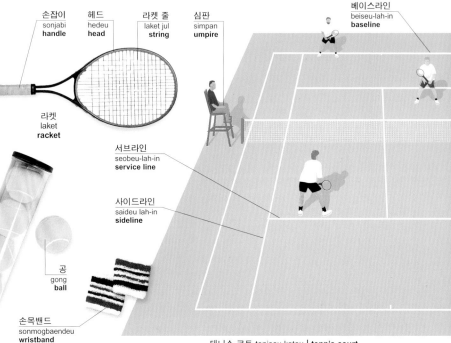

손잡이
sonjabi
handle

헤드
hedeu
head

라켓 줄
laket jul
string

심판
simpan
umpire

베이스라인
beiseu-lah-in
baseline

라켓
laket
racket

서브라인
seobeu-lah-in
service line

사이드라인
saideu lah-in
sideline

공
gong
ball

손목밴드
sonmogbaendeu
wristband

테니스 코트 teniseu koteu | **tennis court**

어휘 eohwi · **vocabulary**

선수권대회 seonsugwondaehoei **championship**	경기 gyeong-gi **game**	무득점 mudeukjeom **love**	어드밴티지 eodeubaentiji **advantage**	드롭샷 deurobshat **dropshot**	레트! leteu! **let!**
싱글 sing-geul **singles**	세트 seteu **set**	듀스 dyuseu **deuce**	서브 실수 seobeu silsu **fault**	슬라이스 seullaiseu **slice**	스핀 seupin **spin**
더블 deobeul **doubles**	매치 maechi **match**	타이브레이크 taibeuraeikeu **tiebreaker**	에이스 eiseu **ace**	랠리 laelli **rally**	선심 seonsim **linesman**

스트로크 seuteurokeu • **strokes**

그물
geumul
net

스매시
seumaesi
smash

볼보이
bolboi
ball boy / ball girl

서브하다
seobeuhada
serve (v)

테니스화
teniseuhwa
tennis shoes

선수 seonsu | **player**

서브
seobeu
serve

발리
balli
volley

되넘기기
doeneomgigi
return

로브
robeu
lob

포핸드
pohaendeu
forehand

백핸드
baekhaendeu
backhand

라켓 게임 laket geim • **racket games**

서틀콕
sheoteulkok
shuttlecock

배드민턴
baedeuminteon
badminton

배트
baeteu
paddle

탁구
takgu
table tennis

스쿼시
seukwosi
squash

라켓볼
laketbol
racquetball

골프 golpeu • **golf**

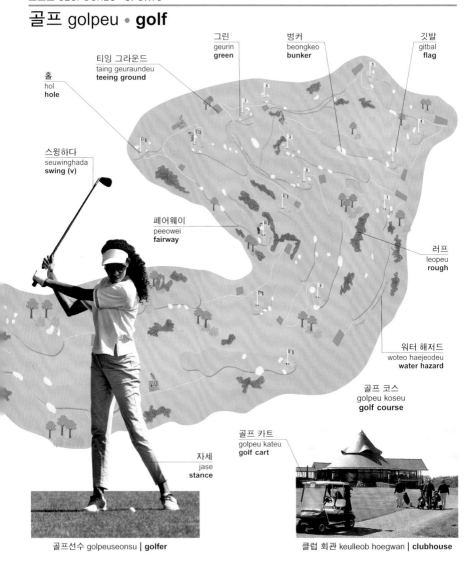

그린
geurin
green

벙커
beongkeo
bunker

깃발
gitbal
flag

티잉 그라운드
taing geuraundeu
teeing ground

홀
hol
hole

스윙하다
seuwinghada
swing (v)

페어웨이
peeowei
fairway

러프
leopeu
rough

워터 해저드
woteo haejeodeu
water hazard

골프 코스
golpeu koseu
golf course

골프 카트
golpeu kateu
golf cart

자세
jase
stance

골프선수 golpeuseonsu | **golfer**

클럽 회관 keulleob hoegwan | **clubhouse**

도구 dogu • **equipment**

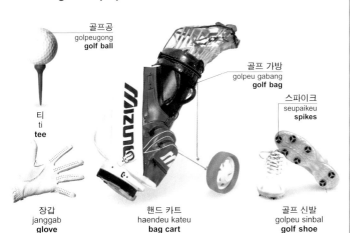

골프공
golpeugong
golf ball

골프 가방
golpeu gabang
golf bag

스파이크
seupaikeu
spikes

티
ti
tee

장갑
janggab
glove

핸드 카트
haendeu kateu
bag cart

골프 신발
golpeu sinbal
golf shoe

골프 클럽
golpeu
keulleob
golf clubs

우드
udeu
wood

퍼터
peoteo
putter

동작 dongjak • **actions**

티에서 공을 치다
tieseo gong-eul chida
tee off (v)

공을 세게 치다
gong-eul sege chida
drive (v)

퍼팅하다
peotinghada
putt (v)

높이 치다
nop-i chida
chip (v)

아이언
aion
iron

웨지
weji
wedge

어휘 eohwi • **vocabulary**

기준 타수 gijoon tasu **par**	오버 파 obeo pa **over par**	핸디캡 haendikaeb **handicap**	캐디 kaedi **caddy**	스윙 연습하다 seuwing yeonseumhada **practice swing**	스트로크 seuteurokeu **stroke**
언더 파 eondeo pa **under par**	홀인원 hol-in-won **hole in one**	토너먼트 toneomeonteu **tournament**	관중 gwanjoong **spectators**	백스윙 baegseuwing **backswing**	플레이 라인 peullei lah-in **line of play**

육상경기 yooksang-gyeong-gi • **track and field**

트랙
teuraeg
track

레인
lein
lane

결승선
gyeolseungseon
finish line

출발선
chulbalseon
starting line

경기장
gyeong-gijang
field

운동 선수
undong
seonsu
athlete

출발대
chulbaldae
**starting
blocks**

단거리 주자
dangeori jooja
sprinter

원반던지기
wonbandeonjigi
discus

투포환
tupohwan
shotput

투창
tuchang
javelin

어휘 eohwi • **vocabulary**

경주 gyeongju **race**	기록 girog **record**	마라톤 maraton **marathon**	개인 최고 기록 gaein choego girog **personal best**
시간 sigan **time**	신기록을 세우다 singirog-eul se-uda **break a record (v)**	사진 판정 sajin panjeong **photo finish**	장대 높이뛰기 jangdae nop-ittwigi **pole vault**

스톱워치
seutob-wochi
stopwatch

바톤
baton
baton

가로대
garodae
crossbar

계주
gyeju
relay race

높이 뛰기
nop-i ttwigi
high jump

멀리 뛰기
meolli ttwigi
long jump

허들 경주
heodeul gyeongju
hurdles

체조 chejo • **gymnastics**

도약판
doyakpan
springboard

체조선수
chejoseonsu
gymnast

공중제비
gongjoongjebi
somersault

평균대 pyeong-gyundae | **balance beam**

리본
libon
ribbon

안마
anma
horse

매트
maeteu
mat

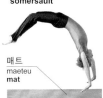

뛰어넘기
ttwie-eo-neom-gi
vault

마루 운동
maru undong
floor exercises

옆으로 재주넘기
yeop-euro jaejoo-neomgi
cartwheel

리듬 체조
lideum chejo
rhythmic gymnastics

어휘 eohwi • **vocabulary**

철봉 경기 cheolbong gyeong-gi **horizontal bar**	안마 anma **pommel horse**	링 ling **rings**	메달 medal **medals**	은 eun **silver**
평행봉 pyeonghaengbong **parallel bars**	이단 평행봉 idan pyeonghaengbong **asymmetric bars**	단상 dansang **podium**	금 geum **gold**	동 dong **bronze**

투기 toogi • **combat sports**

상대방
sangdaebang
opponent

방어 자세
bang-eo jase
guard

장갑
janggab
glove

띠
tti
belt

태권도 taegwondo | **tae kwon do**

가라테 garate | **karate**

호구
hogoo
mask

검
geom
sword

유도 yudo | **judo**

합기도 habgido | **aikido**

검도 geomdo | **kendo**

쿵후 koonghoo | **kung fu**

킥복싱
kikbogsing | **kickboxing**

레슬링 leseulling | **wrestling**

권투 gwontoo | **boxing**

동작 dongjak · **actions**

쓰러짐 sseureojim | **fall**

잡기 jabgi | **hold**

던지기 deonjigi | **throw**

누르기 nooreugi | **pin**

차기
chagi | **kick**

정권치기
jeong-gwonchigi | **punch**

가격
gagyeok | **strike**

막기 makgi | **block**

점프 jeompeu | **jump**

손날치기
nson-nalchigi | **chop**

어휘 eohwi · **vocabulary**

복싱 링
bogsing ling
boxing ring

라운드
laundeu
round

주먹
joomeok
fist

호신술
hosinsul
self-defense

태극권
taegeukgwon
tai chi

마우스피스
mauseupiseu
mouth guard

시합
sihab
bout

녹아웃
nog-aut
knockout

무술
musul
martial arts

카포에이라
kapo-eira
capoeira

권투 장갑
gwontu janggab
boxing gloves

스파링
seuparing
sparring

펀치백
peonchibaeg
punching bag

검은 띠
geom-eun tti
black belt

스모
seumo
sumo wrestling

수영 sooyeong · **swimming**

장비 jangbi · **equipment**

완장형 튜브
wanjanghyeong
tyubeu
water wings

노즈 클립
nojeu keullib
nose clip

물안경
mool-an-gyeong | **goggles**

킥보드 kikbodeu | **kickboard**

여자 수영복
yeoja suyeongbok
swimsuit

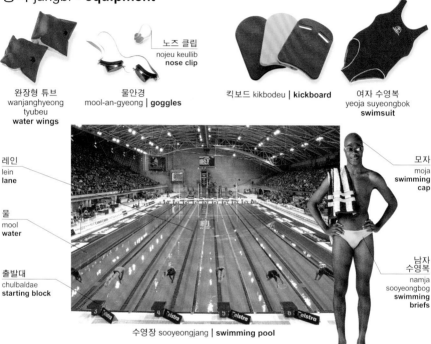

레인
lein
lane

물
mool
water

출발대
chulbaldae
starting block

모자
moja
**swimming
cap**

남자
수영복
namja
sooyeongbog
**swimming
briefs**

수영장 sooyeongjang | **swimming pool**

수영선수 sooyeongseonsu
swimmer

도약판
doyakpan
diving board

다이버
daibeo
diver

다이빙하다 daibinghada | **dive (v)**

수영하다 sooyeonghada
swim (v)

턴 tin | **turn**

수영 동작 sooyeong dongjak • **styles**

자유형 jayoohyeong | **front crawl**

평영 pyeonghyeong | **breaststroke**

스트로크
seuteurokeu
stroke

배영 baeyeong | **backstroke**

차기
chagi
kick

접영 jeobyeong | **butterfly**

스쿠버 다이빙 seukubeo daibing • **scuba diving**

공기 실린더
gong-gi sillindeo
air tank

마스크
maseukeu
mask

잠수복
jamsoobog
wetsuit

오리발
oribal
fin

호흡기
hoheupgi
regulator

웨이트벨트
weiteubelteu
weight belt

스노클
snokeul
snorkel

어휘 eohwi • **vocabulary**

다이빙 daibing **dive**	다이빙 출발 daibing choolbal **racing dive**	수구 sugu **water polo**	얕은 쪽 yat-eun jjog **shallow end**	경련 gyeonglyeon **cramp**	로커 lokeo **lockers**
하이 다이빙 hai daibing **high dive**	선헤엄치다 seonhae-eomchida **tread water (v)**	수중 발레 soojoong ballae **synchronized swimming**	수심이 깊은 쪽 susim-i gipeun jjog **deep end**	익사하다 iksahada **drown (v)**	인명 구조원 inmyeong gujowon **lifeguard**

요트타기 yoteutagi • **sailing**

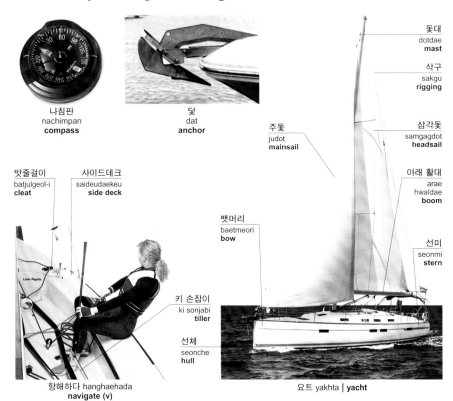

나침판
nachimpan
compass

닻
dat
anchor

돛대
dotdae
mast

삭구
sakgu
rigging

주돛
judot
mainsail

삼각돛
samgagdot
headsail

밧줄걸이
batjulgeol-i
cleat

사이드데크
saideudaekeu
side deck

아래 활대
arae
hwaldae
boom

뱃머리
baetmeori
bow

선미
seonmi
stern

키 손잡이
ki sonjabi
tiller

선체
seonche
hull

항해하다 hanghaehada
navigate (v)

요트 yakhta | **yacht**

안전 anjeon • **safety**

신호탄
sinhotan
flare

구명 부표
goomyeong boopyo
life buoy

구명 조끼
goomyeong jokki
life jacket

구명 보트
goomyeong boteu
life raft

수상스포츠 soosangseupocheu · **watersports**

노 젓는 사람
no jeotneun saram
rower

노
no
oar

배를 젓다 baereul jeotda | **row (v)**

카약
kayak
kayak

짧은 노
jjalbeun no
paddle

카약 타기 kayak tagi | **kayaking**

항해
hanghae
sail

윈드서퍼
windeuseopeo
windsurfer

보드
bodeu
board

서퍼
seopeo
surfer

서핑
seoping
surfing

스키
seuki
ski

수상스키
soosangseuki
water-skiing

고속 모터보트 타기
gosog moteoboteu tagi
speedboating

풋 스트랩
put seuteuraeb
footstrap

윈드서핑 windeuseoping | **windsurfing**

래프팅
laepeuting
rafting

제트스키
jaeteuseuki
jet-skiing

어휘 eohwi · **vocabulary**

서핑 seoping **surf**	바람 baram **wind**	시트 siteu **sheet**	하수용골 hasuyong-gol **centerboard**	빗겨 나아가다 bitgyeo na-a-gada **tack (v)**	급류 geubryu **rapids**
서핑보드 seopingbodeu **surfboard**	파도 pado **wave**	방향타 banghyangta **rudder**	선원 seon-won **crew**	뒤집히다 dwijibhida **capsize (v)**	

승마 seungma • **horseback riding**

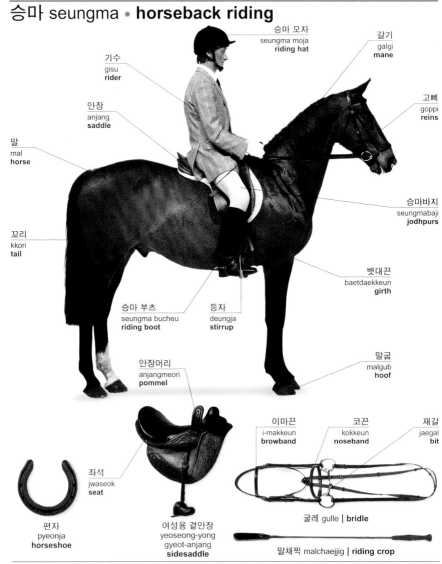

승마 모자
seungma moja
riding hat

갈기
galgi
mane

기수
gisu
rider

고삐
goppi
reins

안장
anjang
saddle

말
mal
horse

승마바지
seungmabaji
jodhpurs

꼬리
kkori
tail

뱃대끈
baetdaekkeun
girth

승마 부츠
seungma bucheu
riding boot

등자
deungja
stirrup

말굽
malgub
hoof

안장머리
anjangmeori
pommel

이마끈
i-makkeun
browband

코끈
kokkeun
noseband

재갈
jaegal
bit

좌석
jwaseok
seat

굴레 gulle | **bridle**

편자
pyeonja
horseshoe

여성용 곁안장
yeoseong-yong
gyeot-anjang
sidesaddle

말채찍 malchaejjig | **riding crop**

경기 gyeong-gi • **events**

경주말
gyeongjoomal
racehorse

담장
damjang
fence

경마
gyeongma
horse race

장애물 경마
jang-aemul gyeongma
steeplechase

하니스 레이스
haniseu leiseu
harness race

로데오
lode-o
rodeo

장애물 뛰어넘기
jang-aemul ttwie-eo-neomgi
showjumping

마차경주
machagyeongju
carriage race

트레킹
teuraeking | **trail riding**

마장마술
majangmasool | **dressage**

폴로 pollo | **polo**

어휘 eohwi • **vocabulary**

구보 gubo **walk**	느린 구보 neurin gubo **canter**	점프 jeompeu **jump**	고삐 goppi **halter**	대기소 daegiso **paddock**	평지 경기 pyeongji gyeong-gi **flat race**
속보 sogbo **trot**	질주 jilju **gallop**	마부 mabu **groom**	마구간 magoogan **stable**	경기장 gyeong-gijang **arena**	경마장 gyeongmajang **racecourse**

낚시 naksi • **fishing**

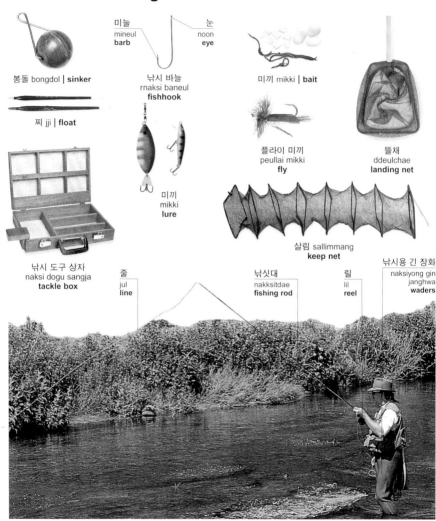

봉돌 bongdol | **sinker**

찌 jji | **float**

미늘
mineul
barb

눈
noon
eye

낚시 바늘
rnaksi baneul
fishhook

미끼
mikki
lure

미끼 mikki | **bait**

플라이 미끼
peullai mikki
fly

뜰채
ddeulchae
landing net

낚시 도구 상자
naksi dogu sangja
tackle box

살림 sallimmang
keep net

줄
jul
line

낚싯대
nakksitdae
fishing rod

릴
lil
reel

낚시용 긴 장화
naksiyong gin
janghwa
waders

낚시꾼 naksi-kkun | **angler**

낚시 유형 naksi yoohyeong • **types of fishing**

민물고기 낚시
minmulgogi naksi
freshwater fishing

플라이 낚시
peullai naksi
fly-fishing

스포츠 피싱
seupocheu pising
sportfishing

원양 어업
won-yang eo-eob
deep-sea fishing

서프캐스팅
seopeukaeseuting
surfcasting

활동 hwaldong • **activities**

던지다
deonjida
cast (v)

잡다
jabda
catch (v)

감다
gamda
reel in (v)

그물을 치다
geumul-eul chida
net (v)

놓아주다
noajooda
release (v)

어휘 eohwi • **vocabulary**

미끼를 물다 mikkireul mulda **bite (v)**	낚시용 태클 naksiyong taekeul **tackle**	낚싯대 nakksitdae **pole**	방수 bangsu **rain gear**	바다 낚시 bada naksi **marine fishing**
미끼를 달다 mikkireul dalda **bait (v)**	실감개 silgamgae **spool**	고기 담는 바구니 gogi damneun baguni **creel**	낚시 허가 naksi heoga **fishing license**	스피어피싱 seupieopising **spearfishing**

스키타기 seukitagi • **skiing**

의자식 리프트
uijasik lipeuteu
chairlift

스키장
seukijang
ski slope

스키 스틱
seuki seutik
ski pole

장갑
janggab
glove

스키 활주로
seuki hwaljooro
ski run

안전벽
anjeonbyeok
safety barrier

끝부분
kkeutbubun
tip

날
nal
edge

스키
seuki
ski

스키 부츠
seuki bucheu
ski boot

스키 자켓
seuki jaket
ski jacket

스키 타는 사람
seuki taneun saram
skier

경기 gyeong-gi • **events**

활강
hwalgang
downhill skiing

게이트
geiteu
gate

회전경기
heojeongyeong-gi
slalom

스키 점프
seuki jeompeu
ski jump

크로스컨트리 스키
keuroseukeonteuri seuki
cross-country skiing

동계 스포츠 dong-gye seupocheu
winter sports

빙벽 등반
bingbyeok deungban
ice climbing

아이스 스케이팅
aiseu seukeiting
ice-skating

피겨 스케이팅
pigyeo seukeiting
figure skating

고글
gogeul
goggles

스케이트
seukeiteu
skate

스노우보딩
seu-nou-boding
snowboarding

봅슬레이
bobseullei
bobsled

루지
looji
luge

스노우모빌
seu-nou mobil
snowmobile

썰매타기
sseolmaetagi
sledding

어휘 eohwi • **vocabulary**

산악 스키
san-ag seuki
alpine skiing

대회전경기
daehoejeongyeong-gi
giant slalom

오프피스트
opeupiseuteu
off-piste

케이블카
kaeibeulka
cable car

컬링
keolling
curling

개 썰매
gae sseolmae
dogsledding

스피드 스케이팅
seupideu seukeiting
speed skating

바이애슬론
bai-ae-seullon
biathlon

눈사태
noonsatae
avalanche

기타 스포츠 gita seupocheu • **other sports**

글라이더
geullaideo
glider

행글라이더
haeng-geullaideo
hang-glider

글라이딩
geullaiding
gliding

낙하산
nakhasan
parachute

행글라이딩
haeng-geullaiding
hang-gliding

로프
lopeu
rope

암벽 등반
ambyeok deungban
rock climbing

패러슈팅
paereoshooting
parachuting

패러글라이딩
paereogeullaiding
paragliding

스카이 다이빙
seukai daibing
skydiving

현수 하강
hyeonsu hagang
rappelling

번지 점프
beonji jeompeu
bungee jumping

랠리 주행
laelli juhaeng
rally driving

레이서
leiseo
race-car driver

자동차 경주
jadongcha gyeongju
auto racing

모토크로스
motokeuroseu
motocross

오토바이 경주
otobai gyeongju
motorcycle racing

스케이트보드
seukeiteubodeu
skateboard

스케이트보드 타기
seukeiteubodeu tagi
skateboarding

인라인스케이트 타기
inlainseukeiteu tagi
inline skating

스틱
seutik
stick

라크로스
lakeuroseu
lacrosse

호구
hogoo
mask

펜싱 검
pensing geom
foil

펜싱
pensing
fencing

핀
pin
pin

볼링공
bolling-gong
bowling ball

볼링
bolling
bowling

화살
hwasal
arrow

활
hwal
bow

화살통
hwasaltong
quiver

양궁
yang-goong
archery

표적
pyojeok
target

사격
sagyeok
target shooting

스누커
seu-nookeo
snooker

포켓볼
poketbol
pool

피트니스 piteuniseu • **fitness**

운동용 자전거
undong-yong
jajeongeo
exercise bike

운동 기계
undong gigye
gym machine

벤치
benchi
bench

프리 웨이트
peuri waeiteu
free weights

바
ba
bar

헬스장
helseujang
gym

로잉 머신
loing meosin
rowing machine

개인 트레이너
gaein teureineo
personal trainer

스텝 머신
seuteb meosin
stair machine

러닝 머신
leoning meosin
treadmill

수영장
sooyeongjang
swimming pool

크로스 트레이너
keuroseu teureineo
elliptical trainer

사우나
sauna
sauna

운동 undong • **exercises**

스트레칭
seuteureching
stretch

런지
leonji
lunge

팔굽혀 펴기
palgubhyeo pyeogi
push-up

아령
aryeong
dumbbell

스쿼트
seu-kwoeteu
squat

윗몸 일으키기
witmom il-eukigi
sit-up

팔뚝 운동
palttug undong
bicep curl

레그 프레스
legeu peureseu
leg press

중량봉
joonglyangbong
weight bar

운동화
undonghwa
sneakers

가슴 운동
gaseum undong
chest press

근력 운동
geunlyeog undong
weight training

달리기
dalligi
jogging

필라테스
pillateseu
Pilates

어휘 eohwi • **vocabulary**

훈련하다
hoonlyeonhada
train (v)

준비 운동을 하다
joonbi undong-eul hada
warm up (v)

제자리 뛰다
jejari ttwida
jog in place (v)

끌어 올리다
kkeureo ollida
pull up (v)

몸을 풀다
mom-eul pulda
flex (v)

몸을 쭉 뻗다
mom-eul jjoog
ppeotda
extend (v)

복서사이즈
bogseosaijeu
boxercise

서킷 트레이닝
seokit
teuraeining
circuit training

줄넘기
julneomgi
jumping rope

스핀 클래스
spin klaesseu
spin class

레저 lejeo
leisure

극장 geugjang • **theater**

커튼
keoteun
curtain

무대 양쪽 끝
moodae
yangjjog kkeut
wings

세트
seteu
set

관중
gwanjoong
audience

오케스트라
okeseuteura
orchestra

무대 mudae | **stage**

이층 정면석
i-cheung
jeongmyeonseok
balcony seats

특별석
teukbyeolseok
box

좌석열
jwaseog-
yeol
row

좌석
jwaseok
seat

발코니석
balkoniseok
balcony

서클
seokeul
mezzanine

통로
tongro
aisle

무대앞
moodae-ap
orchestra seats

오케스트라석
okeseuteuraseok
orchestra pit

좌석
jwaseok | **seating**

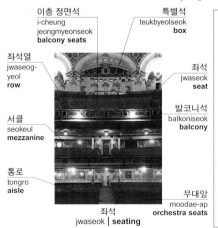

어휘 eohwi • **vocabulary**

연극 yeon-geuk **play**	등장인물 deungjang-inmul **cast**	개막 공연 gaemag gong-yeon **opening night**
대본 daebon **script**	감독 gamdog **director**	프로그램 peurogeuraem **program**
배경 baegyeong **backdrop**	프로듀서 peurodyuseo **producer**	막간 makgan **intermission**
오케스트라석 okeseuteuraseok **orchestra pit**	배우 / 여배우 baewoo *m* yeobaewoo *f* **actor**	

콘서트 konseoteu | **concert**

뮤지컬 myujikeol | **musical**

의상
uisang
costume

발레 balle | **ballet**

어휘 eohwi • **vocabulary**

클래식 음악
keullaesik eum-ak
classical music

악보
akbo
musical score

좌석 안내원
jwaseog annaewon
usher

박수치다
bagsoochida
applaud (v)

앙코르
angkoreu
encore

사운드 트랙
saundeu teuraek
soundtrack

몇 시에 시작합니까?
myeot sie sijakhamnikka?
What time does it start?

오늘 저녁 공연 표 두 장 주세요.
oh-neul jeonyeok gong-yeon
pyo doo jang juseyo
**I'd like two tickets for
tonight's performance.**

오페라
opera | **opera**

영화 yeonghwa • **movies**

팝콘
pabkon
popcorn

포스터
poseuteo
poster

매표소
maepyoso
box office

로비
lobi
lobby

영화관
yeonghwagwan
movie theater

스크린
seukeurin
screen

어휘 eohwi • **vocabulary**

코미디
komidi
comedy

로맨스
lomaenseu
romance

공상과학 영화
gongsang-gwahak yeonghwa
science fiction movie

서부극
seoboogeuk
western

모험 영화
moheom yeonghwa
adventure movie

애니메이션
aenimeisheon
animated movie

스릴러
seulilleo
thriller

공포 영화
gongpo yeonghwa
horror movie

오케스트라 okeseuteura · **orchestra**

현악기 hyeon-akgi · **strings**

하프
hapeu
harp

지휘자
jihwija
conductor

더블 베이스
deobeul beiseu
double bass

바이올린
baiollin
violin

단상
dansang
podium

첼로
chello
cello

비올라
biolla
viola

악보
akbo
score

높은 음자리표
nopeun eumjaripyo
treble clef

음표
eumpyo
note

오선
oseon
staff

낮은 음자리표
najeun eumjaripyo
bass clef

피아노 piano | **piano**

표기법 pyogibeob | **notation**

어휘 eohwi · **vocabulary**

소나타 sonata **sonata**	서곡 seogog **overture**	음계 eumgye **scale**	올림표 ollimpyo **sharp**	숨표 soompyo **rest**	제자리표 jejaripyo **natural**
심포니 simponi **symphony**	악기 akgi **instruments**	음높이 eumnopi **pitch**	내림표 naerimpyo **flat**	마디 madi **bar**	지휘봉 jihwibong **baton**

목관악기 mokgwan-akgi · **woodwind**

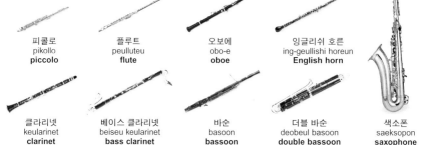

피콜로
pikollo
piccolo

플루트
peulluteu
flute

오보에
obo-e
oboe

잉글리쉬 호른
ing-geullishi horeun
English horn

색소폰
saeksopon
saxophone

클라리넷
keularinet
clarinet

베이스 클라리넷
beiseu keularinet
bass clarinet

바순
basoon
bassoon

더블 바순
deobeul basoon
double bassoon

타악기 ta-akgi · **percussion**

비브라폰
bibeurapon
vibraphone

봉고
bong-go
bongos

스네어드럼
seuneeodeureom
snare drum

팀파니
timpani
kettledrum

공
gong
gong

트라이앵글
teuraiaeng-geul
triangle

마라카스
marakaseu
maracas

심벌즈
simbeoljeu
cymbals

탬버린
taembeorin
tambourine

페달
pedal
foot pedal

금관악기 geumgwan-akgi · **brass**

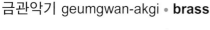

트럼펫
teureompet
trumpet

트롬본
teurombon
trombone

프렌치 호른
peurenchi horeun
French horn

튜바
tyuba
tuba

콘서트 konseoteu • **concert**

스피커
seupikeo
speaker

팬
paen
fans

리드 싱어
lideu sing-eo
lead singer

기타리스트
gitariseuteu
guitarist

마이크
maikeu
microphone

드러머
deureomeo
drummer

록 콘서트 log konseoteu | **rock concert**

악기 akgi • **instruments**

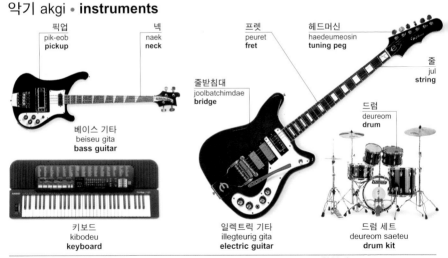

픽업
pik-eob
pickup

넥
naek
neck

프렛
peuret
fret

헤드머신
haedeumeosin
tuning peg

줄
jul
string

줄받침대
joolbatchimdae
bridge

드럼
deureom
drum

베이스 기타
beiseu gita
bass guitar

키보드
kibodeu
keyboard

일렉트릭 기타
illegteurig gita
electric guitar

드럼 세트
deureom saeteu
drum kit

음악 스타일 eum-ak seutail • **musical styles**

재즈 jaejeu | **jazz**

블루스 beulluseu | **blues**

가스펠 gaseupel | **gospel**

포크 음악
pokeu eum-ak | **folk music**

팝
pap | **pop**

댄스
daenseu | **dance music**

랩 laeb | **rap**

헤비 메탈
hebi metal | **heavy metal**

클래식 음악 keullaesik eum-ak
classical music

어휘 eohwi • **vocabulary**

노래	가사	멜로디	비트	레게	컨트리	스포트라이트
norae	gasa	mellodi	biteu	lege	keonteuri	seupoteuraiteu
song	**lyrics**	**melody**	**beat**	**reggae**	**country**	**spotlight**

관광 gwangwang · **sightseeing**

관광객
gwangwang-
gaeg
tourist

관광 명소 gwangwang myeongso
tourist attraction

일정
iljeong
itinerary

오픈 톱
o-peun top
open-top

관광 버스
gwangwang beoseu | **tour bus**

여행안내원
yeohaeng
annaewon
tour guide

작은 조각품
jag-eun jogakpum
figurine

가이드 투어
gaideu too-eo
guided tour

기념품
ginyeompum
souvenirs

어휘 eohwi · **vocabulary**

입장료
ibjangryo
entrance fee

개점
gaejeom
open

폐점
pyaejeom
closed

카메라
kamera
camera

배터리
baeteori
batteries

여행안내서
yeohaeng
annaeseo
guidebook

오디오 가이드
odio gaideu
audioguide

방향
banghyang
directions

왼쪽
oenjjok
left

오른쪽
oreunjjok
right

직진
jigjin
straight ahead

...어디에 있어요?
...eodi-eh isseoyo?
Where is... ?

길을 잃었어요.
gireul il-eosseoyo
I'm lost.

...가는 길을 알려주세요.
...ganeun gireul
allyeojuseyo
**Can you tell me
the way to... ?**

명소 myeongso • **attractions**

그림
geurim
painting

전시
jeonsi
exhibit

조각
jogak
statue

전시회
jeonsihoei
exhibition

유명한 유적
yoomyeonghan yoojeok
famous ruin

미술관
misoolgwan
art gallery

기념비
ginyeombi
monument

박물관
bakmulgwan
museum

역사적 건물
yeoksajeok geonmul
historic building

카지노
kajino
casino

정원
jeong-won
gardens

국립 공원
gooklib gong-won
national park

정보 jeongbo • **information**

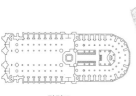

시간
sigan
times

평면도
pyeongmyeondo
floor plan

지도
jido
map

시간표
siganpyo
schedule

관광 안내소
gwangwang annaeso
tourist information

야외 활동 ya-wae hwaldong • **outdoor activities**

산책로
sanchaekro
footpath

해시계
haesigye
sundial

카페
kape
café

공원 gong-won | **park**

잔디밭
jandibat
grass

벤치
benchi
bench

정형식 정원
jeonghyeongsik jeong-won
formal gardens

롤러 코스터
lolleo koseuteo
roller coaster

축제마당
chookjemadang
fairground

테마 파크
teh-ma pakeu
theme park

사파리 공원
sapari gong-won
safari park

동물원
dongmul-won
zoo

활동 hwaldong · **activities**

자전거 타기
jajeongeo tagi
cycling

조깅
joging
jogging

스케이트보드 타기
seukeiteubodeu tagi
skateboarding

롤러블레이드 타기
lolleobeulleideu tagi
rollerblading

승마길
seungmagil
bridle path

탐조 활동
tamjo hwaldong
bird-watching

승마
seungma
horseback riding

하이킹
haiking
hiking

바구니
baguni
picnic basket

소풍
sopoong
picnic

놀이터 nol-iteo · **playground**

모래밭
moraebat
sandbox

간이 수영장
gan-i sooyeongjang
wading pool

그네
geu-nae
swing

시소 siso | **seesaw**

미끄럼틀 mikkeureomteul | **slide**

정글짐 jeong-geuljim
climbing frame

해변 haebyeon • **beach**

호텔
hotel
hotel

비치 파라솔
bichi parasol
beach umbrella

파도
pado
wave

바다
bada
sea

선라운저
seonlaunjeo
sun lounger

모래
morae
sand

비키니
bikini
bikini

남자 수영복
namja
sooyeongbog
swimming briefs

비치백
bichibaeg
beach bag

일광욕하다 ilgwang-yokhada | **sunbathe (v)**

인명 구조원
inmyeong gujowon
lifeguard

안전 감시탑
ianjeon gamsitap
lifeguard tower

방풍막
bangpoongmak
windbreak

해변 산책로
haebyeon sanchaeklo
boardwalk

덱 체어
dek che-eo
deck chair

선글라스
seongeullaseu
sunglasses

챙모자
chaengmoja
sun hat

선탠 로션
seontaen losheon
suntan lotion

자외선 차단제
jawaeseon chadanjae
sunscreen

비치볼
bichibol
beach ball

수영 튜브
suyeong tyubeu
inflatable ring

수영복
sooyeongbok
swimsuit

삽
sab
shovel

양동이
yangdong-i
pail

모래성
moraeseong
sandcastle

조개 껍질
jogae kkeobjil
shell

비치 타올
bichi taol
beach towel

캠핑 kaemping • **camping**

쓰레기장
sseuraegijang
waste disposal

화장실
hwajangsil
restrooms

샤워장
shawojang
shower block

전기 연결대
jeongi yeon-gyeoldae
electric hookup

플라이
peullai
rain fly

텐트팩
taenteupaek
tent peg

버팀줄
beotimjul
guy rope

카라반
karaban
camper

캠프장 kaempeujang | **campground**

어휘 eohwi • **vocabulary**

캠핑하다
kaempinghada
camp (v)

텐트를 치다
tenteureul chida
pitch a tent (v)

피크닉 테이블
pikeunik
picnic bench

불을 지피다
bul-eul jipida
light a fire (v)

시설 관리 사무소
siseol gwanli samuso
site manager's office

자리
jari
site

해먹
haemeog
hammock

캠프파이어
kaempeupaieo
campfire

텐트 자리
tenteu jari
sites available

텐트 폴
taenteu pol
tent pole

캠핑 밴
kaemping baen
camper van

숯
soot
charcoal

빈 자리 없음
bin jari eobseum
full

캠핑 침대
kaemping chimdae
camp bed

트레일러
teureilleo
trailer

불쏘시개
bulssosigae
firelighter

프레임
peureim
frame

바닥 매트
badak maeteu
ground sheet

배낭
baenang
backpack

진공 보온병
jingong
bo-onbyeong
vacuum flask

물병
mulbyeong
water bottle

텐트
tenteu
tent

벌레 퇴치제
beolle toechije
insect repellent

손전등
sonjeondeung
flashlight

모기장
mogijang
mosquito net

보온 내의
bo-on nae-ui
thermal underwear

등산화
deungsanhwa
hiking boots

방수용품
bangsooyongpoom
rain gear

침낭
chimnang
sleeping bag

슬리핑 매트
seulliping maeteu
sleeping mat

캠핑 버너
kaemping beo-nuh
camping stove

바베큐 그릴
babekyu geurill
barbecue grill

에어 매트리스
ae-eo maeteuriseu | **air mattress**

홈 엔터테인먼트 hom aenteotaeinmeonteu
home entertainment

평면 TV
pyeongmyeon tibeu-i
flatscreen TV

앰프
aempeu
amplifier

스피커
seupikeo
speaker

스피커 스탠드
seupikeo seutaendeu
speaker stand

빨리 감기
ppalli gamgi
fast-forward

되감기
doegamgi
rewind

재생
jaesaeng
play

일시 정지
ilsi jeongji
pause

음량
eumryang
volume

녹화
nokhwa
record

정지
jeongji
stop

리모컨
limokeon | **remote control**

DVD 플레이어
dibeu-idi peulleieo
DVD player

독
dok
dock

라디오
ladio
radio

셋톱박스
saetopbokseu
DTV converter box

디지털 라디오
dijiteol ladio
digital radio

위성방송 안테나
wiseongbangsong antaena
satellite dish

아이컵
aikeob
eyecup

스크린
seukeurin
screen

캠코더
kaemkodeo
camcorder

게임기
gaeimgi
console

컨트롤러
keonteurolleo
controller

비디오 게임 bidio geim | **video game**

스마트 스피커
seu-mateu spikeo
smart speaker

케이스
keiseu
case

블루투스 스피커
blutuseu spikeo
Bluetooth speaker

헤드폰
hedeupon
headphones

무선 이어폰
museon i-eopon
wireless earphones

어휘 eohwi • **vocabulary**

와이파이 waipai **Wi-Fi**	프로그램 peurogeuraem **program**	CD 플레이어 ssidi peulleieo **CD player**	텔레비전을 끄다 tellebijyeon-eul kkeuda **turn off the television (v)**	스마트 티비 seu-mateu tibi **smart TV**
스트리밍 seuteuriming **streaming**	장편 영화 jangpyeon yeonghwa **feature film**	스테레오 seutere-oh **stereo**	텔레비전을 켜다 tellebijyeon-eul kyeoda **turn on the television (v)**	노래방 noraebang **karaoke**
디지털 dijiteol **digital**	광고 gwang-go **advertisement**	사운드바 saundeuba **soundbar**	텔레비전을 보다 tellebijeon-eul boda **watch television (v)**	
고화질 gohwajil **high-definition**	케이블 TV keibeul tibeu-i **cable television**		채널을 바꾸다 chaeneol-eul bakkuda **change channel (v)**	

사진술 sajinsul • **photography**

서터 버튼
sheoteo beoteun
shutter release

조리개 다이얼
jorigae daieol
aperture dial

렌즈
lenjeu
lens

필터
pilteo
filter

렌즈 캡
lenjeu kaeb
lens cap

SLR 카메라 eseuel-al kamela | **SLR camera**

외장 플래시
waejang peullaesi
flash gun

노출계
nochoolgye
light meter

줌 렌즈
joom lenjeu
zoom lens

삼각대
samgakdae
tripod

카메라 유형 kamera yoohyeong • **types of camera**

폴라로이드 카메라
pollaloideu kamera
Polaroid camera

플래시
peullaesi
flash

디지털 카메라
dijiteol kamera
digital camera

카메라폰
kamerapon
camera phone

일회용 카메라
ilhoeyong kamera
disposable camera

사진찍다 sajinjjigda · **photograph (v)**

초점을 맞추다
chojeom-eul matchuda
focus (v)

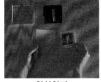

현상하다
hyeonsanghada
develop (v)

음화
eumhwa
negative

셀카
selka
selfie

풍경
poong-gyeong
landscape

인물
inmul
portrait

사진 sajin | **photograph**

사진 앨범
sajin aelbeom
photo album

사진 액자
sajin aekja
picture frame

문제 moonje · **problems**

노출 부족
nochool boojok
underexposed

노출 과다
nochool gwada
overexposed

초점 흐림
chojeom heurim
out of focus

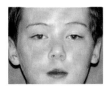

적목 현상
jeokmog hyeonsang
red eye

어휘 eohwi · **vocabulary**

카메라 케이스
kamera keiseu
camera case

뷰파인더
byoopaindeo
viewfinder

필름
pilleum
film

노출
nochul
exposure

인쇄
inswae
print

무광
moogwang
matte

유광
yoogwang
gloss

확대
hwakdae
enlargement

이 필름을 현상해주세요.
i pilleum-eul hyeonsanghaejooseyo
I'd like this film processed.

게임 geim · **games**

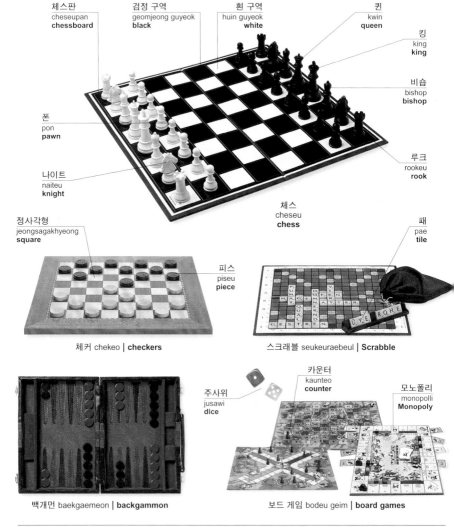

체스판
cheseupan
chessboard

검정 구역
geomjeong guyeok
black

흰 구역
huin guyeok
white

퀸
kwin
queen

킹
king
king

비숍
bishop
bishop

폰
pon
pawn

루크
rookeu
rook

나이트
naiteu
knight

체스
cheseu
chess

정사각형
jeongsagakhyeong
square

피스
piseu
piece

패
pae
tile

체커 chekeo | **checkers**

스크래블 seukeuraebeul | **Scrabble**

주사위
jusawi
dice

카운터
kaunteo
counter

모노폴리
monopolli
Monopoly

백개먼 baekgaemeon | **backgammon**

보드 게임 bodeu geim | **board games**

퍼즐 맞추기
peojeul matchoogi
jigsaw puzzle

도미노
domino | **dominoes**

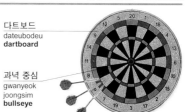

다트보드
dateubodeu
dartboard

과녁 중심
gwanyeok
joongsim
bullseye

다트 dateu | **darts**

조커
jokeo
joker

잭
jaek
jack

퀸
kwin
queen

킹
king
king

에이스
eiseu
ace

카드 kadeu | **cards**

다이아몬드
daiamondeu
diamond

스페이드
seupeideu
spade

하트
hateu
heart

클럽
keulleob
club

섞다 seokkda
shuffle (v)

카드를 돌리다
kadeureul dollida | **deal (v)**

어휘 eohwi · **vocabulary**

플레이어 peulleieo **player**	시합하다 sihabhada **play (v)**	게임 geim **game**	포커 pokeo **poker**	브리지 briji **bridge**	주사위를 던지세요. joosawireul deonjisaeyo **Roll the dice.**
승자 seungja **winner**	이기다 igida **win (v)**	두기 doogi **move**	포인트 pointeu **point**	무늬 moonui **suit**	누구 차례지요? nugu charyejiyo? **Whose turn is it?**
패자 paeja **loser**	지다 jida **lose (v)**	점수 jeomsu **score**	내기 naegi **bet**	카드 한 벌 kadeu han beol **deck of cards**	당신 차례예요. dangsin charyeyeyo **It's your move.**

공예 gong-ye · **arts and crafts (1)**

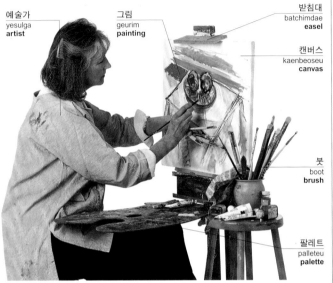

예술가
yesulga
artist

그림
geurim
painting

받침대
batchimdae
easel

캔버스
kaenbeoseu
canvas

붓
boot
brush

팔레트
palleteu
palette

그림 geurim | **painting**

색깔 saegkkal · **colors**

빨강 ppalgang
red

파랑 parang
blue

노랑 norang
yellow

초록 chorog
green

주황 joohwang
orange

자주 jaju
purple

흰색 huinsaek
white

검은색 geom-eunsaek
black

회색 hoeisaek
gray

분홍 boonhong
pink

갈색 galsaek
brown

남색 namsaek
indigo

그림물감 geurimmulgam **paints**

유화 물감
yoohwa mulgam
oil paint

수성 물감
suseong mulgam
watercolor paint

파스텔
paseutel
pastels

아크릴 물감
akeuril mulgam
acrylic paint

포스터 물감
poseuteo mulgam
poster paint

기타 공예 gita gong-ye • **other crafts**

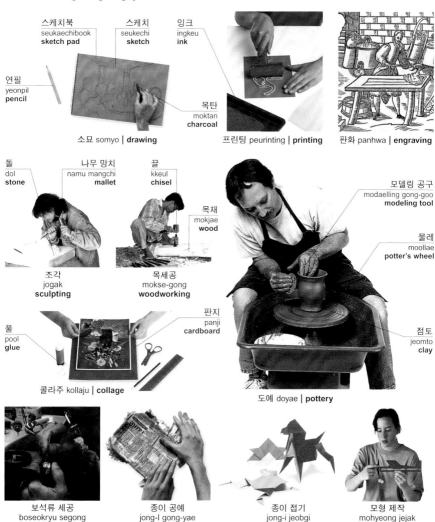

스케치북
seukaechibook
sketch pad

스케치
seukechi
sketch

잉크
ingkeu
ink

연필
yeonpil
pencil

목탄
moktan
charcoal

소묘 somyo | **drawing**

프린팅 peurinting | **printing**

판화 panhwa | **engraving**

돌
dol
stone

나무 망치
namu mangchi
mallet

끌
kkeul
chisel

목재
mokjae
wood

조각
jogak
sculpting

목세공
mokse-gong
woodworking

모델링 공구
modaelling gong-goo
modeling tool

물레
moollae
potter's wheel

풀
pool
glue

판지
panji
cardboard

콜라주 kollaju | **collage**

점토
jeomto
clay

도예 doyae | **pottery**

보석류 세공
boseokryu segong
jewelry-making

종이 공예
jong-I gong-yae
papier-mâché

종이 접기
jong-i jeobgi
origami

모형 제작
mohyeong jejak
model-making

공예 gong-ye · **arts and crafts (2)**

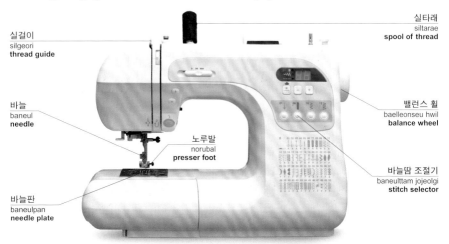

실타래
siltarae
spool of thread

실걸이
silgeori
thread guide

바늘
baneul
needle

밸런스 휠
baelleonseu hwil
balance wheel

노루발
norubal
presser foot

바늘땀 조절기
baneulttam jojeolgi
stitch selector

바늘판
baneulpan
needle plate

재봉틀 jaebongteul | **sewing machine**

가위
gawi
scissors

패턴
paeteon
pattern

핀
pin
pin

바늘 꽂이
baneul kkoji
pincushion

줄자
julja
tape measure

재료
jaeryo
material

바느질 바구니
baneujil baguni | **sewing basket**

실
sil
thread

눈
noon
eye

실패
silpae
bobbin

고리
gori
hook

골무
golmoo
thimble

재단 초크
jaedan chokeu
tailor's chalk

재단 인체 모형
jaedan inche mohyeong
tailor's form

실을 꿰다
sireul kkweda
thread (v)

바느질하다
baneujilhada
sew (v)

바늘땀
baneulttam
stitch

꿰매다
kkwemaeda
darn (v)

시침질하다
sichimjilhada | **tack (v)**

재단하다
jaedanhada
cut (v)

니들포인트 자수
nideulpointeu jasu
needlepoint

자수
jasu
embroidery

코바늘
kobaneul
crochet hook

코바늘 뜨개질
kobaneul tteugaejil
crochet

마크라메
makeurame
macramé

조각보 깁기
jogakbo gibgi
patchwork

누비질하기
nubijilhagi
quilting

레이스 보빈
leiseu bobin
lace bobbin

레이스 만들기
leiseu mandeulgi
lacemaking

베틀
beteul
loom

짜기
jjagi
weaving

뜨개질 바늘
tteugaejil baneul
knitting needle

뜨개질하기 tteugaejilhagi
knitting

타래 tarae
skein

양모
yangmo
yarn

어휘 eohwi • **vocabulary**

면 myeon **cotton**	직물 jigmul **fabric**
리넨 제품 linen jepoom **linen**	지퍼 jipeo **zipper**
폴리에스테르 pollieseutereu **polyester**	패션 paesheon **fashion**
나일론 naillon **nylon**	디자이너 dijaineo **designer**
실크 silkeu **silk**	바늘땀을 풀다 baneulttam-eul pulda **unpick (v)**

환경 hwan-gyeong
environment

우주 ujoo · **space**

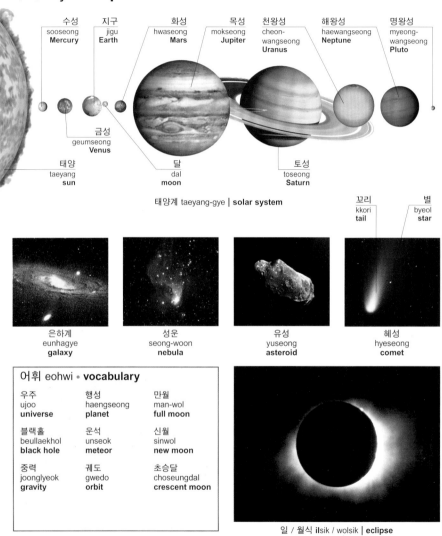

수성
sooseong
Mercury

지구
jigu
Earth

화성
hwaseong
Mars

목성
mokseong
Jupiter

천왕성
cheon-
wangseong
Uranus

해왕성
haewangseong
Neptune

명왕성
myeong-
wangseong
Pluto

금성
geumseong
Venus

태양
taeyang
sun

달
dal
moon

토성
toseong
Saturn

태양계 taeyang-gye | **solar system**

꼬리
kkori
tail

별
byeol
star

은하계
eunhagye
galaxy

성운
seong-woon
nebula

유성
yuseong
asteroid

혜성
hyeseong
comet

어휘 eohwi · **vocabulary**

우주
ujoo
universe

행성
haengseong
planet

만월
man-wol
full moon

블랙홀
beullaekhol
black hole

운석
unseok
meteor

신월
sinwol
new moon

중력
joonglyeok
gravity

궤도
gwedo
orbit

초승달
choseungdal
crescent moon

일 / 월식 ilsik / wolsik | **eclipse**

우주 탐사 ujoo tamsa
space exploration

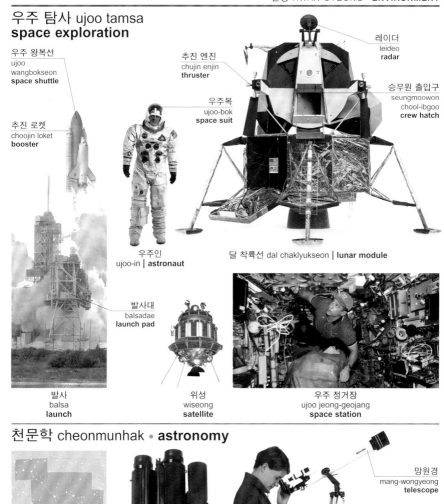

우주 왕복선
ujoo
wangbokseon
space shuttle

추진 로켓
choojin loket
booster

추진 엔진
chujin enjin
thruster

우주복
ujoo-bok
space suit

레이더
leideo
radar

승무원 출입구
seungmoowon
chool-ibgoo
crew hatch

우주인
ujoo-in | **astronaut**

달 착륙선 dal chaklyukseon | **lunar module**

발사대
balsadae
launch pad

발사
balsa
launch

위성
wiseong
satellite

우주 정거장
ujoo jeong-geojang
space station

천문학 cheonmunhak · **astronomy**

별자리
byeoljari
constellation

쌍안경
ssang-ahn-gyeong
binoculars

망원경
mang-wongyeong
telescope

삼각대
samgakdae
tripod

지구 jigu · **Earth**

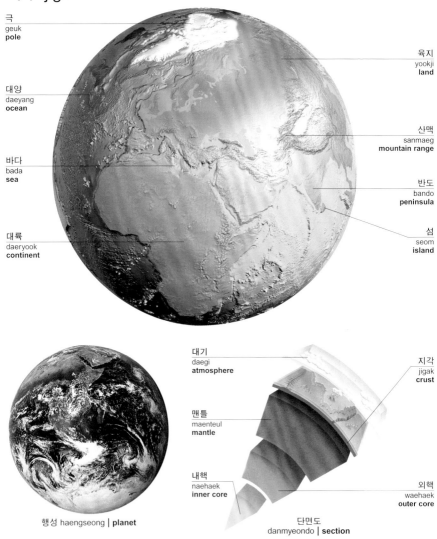

극
geuk
pole

육지
yookji
land

대양
daeyang
ocean

산맥
sanmaeg
mountain range

바다
bada
sea

반도
bando
peninsula

대륙
daeryook
continent

섬
seom
island

대기
daegi
atmosphere

지각
jigak
crust

맨틀
maenteul
mantle

내핵
naehaek
inner core

외핵
waehaek
outer core

행성 haengseong | **planet**

단면도
danmyeondo | **section**

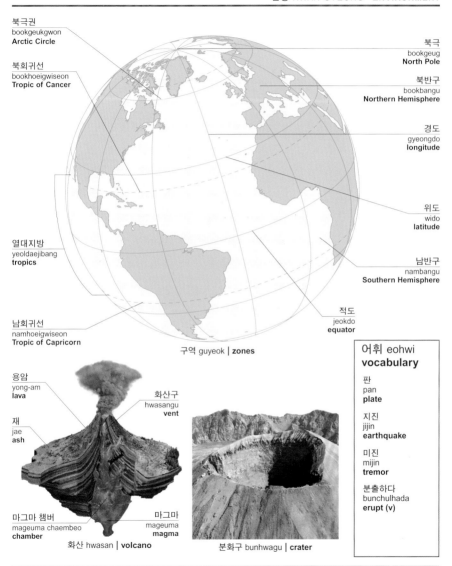

북극권
bookgeukgwon
Arctic Circle

북극
bookgeug
North Pole

북회귀선
bookhoeigwiseon
Tropic of Cancer

북반구
bookbangu
Northern Hemisphere

경도
gyeongdo
longitude

위도
wido
latitude

열대지방
yeoldaejibang
tropics

남반구
nambangu
Southern Hemisphere

남회귀선
namhoeigwiseon
Tropic of Capricorn

적도
jeokdo
equator

구역 guyeok | **zones**

용암
yong-am
lava

화산구
hwasangu
vent

재
jae
ash

마그마 챔버
mageuma chaembeo
chamber

마그마
mageuma
magma

화산 hwasan | **volcano**

분화구 bunhwagu | **crater**

**어휘 eohwi
vocabulary**

판
pan
plate

지진
jijin
earthquake

미진
mijin
tremor

분출하다
bunchulhada
erupt (v)

풍경 poong-gyeong • **landscape**

산
san
mountain

경사지
gyeongsaji
slope

강둑
gangdook
bank

강
gang
river

급류
geubryu
rapids

바위
bawi
rocks

빙하 bingha | **glacier**

계곡 gyegog | **valley**

언덕
eondeok
hill

고원
gowon
plateau

협곡
hyeobgog
gorge

동굴
dong-gul
cave

평원 pyeong-won
plain

사막 samak
desert

삼림지대 samrim jidae
forest

숲 soop
woods

열대우림
yeoldae-urim
rain forest

습지
seupji
swamp

목초지
mogchoji
meadow

초원
chowon
grassland

폭포
pogpo
waterfall

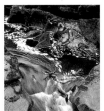

개울
gae-ul
stream

호수
hosoo
lake

간헐천
ganheolcheon
geyser

해안
hae-an
coast

절벽
jeolbyeok
cliff

산호초
sanhocho
coral reef

삼각강
samgakgang
estuary

날씨 nalssi • **weather**

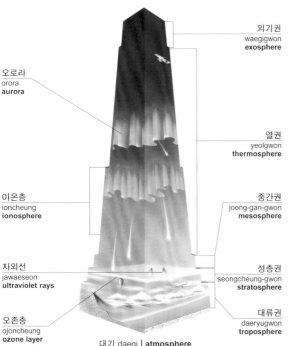

외기권
waegigwon
exosphere

오로라
orora
aurora

열권
yeolgwon
thermosphere

이온층
ioncheung
ionosphere

중간권
joong-gan-gwon
mesosphere

자외선
jawaeseon
ultraviolet rays

성층권
seongcheung-gwon
stratosphere

오존층
ojoncheung
ozone layer

대류권
daeryugwon
troposphere

대기 daegi | **atmosphere**

햇빛 haetbit | **sunshine**

바람 baram | **wind**

어휘 eohwi • **vocabulary**

천둥 cheondoong **thunder**	화창한 hwachanghan **sunny**	바람부는 baramboo-neun **windy**	더운 deo-un **hot**	건조한 geonjohan **dry**	더워요 / 추워요. deowoeyo / chuwoyo **I'm hot / cold.**
우박 woobag **hail**	흐린 heurin **cloudy**	강풍 gangpoong **gale**	추운 choo-un **cold**	축축한 chookchookhan **wet**	비가 와요. biga wayo **It's raining.**
진눈깨비 jinnoonkkaebi **sleet**	소나기 sonagi **shower**	기온 gi-on **temperature**	따뜻한 ttatteutan **warm**	습한 seumhan **humid**	...도예요. ...doyeyo **It's... degrees.**

구름 gooreum
cloud

비 bi
rain

번개
beongae
lightning

폭풍 pogpoong
storm

엷은 안개 yeolbeun angae
mist

안개 angae
fog

무지개 mujigae
rainbow

눈 noon
snow

서리 seori
frost

얼음 eol-eum
ice

고드름
godeureum
icicle

동결 dong-gyeol
freeze

허리케인 heorikein
hurricane

토네이도 tonaeido
tornado

우기 woo-gi
monsoon

홍수 hongsoo
flood

암석 amseok • **rocks**

화성암 hwaseong-am
igneous

화강암
hwagang-am
granite

흑요석
heug-yoseok
obsidian

현무암
hyeonmuam
basalt

부석
buseok
pumice

퇴적암 toejeog-am • **sedimentary**

사암
sa-am
sandstone

석회암
seokhoe-am
limestone

백악
baeg-ak
chalk

수석
suseok
flint

역암
yeog-am
conglomerate

석탄
seoktan
coal

변성암 byeonseong-am
metamorphic

점판암
jeompan-am
slate

편암
pyeon-am
schist

편마암
pyeonma-am
gneiss

대리석
daeriseok
marble

보석 암석 boseog amseog • **gems**

루비
lubi
ruby

남옥
nam-ok
aquamarine

자수정
jasoojeong
amethyst

다이아몬드
daiamondeu
diamond

비취
bichwi
jade

흑옥
heug-ok
jet

에메랄드
emeraldeu
emerald

오팔
opal
opal

사파이어
sapaieo
sapphire

월장석
woljangseok
moonstone

석류석
seogryuseok
garnet

황옥
hwang-ok
topaz

전기석
jeongiseok
tourmaline

광물 gwangmul · **minerals**

석영
seog-yeong
quartz

운모
unmo
mica

유황
yoohwang
sulfur

적철석
jeogcheolseok
hematite

방해석
banghaeseok
calcite

공작석
gongjagseok
malachite

터키석
teokiseok
turquoise

줄마노
julmano
onyx

마노
mano
agate

흑연
heug-yeon
graphite

금속 geumsok · **metals**

금
geum
gold

은
eun
silver

백금
baekgeum
platinum

니켈
nikel
nickel

철
cheol
iron

구리
guri
copper

주석
jooseok
tin

알루미늄
alluminyum
aluminum

수은
sueun
mercury

아연
ayeon
zinc

동물 dongmul • **animals (1)**

포유류 poyuryu • **mammals**

수염
suyeom
whiskers

꼬리
kkori
tail

토끼
tokki
rabbit

햄스터
haemseuteo
hamster

생쥐
saengjwi
mouse

쥐
jwi
rat

고슴도치
goseumdochi
hedgehog

다람쥐
daramjwi
squirrel

박쥐
bagjwi
bat

너구리
neoguri
raccoon

여우
yeo-woo
fox

늑대
neugdae
wolf

강아지
gang-aji
puppy

새끼 고양이
saekki goyang-i
kitten

동물의 새끼
dongmul-ui saekki
pup

개
gae
dog

고양이
goyang-i
cat

수달
sudal
otter

바다표범
badapyobeom
seal

지느러미발
jineureomibal
flipper

분수공
boonsugong
blowhole

바다 사자
bada saja
sea lion

바다코끼리
badakokkiri
walrus

고래
gorae
whale

돌고래
dolgorae
dolphin

가지진 뿔
gajijin ppul
antler

갈기
galgi
mane

말굽
malgub
hoof

혹
hok
hump

사슴
saseum
deer

얼룩말
eollookmal
zebra

기린
girin
giraffe

낙타
nagta
camel

코끼리 코
kokkiri ko
trunk

상아
sang-a
tusk

뿔
ppul
horn

하마
hama
hippopotamus

코끼리
kokkiri
elephant

코뿔소
koppulso
rhinoceros

호랑이
horang-i
tiger

갈기
galgi
mane

사자
saja
lion

원숭이
wonsoong-i
monkey

고릴라
gorilla
gorilla

코알라
koalla
koala

새끼 주머니
saekki jumeoni
pouch

판다
panda
panda

캥거루
kaeng-georu
kangaroo

발톱
baltob
claw

곰
gom
bear

흰곰
huingom
polar bear

동물 dongmul • **animals (2)**

새 sae • **birds**

꼬리
kkori
tail

카나리아
kanaria
canary

참새
chamsae
sparrow

벌새
beolsae
hummingbird

제비
jebi
swallow

까마귀
kkamagwi
crow

비둘기
bidulgi
pigeon

딱따구리
ttakttaguri
woodpecker

매
mae
falcon

부엉이
bueong-i
owl

갈매기
galmaegi
gull

독수리
doksuri
eagle

펠리컨
pellikeon
pelican

플라밍고
peullaming-go
flamingo

황새
hwangsae
stork

두루미
durumi
crane

펭귄
peng-gwin
penguin

타조
tajo
ostrich

파충류 pachungryu ∙ **reptiles**

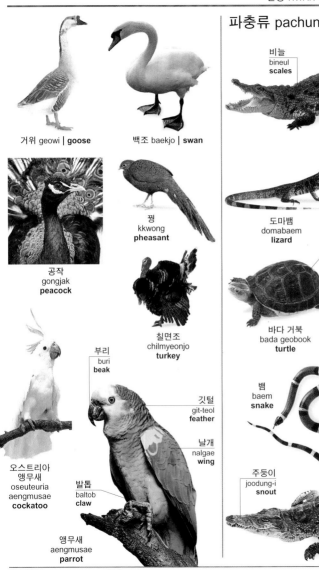

거위 geowi | **goose**

백조 baekjo | **swan**

공작
gongjak
peacock

꿩
kkwong
pheasant

칠면조
chilmyeonjo
turkey

오스트리아
앵무새
oseuteuria
aengmusae
cockatoo

부리
buri
beak

깃털
git-teol
feather

날개
nalgae
wing

발톱
baltob
claw

앵무새
aengmusae
parrot

비늘
bineul
scales

악어 (앨리게이터)
ag-eo (aelligeiteo)
alligator

이구아나
iguana
iguana

도마뱀
domabaem
lizard

껍데기
kkeobdaegi
shell

바다 거북
bada geobook
turtle

거북
geobook
tortoise

뱀
baem
snake

주둥이
joodung-i
snout

악어 (크로커다일)
ag-eo (keurokeodail)
crocodile

동물 dongmul • **animals (3)**
양서류 yangseoryu • **amphibians**

개구리 gaeguri
frog

두꺼비 dukkeobi
toad

올챙이 olchaeng-i
tadpole

도롱뇽 dorongnyong
salamander

어류 eoryu • **fish**

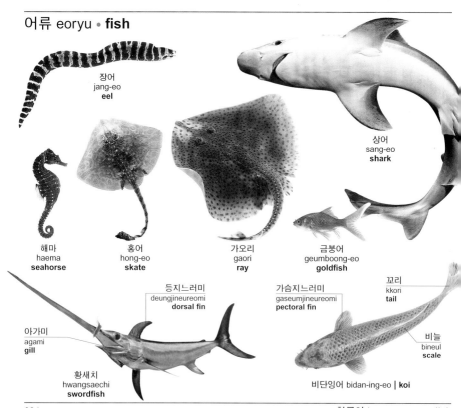

장어
jang-eo
eel

상어
sang-eo
shark

해마
haema
seahorse

홍어
hong-eo
skate

가오리
gaori
ray

금붕어
geumboong-eo
goldfish

등지느러미
deungjineureomi
dorsal fin

가슴지느러미
gaseumjineureomi
pectoral fin

꼬리
kkori
tail

아가미
agami
gill

비늘
bineul
scale

황새치
hwangsaechi
swordfish

비단잉어 bidan-ing-eo | **koi**

무척추 동물 mucheokchu dongmul • **invertebrates**

개미
gaemi
ant

흰개미
huingaemi
termite

벌
beol
bee

말벌
malbeol
wasp

딱정벌레
ttakjeongbeolle
beetle

바퀴벌레
bakwibeolle
cockroach

나방
nabang
moth

더듬이
deodeum-i
antenna

나비
nabi
butterfly

고치
gochi
cocoon

애벌레
aebeolle
caterpillar

귀뚜라미
gwitturami | **cricket**

메뚜기
mettugi
grasshopper

사마귀
samagwi
praying mantis

침
chim
sting

전갈
jeongal
scorpion

지네
jine
centipede

잠자리
jamjari
dragonfly

파리
pari
fly

모기
mogi
mosquito

무당벌레
moodangbeolle
ladybug

거미
geomi
spider

민달팽이
mindalpaeng-i
slug

달팽이
dalpaeng-i
snail

지렁이류
jireong-i-ryu | **worm**

불가사리
bulgasari
starfish

홍합
honghab
mussel

게
ge | **crab**

바닷가재
badatgajae | **lobster**

문어
muneo | **octopus**

오징어
ojing-eo | **squid**

해파리
haepari | **jellyfish**

식물 sikmul • **plants**

나무 namu • **tree**

가지
gaji
branch

잎
ip
leaf

잔가지
jangaji
twig

나무껍질
namukkeobjil
bark

버드나무
beodeunamu
willow

뿌리
ppuri
root

나무 몸통
namu momtong
trunk

참나무 chamnamoo | **oak**

포플러
popeulleo
poplar

유칼립투스
yukallibtuseu
eucalyptus

낙엽송
nagyeobsong
larch

너도밤나무
neodobamnamu
beech

자작나무
jajaknamu
birch

소나무
sonamu
pine

삼나무
samnamu
cedar

단풍나무
danpoongnamu
maple

느릅나무
neureumnamu
elm

라임 나무
laim namu
lime

산딸기류
열매
santtalgiryu
yeolmae
berry

호랑가시나무
horang-gasinamu
holly

야자수
yajasoo
palm

꽃식물 kkotsikmul • **flowering plant**

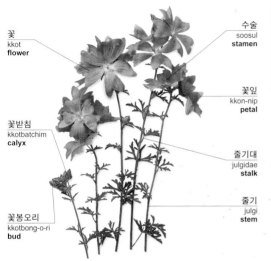

꽃
kkot
flower

수술
soosul
stamen

꽃잎
kkon-nip
petal

꽃받침
kkotbatchim
calyx

줄기대
julgidae
stalk

줄기
julgi
stem

꽃봉오리
kkotbong-o-ri
bud

미나리아재비
minariajaebi
buttercup

데이지
deiji
daisy

엉겅퀴
eong-geongqwi
thistle

민들레
mindeulle
dandelion

헤더
hedeo
heather

양귀비
yang-gwibi
poppy

디기탈리스
digitalliseu
foxglove

인동
indong
honeysuckle

해바라기
haebaragi
sunflower

클로버
keullobeo
clover

블루벨
beullubel
bluebells

프림로즈
peurimlojeu
primrose

루핀
lupin
lupines

쐐기풀
sswaegipul
nettle

도시 dosi • **city**

골목
golmog
alley

아파트 단지
apateu danji
apartment building

거리
geori
street

차량 진입 방지 말뚝
charyang jin-ib
bangji malttuk
barrier

광장
gwangjang
square

상점
sangjeom
store

길모퉁이
gilmotung-i
street corner

가로등
garodeung
streetlight

연석
yeonseok
curb

보도
bodo
sidewalk

주차장
juchajang
parking lot

일방 통행 시스템
ilbang tonghaeng
siseutem
one-way system

건물 geonmool · **buildings**

시청
sicheong
town hall

도서관
doseogwan
library

영화관
yeonghwagwan
movie theater

극장
geugjang
theater

대학
daehak
university

고층 건물
gocheung geonmul
skyscraper

지역 jiyeok · **areas**

산업 단지
san-eob danji
industrial park

도심
doshim
downtown

교외
gyo-wae
suburb

마을
ma-eul
village

학교
hakgyo
school

어휘 eohwi · **vocabulary**

거리 geori **avenue**	배수구 baesoogoo **gutter**	맨홀 maenhol **manhole**	보행자 구역 bohaengja gooyeok **pedestrian zone**	공장 gongjang **factory**
골목 golmog **side street**	배수관 baesugwan **drain**	버스 정류장 beoseu jeongryujang **bus stop**	사무실 밀집 구역 amusil miljib guyeok **office building**	교회 gyohoei **church**

건축물 geonchookmool · **architecture**

건물 및 구조 geonmul mit goojo · **buildings and structures**

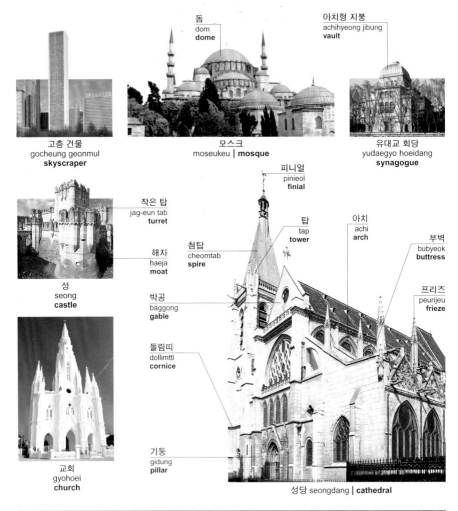

돔
dom
dome

아치형 지붕
achihyeong jibung
vault

고층 건물
gocheung geonmul
skyscraper

모스크
moseukeu | **mosque**

유대교 회당
yudaegyo hoeidang
synagogue

피니얼
pinieol
finial

작은 탑
jag-eun tab
turret

탑
tap
tower

아치
achi
arch

부벽
bubyeok
buttress

해자
haeja
moat

첨탑
cheomtab
spire

박공
baggong
gable

성
seong
castle

돌림띠
dollimtti
cornice

프리즈
peurijeu
frieze

기둥
gidung
pillar

교회
gyohoei
church

성당 seongdang | **cathedral**

사원 sawon | **temple**

댐 daem | **dam**

다리 dari | **bridge**

양식 yangshik • **styles**

고딕 godig | **Gothic**

처마도리
cheomadori
architrave

르네상스
leunesangseu
Renaissance

바로크 barokeu
Baroque

성가대석
seong-
gadaeseok
choir

로코코 lokoko
Rococo

페디먼트
pedimeonteu
pediment

신고전주의 singojeonju-ui
Neoclassical

아르 누보 areu nubo
Art Nouveau

아르 데코 areu deko
Art Deco

참고 chamgo
reference

시간 sigan · **time**

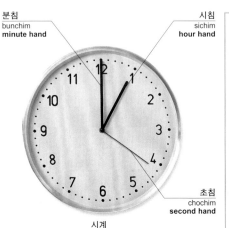

분침
bunchim
minute hand

시침
sichim
hour hand

초침
chochim
second hand

시계
sigye
clock

어휘 eohwi · **vocabulary**

초
cho
second

분
bun
minute

시간
sigan
hour

지금
jigeum
now

나중에
najoong-eh
later

15분
sib-oh-bun
**a quarter
of an hour**

20분
i-sib-bun
twenty minutes

30분
sam-sib bun
half an hour

40분
sa-sib-bun
forty minutes

몇 시예요?
myeot si yeyo?
What time is it?

3시 정각이에요.
sae-si jeong-gag-ieyo
It's three o'clock.

1시 5분
han-si oh-bun
five past one

1시 10분
han-si sib-bun
ten past one

1시 15분
han-si sib-oh-bun
quarter past one

1시 20분
han-si i-sib-bun
twenty past one

1시 25분
han-si i-sib-oh-bun
twenty-five past one

1시 30분
han-si sam-sib-bun
one thirty

2시 25분 전
du-si i-sib-oh-bun jeon
twenty-five to two

2시 20분 전
du-si i-sib-bun jeon
twenty to two

2시 15분 전
du-si sib-oh-bun jeon
quarter to two

2시 10분 전
du-si sib-bun jeon
ten to two

2시 5분 전
du-si oh-bun jeon
five to two

2시 정각
du-si jeong-gag
two o'clock

밤과 낮 bamgwa nat • **night and day**

자정 polnoch | **midnight**

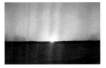

일출 ilchool | **sunrise**

새벽 saebyeok | **dawn**

아침 achim | **morning**

일몰
ilmol
sunset

정오
jeong-oh
noon

황혼 hwanghon | **dusk**

저녁 jeonyeok | **evening**

오후 ohu | **afternoon**

어휘 eohwi • **vocabulary**

이른
ireun
early

정시
jeongsi
on time

늦은
neujeun
late

일찍 오셨네요.
iljjig osheotneyo
You're early.

늦으셨네요.
neujeusheotneyo
You're late.

시간 맞춰서 오세요.
sigan matchuoseo osaeyo
Please be on time.

곧 도착할 거예요.
got dochakhal geoyeyo
I'll be there soon.

다음에 봐요.
da-eum-e bwayo
I'll see you later.

밤이 깊어지고 있어요.
bam-i gipeojigo isseoyo
It's getting late.

몇 시에 시작합니까?
myeot sie sijakhamnikka?
What time does it start?

언제 끝나요?
eonje kkeutnayo?
What time does it end?

얼마나 걸려요?
eolmana geollyeoyo?
How long will it last?

달력 dallyeok • **calendar**

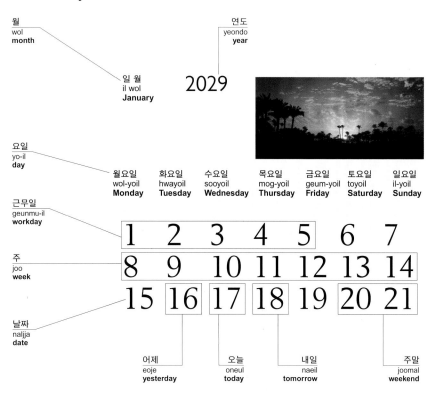

월
wol
month

연도
yeondo
year

일 월
il wol
January

2029

요일
yo-il
day

근무일
geunmu-il
workday

주
joo
week

날짜
naljja
date

월요일	화요일	수요일	목요일	금요일	토요일	일요일
wol-yoil	hwayoil	sooyoil	mog-yoil	geum-yoil	toyoil	il-yoil
Monday	**Tuesday**	**Wednesday**	**Thursday**	**Friday**	**Saturday**	**Sunday**
1	2	3	4	5	6	7
8	9	10	11	12	13	14
15	16	17	18	19	20	21

어제
eoje
yesterday

오늘
oneul
today

내일
naeil
tomorrow

주말
joomal
weekend

어휘 eohwi • **vocabulary**

일월	삼월	오월	칠월	구월	십일월
il-wol	sam-wol	o-wol	chil-wol	goo-wol	sib-il-wol
January	**March**	**May**	**July**	**September**	**November**
이월	사월	유월	팔월	시월	십이월
i-wol	sa-wol	yoo-wol	pal-wol	si-wol	sib-i-wol
February	**April**	**June**	**August**	**October**	**December**

년 nyeon • **years**

1900 천구백 cheongoobaeg • **nineteen hundred**

1901 천구백일 cheongoobaeg-il • **nineteen oh one**

1910 천구백십 cheongoobaegsib • **nineteen ten**

2000 이천 icheon • **two thousand**

2001 이천일 icheon-il • **two thousand and one**

계절 gyejeol • **seasons**

봄
bom
spring

여름
yeoreum
summer

가을
ga-eul
fall

겨울
gyeowool
winter

어휘 eohwi • **vocabulary**

천년 cheonnyeon **millennium**	지난 주 jinan joo **last week**	매월 maewol **monthly**	오늘이 며칠이에요? oh-neul-i myeochil-ieyo? **What's the date today?**
세기 segi **century**	이번 주 i-beon joo **this week**	매년 maenyeon **annual**	2월 7일입니다. i-wol chiril-ipnida **It's February the seventh.**
십년 sib-nyeon **decade**	다음 주 da-eum joo **next week**	그저께 geujeokke **the day before yesterday**	
이 주 동안 i joo dong-an **two weeks**	매주 maejoo **weekly**	모레 more **the day after tomorrow**	

숫자 sutja • **numbers**

0	영(공) yeong (gong) • **zero**	20	이십(스물) isib (seumul) • **twenty**
1	일(하나) il (hana) • **one**	21	이십일(스물하나) isib-il (seumulhana) **twenty-one**
2	이(둘) I (dool) • **two**	22	이십이(스물둘) isib-I (seumuldool) **twenty-two**
3	삼(셋) sam (set) • **three**	30	삼십(서른) samsib (seoreun) • **thirty**
4	사(넷) sa (net) • **four**	40	사십(마흔) sasib (maheun) • **forty**
5	오(다섯) oh (daseot) • **five**	50	오십(쉰) oh-sib (shin) • **fifty**
6	육(여섯) yook (yeoseot) • **six**	60	육십(예순) yooksib (yesoon) • **sixty**
7	칠(일곱) chil (ilgob) • **seven**	70	칠십(일흔) chilsib (ilheun) • **seventy**
8	팔(여덟) pal (yeodeol) • **eight**	80	팔십(여든) palsib (yeodeun) • **eighty**
9	구(아홉) goo (ah-hob) • **nine**	90	구십(아흔) goosib (aheun) • **ninety**
10	십(열) sib (yeol) • **ten**	100	백 baeg • **one hundred**
11	십일(열하나) sib-il (yeolhana) • **eleven**	110	백십 baegsib • **one hundred ten**
12	십이(열둘) sib-I (yeoldul) • **twelve**	200	이백 i-baeg • **two hundred**
13	십삼(열셋) sibsam (yeolset) • **thirteen**	300	삼백 sambaeg • **three hundred**
14	십사(열넷) sibsa (yeolnet) • **fourteen**	400	사백 sabaeg • **four hundred**
15	십오(열다섯) sib-oh (yeoldaseot) • **fifteen**	500	오백 oh-baeg • **five hundred**
16	십육(열여섯) sib-yook (yeol-yeoseot) • **sixteen**	600	육백 yookbaeg • **six hundred**
17	십칠(열일곱) sibchil (yeol-ilgob) • **seventeen**	700	칠백 chilbaeg • **seven hundred**
18	십팔(열여덟) sibpal (yeol-yeodeol) • **eighteen**	800	팔백 palbaeg • **eight hundred**
19	십구(열아홉) sibgoo (yeol-ahob) • **nineteen**	900	구백 goobaeg • **nine hundred**

1,000 천 cheon · **one thousand**

10,000 만 man · **ten thousand**

20,000 이만 i-man · **twenty thousand**

50,000 오만 oh-man · **fifty thousand**

55,500 오만 오천오백 oh-man oh-cheon-oh-baeg
fifty-five thousand five hundred

100,000 십만 sibman · **one hundred thousand**

1,000,000 백만 baegman · **one million**

1,000,000,000 십억 sib-eog · **one billion**

첫 번째 cheot beonjjae **first**

두 번째 doo beonjjae **second**

세 번째 sae beonjjae **third**

네 번째 nae beonjjae **fourth**

다섯 번째 daseot beonjjae **fifth**

여섯 번째 yeoseot beonjjae **sixth**

일곱 번째 ilgob beonjjae **seventh**

여덟 번째 yeodeol beonjjae **eighth**

아홉 번째 ahob beonjjae **ninth**

열 번째 yeol beonjjae **tenth**

열한 번째 yeolhan beonjjae · **eleventh**

열두 번째 yeoldu beonjjae **twelfth**

열세 번째 yeolsae beonjjae **thirteenth**

열네 번째 yeolnae beonjjae · **fourteenth**

열다섯 번째 yeoldaseot beonjjae · **fifteenth**

열여섯 번째 yeol-yeoseot beonjjae · **sixteenth**

열일곱 번째 yeol-ilgob beonjjae **seventeenth**

열여덟 번째 yeol-yeodeol beonjjae · **eighteenth**

열아홉 번째 yeol-ahob beonjjae · **nineteenth**

스무 번째 seumoo beonjjae · **twentieth**

스물한 번째 seumulhan beonjjae · **twenty-first**

스물두 번째 seumuldoo beonjjae · **twenty-second**

스물세 번째 seumulsae beonjjae **twenty-third**

서른 번째 seoreun beonjjae · **thirtieth**

마흔 번째 maheun beonjjae · **fortieth**

쉰 번째 shin beonjjae **fiftieth**

예순 번째 yesoon beonjjae · **sixtieth**

일흔 번째 ilheun beonjjae · **seventieth**

여든 번째 yeodeun beonjjae · **eightieth**

아흔 번째 aheun beonjjae **ninetieth**

백 번째 baeg beonjjae **(one) hundredth**

무게 및 치수 mooge mit chitsu
weights and measures

면적 myeonjeok
area

제곱피트
jaegobpiteu
square foot

제곱미터
jaegobmiteo
square meter

거리 geori
distance

킬로미터
killomiteo
kilometer

마일
mail
mile

저울판
jeo-woolpan
pan

파운드
paundeu
pound

온스
onseu
ounce

킬로그램
killogeuraem
kilogram

그램
geuraem
gram

저울 jeowool | **scale**

어휘 eohwi · **vocabulary**

야드	밀리그램	측정하다
yadeu	milligeuraem	cheugjeonghada
yard	**milligram**	**measure (v)**
미터	톤	무게를 달다
miteo	ton	mugereul dalda
meter	**ton**	**weigh (v)**

길이 giri · **length**

피트
piteu
foot

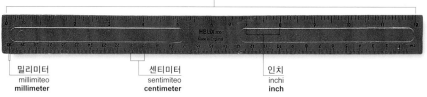

밀리미터
millimiteo
millimeter

센티미터
sentimiteo
centimeter

인치
inchi
inch

용량 yongryang • **capacity**

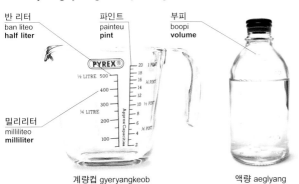

반 리터
ban liteo
half liter

파인트
painteu
pint

부피
boopi
volume

밀리리터
milliliteo
milliliter

계량컵 gyeryangkeob
measuring cup

액량 aeglyang
liquid measure

어휘 eohwi
vocabulary

갤런
gaelleon
gallon

쿼트
qwoteu
quart

리터
liteo
liter

용기 yonggi • **container**

갑
gab
carton

통
tong
packet

병
byeong
bottle

봉지
bongji
bag

통 tong | **tub**

병 byeong | **jar**

깡통 kkangtong | **tin**

분무기 bunmugi
spray bottle

덩어리
deong-eori
bar

튜브
tyubeu
tube

두루마리
durumari
roll

캔
kaen
can

스프레이 통
seupeurei tong
spray can

세계 지도 segye jido · **world map**

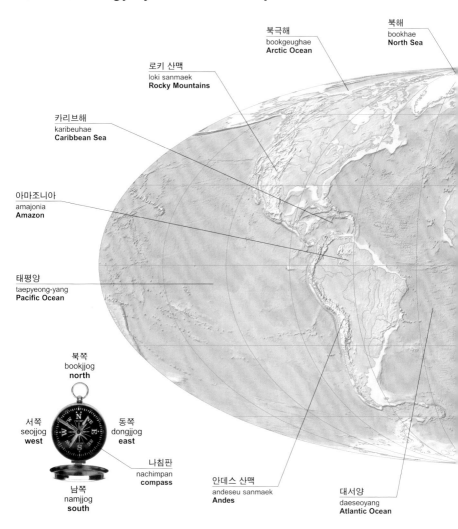

북극해
bookgeughae
Arctic Ocean

북해
bookhae
North Sea

로키 산맥
loki sanmaek
Rocky Mountains

카리브해
karibeuhae
Caribbean Sea

아마조니아
amajonia
Amazon

태평양
taepyeong-yang
Pacific Ocean

북쪽
bookjjog
north

서쪽
seojjog
west

동쪽
dongjjog
east

나침판
nachimpan
compass

남쪽
namjjog
south

안데스 산맥
andeseu sanmaek
Andes

대서양
daeseoyang
Atlantic Ocean

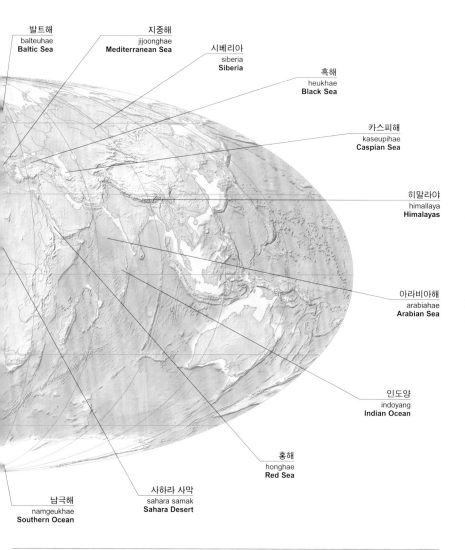

발트해
balteuhae
Baltic Sea

지중해
jijoonghae
Mediterranean Sea

시베리아
siberia
Siberia

흑해
heukhae
Black Sea

카스피해
kaseupihae
Caspian Sea

히말라야
himallaya
Himalayas

아라비아해
arabiahae
Arabian Sea

인도양
indoyang
Indian Ocean

홍해
honghae
Red Sea

남극해
namgeukhae
Southern Ocean

사하라 사막
sahara samak
Sahara Desert

북 아메리카 및 중앙 아메리카 book amerika
mit joong-ang amerika · **North and Central America**

바베이도스 babeidoseu
Barbados

캐나다 kaenada
Canada

코스타리카 koseutarika
Costa Rica

쿠바 kuba
Cuba

자메이카 jameika
Jamaica

멕시코 megsiko
Mexico

파나마
panama
Panama

트리니다드토바고
teurinidadeutobago
Trinidad and Tobago

미국 migook
United States of America

앤티가 바부다 aentiga babuda
Antigua and Barbuda

바하마 bahama · **Bahamas**

바베이도스 babeidoseu
Barbados

벨리즈 bellijeu · **Belize**

캐나다 kaenada · **Canada**

코스타리카 koseutarika
Costa Rica

쿠바 kuba · **Cuba**

도미니카연방 dominikayeonbang
Dominica

도미니카 공화국
dominika gonghwagook
Dominican Republic

엘살바도르 elsalbadoreu
El Salvador

그린란드 geurinlandeu · **Greenland**

그레나다 geurenada · **Grenada**

과테말라 gwatemalla · **Guatemala**

아이티 aiti · **Haiti**

하와이 · hawai · **Hawaii**

온두라스 ondooraseu · **Honduras**

자메이카 jameika · **Jamaica**

멕시코 megsiko · **Mexico**

니카라과 nikaragwa · **Nicaragua**

파나마 panama · **Panama**

푸에르토리코 puereutoriko
Puerto Rico

세인트키츠 네비스 saeinteukicheu
naebiseu · **St. Kitts and Nevis**

세인트루시아 saeinteuroosia
St. Lucia

세인트빈센트 그레나딘 제도
seinteubinsenteu geurenadin jedo
St. Vincent and the Grenadines

트리니다드토바고
teurinidadeutobago
Trinidad and Tobago

미국 migook
United States of America

남아메리카 nam-amerika • **South America**

아르헨티나 areuhentina
Argentina

볼리비아 bollibia
Bolivia

브라질 beurajil
Brazil

칠레 chillae
Chile

콜롬비아 kollombia
Colombia

에콰도르 ekwadoreu
Ecuador

페루 peru
Peru

우루과이 urugwai
Uruguay

베네수엘라 benesuella
Venezuela

아르헨티나 areuhentina • **Argentina**

볼리비아 bollibia • **Bolivia**

브라질 beurajil • **Brazil**

칠레 chillae • **Chile**

콜롬비아 kollombia • **Colombia**

에콰도르 ekwadoreu • **Ecuador**

포클랜드 제도 pokeullaendeu jedo
Falkland Islands

프랑스령 기아나 peurangseuryeong
giana • **French Guiana**

갈라파고스 제도 gallapagoseu jedo
Galápagos Islands

가이아나 gaiana • **Guyana**

파라과이 paragwai • **Paraguay**

페루 peru • **Peru**

수리남 surinam • **Suriname**

우루과이 urugwai • **Uruguay**

베네수엘라 benesuella • **Venezuela**

어휘 eohwi • **vocabulary**

대륙 daeryook **continent**	지방 jibang **province**	구역 guyeok **zone**
국가 gookga **country**	영토 yeongto **territory**	지구 jigu **district**
나라 nara **nation**	식민지 sikminji **colony**	지역 jiyeok **region**
주 joo **state**	공국 gong-gook **principality**	수도 sudo **capital**

유럽 yureob · **Europe**

프랑스 peurangseu
France

독일 dog-il
Germany

이탈리아 itallia
Italy

폴란드 pollandeu
Poland

포르투갈 poreutugal
Portugal

스페인 seupein
Spain

알바니아 albania · **Albania**

안도라 andora · **Andorra**

오스트리아 oseuteuria · **Austria**

발레아레스 제도 balleareseu jedo
Balearic Islands

벨라루스 bellaluseu · **Belarus**

벨기에 belgie · **Belgium**

보스니아 헤르체코비나 boseunia
hereuchekobina · **Bosnia and
Herzegovina**

불가리아 bulgaria · **Bulgaria**

코르시카 koreusika · **Corsica**

크로아티아 keuroatia · **Croatia**

키프로스 kipeuroseu · **Cyprus**

체코 공화국 checo gonghwagook
Czech Republic

덴마크 denmakeu · **Denmark**

잉글랜드 ing-geulandeu · **England**

에스토니아 eseutonia · **Estonia**

핀란드 pinlandeu · **Finland**

프랑스 peurangseu · **France**

독일 dog-il · **Germany**

그리스 geuriseu · **Greece**

헝가리 heong-gari · **Hungary**

아이스란드 aiseurandeu · **Iceland**

아일랜드 aillaendeu · **Ireland**

이탈리아 itallia · **Italy**

칼리닌그라드 kallinin-geuradeu
Kaliningrad

코소보 kosobo · **Kosovo**

라트비아 lateubia · **Latvia**

리히텐슈타인 lihitenshootain
Liechtenstein

리투아니아 lituania · **Lithuania**

룩셈부르크 looksembureukeu
Luxembourg

몰타 molta · **Malta**

몰도바 moldoba · **Moldova**

모나코 monako · **Monaco**

몬테네그로 montenegeuro
Montenegro

네덜란드 nedellandeu
Netherlands

북마케도니아 buk-makedonia
North Macedonia

북아일랜드 buk-ailaendeu
Northern Ireland

노르웨이 noreuwei · **Norway**

폴란드 pollandeu · **Poland**

포르투갈 poreutugal · **Portugal**

루마니아 loo-mania · **Romania**

러시아 연방 leosia yeonbang
Russian Federation

산마리노 sanmarino · **San Marino**

사르디니아 sareudinia · **Sardinia**

스코틀랜드 seukoteul-landeu
Scotland

세르비아 sereumia · **Serbia**

시실리 sisilli · **Sicily**

슬로바키아 seullobakia · **Slovakia**

슬로베니아 seullobenia · **Slovenia**

스페인 seupein · **Spain**

스웨덴 seuweden · **Sweden**

스위스 seuwiseu · **Switzerland**

우크라이나 ukeuraina · **Ukraine**

영국 yeong-gook
United Kingdom

바티칸 시티 batikan siti
Vatican City

웨일즈 weil-jeu · **Wales**

아프리카 apeurika · **Africa**

이집트 ijibteu
Egypt

에티오피아 etiopia
Ethiopia

케냐 kenya
Kenya

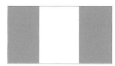

나이지리아 nai-jiria
Nigeria

남아프리카공화국 nam-
apeurikagonghwagook · **South Africa**

우간다 woo-ganda
Uganda

알제리 aljeri · **Algeria**

앙골라 ang-golla · **Angola**

베냉 benaeng · **Benin**

보츠와나 bocheuwana · **Botswana**

부르키나 파소 bureukina paso
Burkina Faso

부룬디 buroondi · **Burundi**

카메룬 kameroon · **Cameroon**

중앙아프리카 공화국 joong-ang-
apeurika gonghwagook
Central African Republic

차드 chadeu · **Chad**

코모로 komoro · **Comoros**

콩고 kong-go · **Congo**

콩고민주공화국
kong-gominjoogonghwagook
Democratic Republic of the Congo

지부티 jibuti · **Djibouti**

이집트 ijibteu · **Egypt**

적도 기니 jeogdo gini
Equatorial Guinea

에리트레아 eriteurea · **Eritrea**

에스와티니 eswatini · **Eswatini**

에티오피아 etiopia · **Ethiopia**

가봉 gabong · **Gabon**

감비아 gambia · **Gambia**

가나 gana · **Ghana**

기니 gini · **Guinea**

기니비사우 ginibisau
Guinea-Bissau

코트디부아르 koteudibuareu
Ivory Coast

케냐 kenya · **Kenya**

레소토 lesoto · **Lesotho**

라이베리아 laiberia · **Liberia**

리비아 libia · **Libya**

마다가스카르 madagaseukareu
Madagascar

말라위 mallawi · **Malawi**

말리 malli · **Mali**

모리타니아 moritania · **Mauritania**

모리셔스 morisheoseu · **Mauritius**

모로코 moroko · **Morocco**

모잠비크 mojambikeu
Mozambique

나미비아 namibia · **Namibia**

니제르 nijereu · **Niger**

나이지리아 nai-jiria · **Nigeria**

르완다 leuwanda · **Rwanda**

상투메 프린시페
sangtume peurinsipei
São Tomé and Príncipe

세네갈 senegal · **Senegal**

시에라리온 sierarion · **Sierra Leone**

소말리아 somallia · **Somalia**

남아프리카공화국 nam-
apeurikagonghwagook
South Africa

남수단 namsudan · **South Sudan**

수단 sudan · **Sudan**

탄자니아 tanjania · **Tanzania**

토고 togo · **Togo**

튀니지 twiniji · **Tunisia**

우간다 woo-ganda · **Uganda**

서사하라 seosahara
Western Sahara

잠비아 jambia · **Zambia**

짐바브웨 jimbabeuwae
Zimbabwe

아시아 asia • **Asia**

방글라데시 bang-geulladesi
Bangladesh

중국 joong-gook
China

인도 indo
India

일본 ilbon
Japan

요르단 yoreudan
Jordan

필리핀 pillipin
Philippines

대한민국 daehanmingook
South Korea

태국 taegook
Thailand

튀르키예 (터키) twireukiye (teoki)
Türkiye (Turkey)

아프가니스탄 apeuganiseutan
Afghanistan

아르메니아 areumenia • **Armenia**

아제르바이잔 ajereumaijan
Azerbaijan

바레인 barein • **Bahrain**

방글라데시 bang-geulladesi
Bangladesh

부탄 bootan • **Bhutan**

브루나이 beurunai • **Brunei**

캄보디아 kambodia • **Cambodia**

중국 joong-gook • **China**

동티모르 dongtimoreu • **East Timor**

조지아 jojia • **Georgia**

인도 indo • **India**

인도네시아 indonesia • **Indonesia**

이란 iran • **Iran**

이라크 irakeu • **Iraq**

이스라엘 iseura-el • **Israel**

일본 ilbon • **Japan**

요르단 yoreudan • **Jordan**

카자흐스탄 kajaheuseutan
Kazakhstan

쿠웨이트 kuweiteu • **Kuwait**

키르기스스탄 kireugiseuseutan
Kyrgyzstan

라오스 laoseu • **Laos**

레바논 lebanon • **Lebanon**

말레이시아 malleisia • **Malaysia**

몰디브 moldibeu • **Maldives**

몽고 mong-go • **Mongolia**

미얀마 (버마) miyanma
(beoma) • **Myanmar (Burma)**

네팔 nepal • **Nepal**

북한 bookhan • **North Korea**

오만 oh-man • **Oman**

파키스탄 pakiseutan • **Pakistan**

필리핀 pillipin • **Philippines**

카타르 katareu • **Qatar**

사우디아라비아 saudiarabia
Saudi Arabia

싱가폴 sing-gapol • **Singapore**

대한민국 daehanmingook
South Korea

스리랑카 seurirangka • **Sri Lanka**

시리아 siri-a • **Syria**

타지키스탄 tajikiseutan • **Tajikistan**

태국 taegook • **Thailand**

튀르키예 (터키) twireukiye (teoki)
Türkiye (Turkey)

투르크메니스탄 tureukeumeniseutan
Turkmenistan

인도네시아 indonesia
Indonesia

사우디아라비아 saudiarabia
Saudi Arabia

베트남 beteunam
Vietnam

아랍 에미리트 연합국 arab emiriteu
yeonhabgook · **United Arab Emirates**

우즈베키스탄 ujeubekiseutan
Uzbekistan

베트남 beteunam · **Vietnam**

예멘 yemen · **Yemen**

오세아니아 oseania
Oceania

호주 hojoo
Australia

뉴질랜드 newjillaendeu
New Zealand

호주 hojoo · **Australia**

피지 piji · **Fiji**

뉴질랜드 newjillaendeu
New Zealand

파푸아뉴기니 papua-newgini
Papua New Guinea

솔로몬제도 sollomonjedo
Solomon Islands

태즈메이니아 taejeumeinia
Tasmania

바누아투 banuatu · **Vanuatu**

불변화사 및 반의어 bulbyeonhwasa mit ban-ui-eo
particles and antonyms

까지
kkaji
to

위
wi
over

앞에
ape
in front of

위에
wi-eh
onto

안에
an-eh
in

위에
wi-eh
above

안
an
inside

위
wi
up

...에
...eh
at

...을(를) 관통해서
...eul (reul)
gwantonghaeseo
through

...의 위에
...ui wi-eh
on top of

사이
sa-i
between

가까운
gakkaun
near

여기
yeogi
here

부터
buteo
from

아래
arae
under

뒤에
dwi-eh
behind

...(안)으로
...(an)euro
into

밖에
bakk-eh
out

아래에
arae-eh
below

바깥
bakkat
outside

아래
arae
down

...을(를) 넘어서
...eul (reul) neom-eoseo
beyond

...을(를) 돌아서
...eul (reul) dol-ah-seo
around

...의 옆에
...ui yeop-eh
beside

반대편의
bandaepyeon-ui
opposite

먼
meon
far

저기
jeogi
there

...을(를) 위해
...eu(reul) wuihae
for

따라서
ttaraseo
along

...함께
...hamkke
with

전에
jeon-eh
before

...에 의해
...e euihe
by

이른
ireun
early

지금
jigeum
now

항상 ...하다
hangsang ...hada
always

종종
jongjong
often

어제
eoje
yesterday

처음
cheo-eum
first

모두
modoo
every

대략
daeryak
about

약간
yakgan
a little

...을(를) 향해서
...eul (reul) hyanghaeseo
toward

건너서
geonneoseo
across

...없이
...eobsi
without

후에
hoo-eh
after

...까지
...kkaji
until

늦은
neujeun
late

나중에
najoong-eh
later

결코 ...않다
gyeolko ...anta
never

드물게
deumulge
rarely

내일
naeil
tomorrow

마지막
majimak
last

일부
ilboo
some

정확히
jeonghwakhi
exactly

많이
man-i
a lot

큰
keun
large

작은
jageun
small

넓은
neolbeun
wide

좁은
jobeun
narrow

긴
gin
tall

짧은
jjalbeun
short

높은
nopeun
high

낮은
najeun
low

두꺼운
dukkeoun
thick

얇은
yalbeun
thin

가벼운
balgeun
light

무거운
moogeo-un
heavy

딱딱한
ttakttakhan
hard

부드러운
budeureoun
soft

젖은
jeojeun
wet

마른
mareun
dry

좋은
jo-eun
good

나쁜
nappeun
bad

빠른
ppareun
fast

느린
neurin
slow

맞는
matneun
correct

틀린
teullin
wrong

깨끗한
kkaekkeuthan
clean

더러운
deoreoun
dirty

아름다운
areumdaun
beautiful

추한
choohan
ugly

비싼
bissan
expensive

싼
ssan
cheap

조용한
joyonghan
quiet

시끄러운
sikkeureoun
noisy

더운
deo-un
hot

추운
choo-un
cold

열린
yeollin
open

닫힌
datchin
closed

가득 찬
gadeuk chan
full

텅 빈
teong bin
empty

새로운
saero-un
new

오래된
o-raedoen
old

밝은
gabyeo-un
light

어두운
eodoo-un
dark

쉬운
she-un
easy

어려운
eoryeo-un
difficult

비어 있는
bieo itneun
free

사용 중인
sayong joong-in
occupied

강한
ganghan
strong

약한
yakhan
weak

뚱뚱한
ddoongddoonghan
fat

마른
mareun
thin

어린
eorin
young

늙은
neulgeun
old

더 좋은
deo joh-eun
better

더 나쁜
deo nappeun
worse

검정색
geomjeongsaek
black

흰색
huinsaek
white

재미있는
jaemi-itneun
interesting

지루한
jiroohan
boring

아픈
apeun
sick

건강한
geonganghan
well

시작
sijak
beginning

끝
kkeut
end

유용한 표현 yuyonghan pyohyeon · **useful phrases**

필수 표현
pilsoo pyohyeon
essential phrases

네
ne
Yes

아니요
aniyo
No

아마
ah-ma
Maybe

부탁합니다
butakhamnida
Please

감사합니다
gamsahamnida
Thank you

천만에요
cheonman-eyo
You're welcome

실례합니다
sillyehamnida
Excuse me

죄송합니다
joesonghamnida
I'm sorry

하지 마세요
haji maseyo
Don't

좋아요
joayo
OK

괜찮아요
gwaenchanayo
That's fine

맞아요
majayo
That's correct

틀려요
teullyeoyo
That's wrong

인사 insa · **greetings**

안녕하세요
annyeonghaseyo
Hello

잘 가세요
jal gaseyo
Goodbye

안녕하세요
annyeonghaseyo
Good morning

안녕하세요
annyeonghaseyo
Good afternoon

안녕하세요
annyeonghaseyo
Good evening

안녕히 주무세요
annyeonghi jumuseyo
Good night

잘 지내셨어요?
jal jinaesheosseoyo?
How are you?

제 이름은... 입니다
je ireum-eun... imnida
My name is...

이름이 뭐예요?
ireum-i mwoyaeyo?
What is your name?

저 사람 이름이 뭐예요?
jeo salam ileum-i mwoyeyo?
What is his / her name?

...을(를) 소개하겠습니다.
...eul (reul) sogaehagesseumnida
May I introduce...

이 분은... 입니다
i boon-eun... imnida
This is...

만나서 반갑습니다
mannaseo bangabseumnida
Pleased to meet you

다음에 만나요
da-eum-eh mannayo
See you later

표지판 pyojipan
signs

관광 안내소
gwangwang annaeso
Tourist information

입구
ibgu
Entrance

출구
chulgu
Exit

비상구
bisang-gu
Emergency exit

미세요
miseyo
Push

위험
wiheom
Danger

금연
geum-yeon
No smoking

고장
gojang
Out of order

영업 시간
yeong-eob sigan
Opening times

무료 입장
muryo ibjang
Free admission

할인
hal-in
Reduced

세일
seil
Sale

휠체어 접근
hwilcha-eo jeobgeun
Wheelchair access

도와주세요
dowajooseyo · **help**

청각 장애인입니다
cheong-gak jang-aeinipnida
I'm deaf

시각 장애인입니다
shigak jang-aeinipnida
I'm blind

도와주세요
dowajooseyo
Can you help me?

이해할 수 없어요
i-haehal su eobseoyo
I don't understand

모르겠어요
moreugesseoyo
I don't know

영어할 줄 아세요?
yeong-eo-hal jul aseyo?
Do you speak English?

저는 영어를 할 수 있어요
jeo-neun yeong-eoreul hal su isseoyo
I speak English

천천히 말해 주세요
cheoncheonhi malhae juseyo
Please speak more slowly

글로 써 주세요
geullo sseo juseyo
Please write it down for me

...을(를) 잃어버렸어요
...eul (reul) ilh-eobeoryeosseoyo
I have lost...

방향 banghyang
directions

길을 잃어버렸어요
gireul il-eobeoryeosseoyo
I am lost

...이(가) 어디에 있어요?
...i(ga) eodi-eh isseoyo?
Where is the... ?

가장 가까운... 이(가)
어디에 있어요?
gajang gakkaun... i(ga)
eodi-eh isseoyo?
**Where is the
nearest... ?**

화장실이 어디예요?
hwajangsil-i eodiyaeyo?
Where is the restroom?

...에 어떻게 가요?
...e eotteoke gayo?
How do I get to... ?

오른쪽으로
oreunjjog-euro
To the right

왼쪽으로
waenjjog-euro
To the left

곧장 앞으로
gotjang apeuro
Straight ahead

...이(가) 얼마나 멀어요?
...i(ga) eolmana
meoreoyo?
How far is... ?

도로 표지판
doro pyojipan
road signs

주의
joo-ui
Caution

진입 금지
jin-ib geumji
Do not enter

천천히
cheoncheonhi
Slow down

우회
uhoe
Detour

우측 통행
ucheuk tonghaeng
Keep right

고속도로
gosokdoro
Freeway

주차 금지
joocha geumji
No parking

통과 못함
tong-gwa motham
Dead end

일방통행
ilbangtonghaeng
One-way street

거주자 전용
geojooja jeon-yong
Residents only

양보
yangbo
Yield

공사 중
gongsa joong
Roadwork

급커브
geubkeobeu
Dangerous curve

숙박시설
sookbaksiseol
accommodations

예약했습니다
yeyakhaetseumnida
I have a reservation

식당이 어디입니까?
sikdang-i eodi-imnikka?
**Where is the dining
room?**

아침 식사가 언제입니까?
achim siksaga
eonjeimnikka?
**What time is
breakfast?**

...까지 돌아오겠습니다
...kkaji dol-ah-
ogeseumnida
I'll be back at... o'clock

내일 떠납니다
naeil tteonamnida
I'm leaving tomorrow

먹고 마시기
meokgo masigi
eating and drinking

건배!
geonbae!
Cheers!

맛있어요 / 맛없어요
mas-isseoyo /
mat-eobseoyo
It's delicious / awful

술 / 담배를 안 합니다
sool / dambaereul an
hamnida
I don't drink / smoke

저는 고기를 안 먹습니다
jeoneun gogireul an
meokseumnida
I don't eat meat

저는 다 먹었어요
감사합니다
jeoneun da
meog-eosseoyo.
gamsahamnida
**No more for me,
thank you**

더 먹어도 돼?
deo meog-eodo
dwaeyo?
**May I have some
more?**

계산서 주세요
gyesanseo juseyo
May we have the check?

영수증 주세요
yeongsujeung juseyo
Can I have a receipt?

흡연 구역
heub-yeon guyeok
Smoking area

건강 geongang
health

몸이 안 좋아요
mom-i an joh-ayo
I don't feel well

속이 안 좋아요
sok-i an joa-yo
I feel sick

여기가 아파요
yeogiga apayo
It hurts here

열이 있어요
yeorii isseoyo
I have a fever

저는 임신... 개월입니다
jeoneun imsin... gaewol-
ibnida
I'm... months pregnant

...약 처방해 주세요
...yak cheobanghae
juseyo
**I need a prescription
for...**

보통... 을(를) 복용해요
botong... eul(reul) bog-
yonghaeyo
I normally take...

...에 알레르기가 있어요
...e alleleugiga isseoyo
I'm allergic to...

그 사람 괜찮을까요?
geu saram
gwaenchan-eulkkayo?
Will he / she be alright?

한국어 색인 hangugeo saegin • **Korean index**

hangugeo

hangugeo

hangugeo

hangugeo

hangugeo

hangugeo

hangugeo

hangugeo

hangugeo

hangugeo

영어 색인 yeongeo saekin · English index

english

english

english

english

english

english

english

english

english

english

english

english

english

english

감사 gamsa • **Acknowledgments**

DORLING KINDERSLEY would like to thank senior picture researchers Deepak Negi and Sumedha Chopra, assistant picture researcher Samrajkumar S, DTP Designer Raman Panwar, and proofreaders Diana Vowles, Heather Wilcox, Catharine Robertson, Chuck Hutchinson, Sam Cooke, Ruth Raisenberger, Manju Gupta and Mika Jin.

The publisher would like to thank the following for their kind permission to reproduce their photographs:
Abbreviations key: (a-above; b-below/bottom; c-centre; f-far; l-left; r-right; t-top)

123RF.com: Aicandy 188fbr; Andriy Popov 34tl; Arthousestudio 265fcla; Astemmer 208c; avigatorphotographer 216bl; Brad Wynnyk 172bc; Cladanifer 25fclb; Daniel Ernst 179tc; Hongqi Zhang 24cla; 175cr; Ingvar Bjork 60c; Koonsiri Scla, 92-93; Kobby Dagan 259c; Kritchanut 25ftl; Lightfieldstudios 35tr; Liubov Vadimovna (Luba) Nel 39cla; Ljupco Smokovski 75crb; Olegtriono 176fcl; Olga Popova 33c; Peopleimages12 41tl; Robert Churchill 94c; Roman Gorielov 33bc; Ruslan Kudrin 33bc, 35tr; Subbotina 39cra; Sutichak Yachaingkham 39tc; Tarzhanova 37tc; Vitaly Valua 39tl; Wilawan Khasawong 75cb. **Action Plus:** 224bc; **Alamy Images:** 154t; Alex Segre 150t; A.T. Willett 287bcl; Alex Segre 105ca; Andrew Barker 195fcl; Ambrophoto 24cra; Art Directors & TRIP / Helene Rogers 115bl; artpartner-images.com 181tc; Ben Queenborough 231crb; Boaz Rottem 209cr; Cultura RM 33r; Bernhard Classen 97bc; David Burton 177clb; Carl DeAbreu 264c; Canan Images 247fcla; Chicken Strip 112fbr; Chris George 271bc; Destina 176crb; Dorling Kindersley Ltd 266t; Dorling Kindersley Ltd / Vanessa Davies 74ftr; dpa picture alliance 112c; Doug Houghton 107fbr; Doug Houghton 213fclb; Gianni Muratore 193ftr; Henri Martin 182ca; Hideo 176tl; Sasa Huzjak 258t; Sergey Kravchenko 37ca; Sergio Azenha 270bc; Stock Connection 287bcr; tarczas 35cr; Tom Koene 213cra; Transport Infrastructures / Paul White 216t; Trekandshoot 194c; Robert Stainforth 98tl; vitaly suprun 176cl; Wavebreak Media Ltd 39cl, 174b, 175tr; Wavebreakmedia Ltd IP-200810 234fcl; **Allsport/Getty Images:** 238cl; **Arcaid:** John Edward Linden 301bl; Martine Hamilton Knight, Architects: Richard Bryant 301br; **Bosch:** 76tc, 76tcl; **Camera Press:** 38tr, 257cr; Barry J. Holmes 148tr; Jane Hanger 159cr; Mary Germanou 259bc; **Corbis:** 78b; Anna Clopet 247tr; Ariel Skelley / Blend Images 52l; Bettmann 181tr; Bo Zauders 156t; Bob Winsett 247cbl; Brian Bailey 247br; Craig Aurness 215bl; David H.Wells 249cbr; Dennis Marsico 274bl; Dimitri Lundt 236bc; Duomo 211tl; Gail Mooney 277ccr; George Lepp 248c; Gerald Nowak 239b; Gunter Marx 248cr; Jack Hollingsworth 231bl; James L. Amos 247bl, 191cr, 220bcr; Jan Butchofsky 277cbc; Johnathan Blair 243cr; Jose F. Poblete 191br; Jose Luis Pelaez.Inc 153tc; Karl Weatherly 220bl, 247tcr; Kelly Mooney Photography 259tl; Kevin Fleming 249bc; Kevin R. Morris 105tr, 243tl, 243tc; Kim Sayer 249tcr; Lynn Goldsmith 258t; Macduff Everton 231bcl; Mark Gibson 249bl; Mark L. Stephenson 249tcl; Mike King 247cbl; Pablo Corral 115bc; 249cctcl; Paul J. Sutton 224cc, 224br; Phil Schermeister 227b; 248tr; R. W Jones 309; Rick Doyle 241ctr; Robert Holmes 97br, 277ctc; Roger Ressmeyer 169tr; Ross Schlejepman 229; The Purcell Team 211clr; Wally McNamee 220br, 220bcl; 224bl; Wavebreak Media Ltd 191bc; Yann Arhus-Bertrand 249tl; **Depositphotos Inc**: Londondeposit 262br; **Demetrio Carrasco / Dorling Kindersley (c) Herge / Les Editions Casterman:** 112ccl; **Dixons:** 270cl, 270cr, 270bl, 270bcl, 270bcr, 270ccr; **Dorling Kindersley:** Banbury Museum 35c; Five Napkin Burger 132t; **Dreamstime.com:** Adempercem 197cb; Akesin 191td; 191cr; Aleksandar Todorovic 300bl; Anan Budtviengpunth 299cra; Andersastphoto 176tc; Andrey Popov 191bl, 55fcra, 190ftr; Anna Eremeeva 82crb; Anna Griessel 25cra; Anna Tolipova 277ftr; Anatoliy Samara 31 1tc; Anton Matveev 2bl; Arenaphotouk 209tr; Arne9001 190tl; Arnel Manalang 195fbr; Artzzz 201b; Avagyanlevon 269cla; Birgit Reitz Hofmann 144ca; Bonandbon Dw 154bc; Bright 199tr; Chaoss 26c; Chernetskaya 60tc, 240tc; Christian Offenberg 99tl; Colicaranica 210t; Dimaberkut 240cr; Dmitry Markov 5fcla, 56-57; Dvmsimages 196bc; Dzmitry Rishchuk 152t; Eakkachai Halang 101ftl; Ekostsov 198fbl; Elena Masiutkina 105fcls; Ellesi 197br; Evgeny Karandaev 145br; Exiledphoto 1ca (Golf Balls), 85crb, 231cr; Gradts 76ftr; Grigor Ivanov 82bl; Gutaper 176br; Hasan Can Balcioglu 261c; Hxdbzxy 5cra, 102-103; Hywit Dimyadi 184clb; Iakov Filimonov 115tr; Ivan Danik 4fcrb, 146-147; Ivan Katsarov 201t; Ilfede 215clb; Imicco 269tc; Isselee 292fcrb; Jamesteohart 290br; Jiri Hera 26tc; Joe Sohm 259tr; Johncox1958 243ca; Kaspars Grinvalds 177crb; Kenny Tong 5tr, 10-11; Kineticimagery 5bl, 302-303; Konstantinos Moraitis 199tl; Lah 249crb; Larry Gevert 1ca (peppers), 5fcra, 116-117; Leonid Andronov 208clb; Leo Daphne 145cb; Leen Beunens 299tl; Iuliia Diakova 15tr; Natalia Bratslavsky 101cl; Natvishenka 269tr; Njnightsky 70bl; Nuwan Fernandez 177tr; Maciej Bledowski 95c, 206br; Madrugadaverde 298; Maksim Toome 199ftr; Maniapixel 215tr; Matthias Ziegler 191ftl; Mholod 4fcra, 42-43; Micha Rojek 177fcl; Miff32 197bl; Mike_Kiev 199cr; Mikeal Keal 269cra; Mohamed Osama 75fbl; Monkey Business Images 26clb, 100t, 169tl; Monticello 145btl; Olena Turovtseva 216br; Olga Plugatar 271clb (X2), 271fclca; Pac 268clb; Paolo De Santis 261ftr; Patricia Hofmeester 233cra; Paul Michael Hughes

162tr; Petro Perutskyy 199bl; Phanuwatn 269cl; Photka 213fcra; Ponomarencko 152cr; Roza 300tc; Ryzhov Sergey 138t; Schamie 176cl; Seanlockephotography 189clb; Sean Pavone 301tl; Shariff Che\' Sjors737 277tc; Serghei Starus 190bc; Sergey Galushko 77ftl; Sergey Tolmachyov 209tr; Sereeniy 48crb; Steafpong 97bl; Sutsaiy 66bl; Takcrane3 198t; Tatiana3337 1ca (multicolor); Theerasak Tammachuen 269cr; 5fclb, 160-161; Trak 256t;Tyler Olson 168crb; Vetkit 189fclb; Volodymyr Melnyk 231ca, 235fcrb; Wang Song 250br, 261cr; Wirestock 169c; Zerbor 296tr; **Education Photos:** John Walmsley 26tl; **Getty Images:** 287tr; 94tr; Corbis Historical / Christopher Pillitz 169cr; George Doyle & Ciaran Griffin 22cr; David Leahy 162tl; DigitalVision / David Leahy 162cla; DigitalVision / We Are 227cra; Don Farrall / Digital Vision 176c; Ethan Miller 270bl; Inti St Clair 179bl; Jeff Bottari 236br; LightRocket / SOPA Images 227ftl; Sean Justice / Digital Vision 24br; The Image Bank / Michael Dunning 235cra; **Getty Images / iStock**: ake1150sb 154bl, Andy0man 304 (Digital Clock X3), Archiedaphoto 268t, Babayev 76fcrb, Bluesky85 213tl, Bluestocking 268cb, Bonetta 66fbr, Svetlana Borisova 286cr, Bulgnn 112br; Hadzhi Hristo Chorbadzhi 260tl, DigitalVision Vectors / youngID 96cl, E+ / Adamkaz 206bl, E+ / Aldomurillo 189cra, E+ / AnVr 144bl, E+ / BraunS 231br, E+ / Dean Mitchell 55ftr; E+ / FG Trade 179ftl, E+ / Fly View Productions 96t, E+ / Ivan Pantic 206bc, E+ / Joel Carillet 215br, E+ / JohnnyGreig 104t, E+ / Jondpatton 196br, E+ / Kali9 186bl, 190clb, E+ / Lorado 115bc, E+ / Mbbirdy 66fclb, E+ / Pagadesign 97tr, E+ / Petko Ninov 198fbr, E+ / Satoshi-K 259crb, E+ / SDI Productions 55fbl, E+ / SolStock 212clb, E+ / South_agency 114br, E+ / Studiocasper 270tc, E+ / Sturti 186bc, E+ / Tashi-Delek 179ftr, E+ / Tempura 48clb, E+ / Tolgart 34br, FamVeld 246tr, Farakos 176cr, FG Trade 188fbl, Gannet77 96c, Grinvalds 99cr, Gumpanat 97cl, Kckate16 188fcla, Kommercialize 208cb, Leedsn 241cra, Sompong Lekhawattana 97tl, LeventKonuk 7c, Liz Leyden 115tc, LightFieldStudios 169cl, Andrii Lysenko 114tl, Karan Mathur 191cra, MicroStockHub 96clb, Mladn61 196cla, 196-197ca, Moumita Mondal 27fcr, Monkeybusinessimages 49crb, Yaman Mutart 105bl, Nojman 276t, OfirPeretz 195ftl, Prostock-Studio 5clb, 170-171, 188crb, RuslanDashinsky 83tl, Scaliger 208t, Kazuma Seki 188bl, Deepak Sethi 271ftr, SimonSkafar 1ca (Cornflowers), 5fbl, 278-279, Stocktrek Images 215bl, TACrafts 199tra, Teamtime 210b, The Image Bank / Ryan McVay 247cra, Tilo 69ftr, Toxitz 99cl, Alla Tsyganova 148tl, Tunatura 287tc, Universal Images Group / Andia 106t, Andik Tri Witanto 209cra, Chunyip Wong 5crb, 192-193, YakubovAlim 55crb, Zdenkam 23bl, Drazen Zigic 49ftr; Sofia Zhuravets 40l; **Hulsta:** 70t; **Ideal Standard Ltd:** 72r; **The Image Bank/Getty Images:** 181tr; **iStockphoto.com:** asterix0597 163tl; EdStock 190br; RichLegg 26bc; **MP Visual.com:** Mark Swallow 202t; **NASA:** 280cr, 280ccl, 281tl; **P A Photos:** 181br; **Plain and Simple Kitchens:** 66t; **Red Consultancy:** Odeon cinemas 257br; **Rex Features:** 106br, 259tc, 259bl, 280b; Charles Ommaney 114tcr; J.F.F Whitehead 243cl; Scott Wiseman 287bl; **Science & Society Picture Library:** Science Museum 202b; **Science Photo Library:** IBM Research 190cla; NASA 281cr; **Shutterstock.com:** Africa Studio 198bl, Akkalak Aiempradit 26cla, BearFotos 245clb, BearFotos 246t, Radu Bercan 213fbl, Comeback Images 24bl, Creative Lab 115ca, Odin Daniel 214bl, Diamant24 60fclb, Early Spring 100br, Dmytro Falkowskyi 196-197cb, freevideophotoagency 241cr, Giuseppe_R 4fbr, 252-253, Kaspars Grinvalds 1ca (Shirts), 5ftr, 28-29, 175clb, Michal Karpinski 114cl, Ground Picture 26ftr, 100fbr, Haveseen 264b, HelloRF Zcool 168t, Joseph Hendrickson 59tl, Nigel Jarvis 214bc, Mkfilm 287br, New Africa 71tr, 75ftr, 77cra, Eline Oostingh 215cb, SeventyFour 232bl, Ilya Sviridenko 185fbr, Alla Tsyganova 114fbl, zcw 77ca; **SuperStock:** Ingram Publishing 62; Juanma Aparicio / age fotostock 172t; **Sony:** 268bc; **Neil Sutherland:** 82tr, 90t, 118, 188ctr, 196tr, 299cl, 299bl; **Vauxhall:** 191cl, 200.

DK PICTURE LIBRARY:
Akhil Bahkshi; Patrick Baldwin; Geoff Brightling; British Museum; John Bulmer; Andrew Butler; Joe Cornish; Brian Cosgrove; Andy Crawford and Kit Hougton; Philip Dowell; Alistair Duncan; Gables; Bob Gathany; Norman Hollands; Kew Gardens; Peter James Kindersley; Vladimir Kozlik; Sam Lloyd; London Northern Bus Company Ltd; Tracy Morgan; David Murray and Jules Selmes; Musée Vivant du Cheval, France; Museum of Broadcast Communications; Museum of Natural History; NASA; National History Museum; Norfolk Rural Life Museum; Stephen Oliver; RNLI; Royal Ballet School; Guy Ryecart; Science Museum; Neil Setchfield; Ross Simms and the Winchcombe Folk Police Museum; Singapore Symphony Orchestra; Smart Museum of Art; Tony Souter; Erik Svensson and Jeppe Wikstrom; Sam Tree of Keygrove Marketing Ltd; Barrie Watts; Alan Williams; Jerry Young.

Additional photography by Colin Walton.

Colin Walton would like to thank:
A&A News, Uckfield; Abbey Music, Tunbridge Wells; Arena Mens Clothing, Tunbridge Wells; Burrells of Tunbridge Wells; Gary at Di Marco's; Jeremy's Home Store, Tunbridge Wells; Noakes of Tunbridge Wells; Ottakar's, Tunbridge Wells; Selby's of Uckfield; Sevenoaks Sound and Vision; Westfield, Royal Victoria Place, Tunbridge Wells.